Pimple's Progress

Pimple's Progress

Fred Evans, Britain's First Film Comedy Star

BARRY ANTHONY

McFarland & Company, Inc., Publishers

Jefferson, North Carolina

ISBN (print) 978-1-4766-8831-2
ISBN (ebook) 978-1-4766-4647-3

LIBRARY OF CONGRESS AND BRITISH LIBRARY
CATALOGUING DATA ARE AVAILABLE

Library of Congress Control Number 2022038285

Front cover image: Fred Evans in *Pimple Has One*, 1915
(courtesy of the British Film Institute)

Printed in the United States of America

*McFarland & Company, Inc., Publishers
Box 611, Jefferson, North Carolina 28640
www.mcfarlandpub.com*

Acknowledgments

Thanks are due to my wife, Jean Anthony; Tony Barker; Stephen Bottomore; Bryony Dixon of the British Film Institute; Tony Fletcher who rescued many audio tapes and letters from Denis Gifford's collection before donating them to the BFI; Bob Geoghegan of Archive Film Agency; Ronald Grant and Martin Humphries of the Cinema Museum, Kennington; Glenn Mitchell; the late Michael Pointon; Tony Scott; and Joy and John Relph. Most of the historic newspapers used were accessed via www.britishnewspaperarchive.co.uk. Above all I would like to acknowledge the late Denis Gifford whose indefatigable research and willingness to share the results has contributed so much to this book.

Contents

Preface

I HAVE INTENDED TO WRITE a biography of Fred Evans for longer than I care to remember. How a film comedian named "Pimple" rivaled the popularity of the great Charles Chaplin in Britain for an extended period yet received so little coverage in the standard histories of cinema was intriguing, even perplexing.

As a theater historian specializing in popular entertainment, I have long been aware of Fred's famous family. His grandfather, also Fred Evans, was celebrated as clown in many of the country's leading pantomimes, while parents Minnie and Fred Evans (yes, another Fred) were top music-hall performers who had toured Europe. His uncles Will Evans and Seth and Albert Jee were long-term stalwarts of the variety theater. But Fred Evans never reached such heights in "The Profession" and his career, despite extending over fifty-years, was largely unrecorded and obscure.

From the time of my earliest interest in silent cinema, I had understood that Fred made over 200 short comedies between 1910 and 1922. In an epic trawl though the trade press of the time film historian Denis Gifford had recorded their titles and included them in his seminal work *The British Film Catalogue, 1895–1970* (1973). In later years I got to know Denis and he revealed that he had interviewed Fred's surviving bother Joe Evans, significant because the siblings had worked together for most of their lives. Denis was happy to discuss his ground-breaking research, but there were still many questions concerning Fred's film career that needed to be resolved. What were the central themes of his films? How and where did he make them? How many films did he make? Why have so few survived? What was it that so endeared him to the British public and what led to him being cold-shouldered by generations of film historians? Why did he suddenly stop making movies to return to the variety stage? Why was he called "Pimple"?

There was little to go on in film literature. As long ago as 1949 Rachael Low had made a few perceptive comments about Pimple comedies in *The History of the British Film, 1906–1914*. In subsequent publications Fred either received a passing mention or was completely ignored. Denis Gifford transcribed some of his taped interview with Joe for *The Silent Picture* magazine in 1970, while in 1988 Catherine Lamb contributed the single page "Britain's Greatest Star" to the

1

Call Boy based on research undertaken for an unpublished MA thesis. It was not until 2000 that Michael Hammond's "'Cultivating Pimple': Performance Traditions and the Film Comedy of Fred and Joe Evans" appeared in *Pimple, Pranks and Pratfalls: British Film Comedy Before 1930,* an insightful account which derived from his presentation at the previous year's British Silent Cinema Weekend. Among the British Film Institute films that Hammond showed was *Pimple Has One* in which the drunken Pimple paints out half the screen to prevent the audience from looking at a woman's ankle. The scene's meta-film propensities were mirrored at the 2013 Silent Film Weekend, when the privately owned *Oliver Twisted* featured Pimple arguing with the supposed director and then murdering him on screen. We were, perhaps, seeing a reason why Pimple and the cinema industry went their separate ways.

By 2006 I had gleaned enough about Fred and Joe Evans to be able to contribute short biographies and a filmography to *Directors in British and Irish Cinema: A Reference Companion,* an entry which was also published as part of the BFI Screenline web site. Three years later Paul Matthew St. Pierre provided the most extensive discussion of Pimple films to date in his *Music Hall Mimesis in British Film, 1895–1960.* It was not, however, until the mass digitization of periodicals undertaken by the British Newspaper Archive that that it became possible to fill in many of the gaps in our knowledge. Research carried out over several years finally demonstrated the richness and diversity of Fred's life and various careers. Several of Fred's surviving films preserved in the BFI and other collections also became available for online study.

As the book developed it became clear that it could not be restricted to telling Fred's life story and attempting to explain his films. It was important to look closely at the entertainment conventions that he inherited; the contemporary issues he reflected; and at the performers with whom he interacted. Brother Joe and uncles Will, Seth and Albert were all known to be influential, but I was also able to resurrect forgotten fellow performers Jimmy Reed and Geraldine Maxwell, both of whom went on to pursue separate and successful film careers. More than anything the book began to expose the tensions and accommodations that were created as cinema became part of an older and more traditional world of entertainment.

I am hoping that this work will explain why Britain's first film comedy star became a mere footnote in cinema history. In his simple capers Pimple employed the broad humor associated with the declining music hall. But in his many parodies of the new feature films, he encouraged an unsophisticated public not to be intimidated by spectacle and complexity. Eventually his patrons found they had no need of such support and Pimple also moved on to pastures new.

Introduction

DENIS GIFFORD PRESSED "RECORD." Rejoicing in the nickname "Mr. Nostalgia" he was dedicated to preserving the history of popular entertainment in all its varied forms. Once-familiar features of his South London home had long-since disappeared under piles of books, newspapers, and vintage comics, leaving just enough room for the most basic requirements. Out of chaos came order. Picking away at his typewriter Denis produced book after book on horror movies, silent films, science fiction, animation, superheroes, and radio comedy. Now he had begun to seek out flesh and blood survivals for his collection, taping their sometimes-faltering reminiscences for future examination and exploitation. For many years he had nursed a project that only he was capable of fulfilling. *The British Film Catalogue*, finally published in 1973, set out to provide detailed information on every UK entertainment film made between 1895 and 1970. Of the thousands of performers listed in the work, one of Denis's favorites was Fred Evans, a music-hall performer whose many appearances as the clownish "Pimple" resulted in him becoming one of Britain's first film stars. He had died before Denis started his research, but his younger brother Joe Evans was still alive and keen to cooperate.

Just before their first recording session in 1965 Denis and Joe probably exchanged a few pleasantries about the world of show business. Joe had spent virtually all his 70 years as a performer, often appearing alongside his brother Fred on the music-hall stage and in early film comedies. Back in the late 1940s Denis had also been part of a double act, playing in a concert party with his childhood friend Bob Monkhouse. After acting as Denis's straight man Bob went on to become one of the country's most popular stand-up comedians. "When I said I wanted to be a comedian they all laughed" he cracked, "they're not laughing now!" Denis and Bob shared a passion for jokes, cartoons, and old films and both presented TV programs which featured vintage popular entertainment. Where national institutions failed to preserve material rated as unimportant because of its ephemeral nature, Denis and Bob amassed huge personal archives relating to cinema, television, radio, and live performance.

The taped interview with Joe was part of Denis's mission to talk to "every last pioneer of the British film industry—producer, director, writer, photographer or actor" to gather information for *The British Film Catalogue*. It was an enormous task of cross-referencing and double-checking, made even more difficult by what exactly his interviewees could, or chose, to recall. Like survivors of Shakespeare's Battle of Agincourt, veterans of the British film industry tended to "remember with advantages" the feats they did in the early days of cinema. With the limited availability of original sources and a general lack of critical examination some pioneers were left to create their own egocentric narratives. But Joe's potential for inflating his own part in the development of the movies was limited, always qualified by his brother's fame. Despite his own talents as a director, writer of screenplays, scene painter and comedian Joe had been ascribed a secondary role, fated always to exist in the shadow of "Pimple." By the time of his interview with Denis Gifford, Joe's personal horizons had become severely limited. Thrombosis had led to the amputation of both legs, confining him to the basement flat of a red-brick Victorian villa in the Sussex seaside town of Hove. He remained stoical in his tiny apartment, however, and was intent on telling his and Fred's epic story. The tape wound on: "This is Joe Evans speaking" he announced.

Joe's recorded narrative, supplemented by letters to Denis, told the life story of both brothers. There were tales of their apprenticeships as circus performers and as youthful members of their parents' music-hall act. There was the shock of their mother's sudden death, followed by their father's immediate re-marriage to a young performer. A troubled childhood was made more traumatic when their father and stepmother left them to pursue a career in the United States. Joe remembered their teenage years working as comedians in a golden age of variety and an early friendship with a young "artiste" named Charles Chaplin. He recalled how they became part of the early cinema industry—devising and appearing in over 200 silent films. And he did his best to describe their extended family, a bewilderingly complex network of individuals whose shared profession frequently resulted in flamboyant and unpredictable behavior. Underlying all of Joe's recollections was a sense of theatrical tradition, the informing presence of a myriad of clowns, dancers, acrobats, bareback riders, puppeteers, musicians, and, above all, comedians.

CHAPTER 1

Pimple's Pantomime Tradition

ONE OF THE STORIES THAT JOE TOLD about his early days concerned Fred and himself setting out in search of their father. They had tramped for several days to get from London to Southampton, hoping to work their passage to the United States. Joe painted a bleak picture, richly deserving of a tear-jerking violin accompaniment. Two little waifs arriving hungry and footsore in a large, uncaring city; Fred and his younger brother in search of a heartless father who had abandoned them to fend for themselves. They were tired and dirty after the long walk, their clothes disheveled and their footwear in a state of imminent collapse. As experienced variety performers, the boys knew that on stage such a threadbare costume was bound to raise unqualified merriment. In real life, this shabby appearance was painfully different. As an old man Joe related the story with relish, presenting the well-honed memory to anyone expressing an interest in his or Fred's formative years. It was a dramatic tale which owed more to generalized feelings of loss and insecurity than it did to hard facts.

The road to Southampton ran through time as well as space. Theirs was a family history that was less a genealogical record and more a continuous performance, a show that was frequently edited and amended to reflect personal circumstances. With so many of the family engaged in the business of fantasy and make-believe, the truth was seldom allowed to get in the way of a good story. A Native American chief here, a few generations of puppeteers there—what did it matter if such barely credible characters made guest appearances. While aware of their rich theatrical pedigree, Fred and Joe were less mindful of destiny's shaping hand than the need to rationalize and re-interpret aspects of their own chaotic lives. A father's heartlessness, an uncle's support, old loves, new loves, sudden successes, and protracted failures were subjected to re-examination and re-interpretation. It was a tragi-comic procedure whose ironies and inconsistencies had much in common with their approach to humor.

From an early age, the brothers had been masters of burlesque. Their paternal grandfather Fred Evans, a famous pantomime clown, had employed comic inversion, substitution, and distortion to satirize the foibles of mid–19th-century audiences. And uncle Will Evans (1868–1931) had become a star of music hall with shrill sendups of such figures as Lady Godiva, "The Suffragette" and the scandalously under-dressed dancer Maud Allan in "Salome." Burlesque had been a dominant feature of popular theater for most of the Victorian period, presenting a topsy-turvy take on contemporary society which the brothers were quick to resurrect in their film comedies.

Frederick the First

Joe was incorrect when he sometimes claimed that W.C. Evans, proprietor of the celebrated proto-music hall, Evans' Song and Supper Rooms, was their great-great grandfather. While the family tree did not include this illustrious entrepreneur, it was heavily laden with other theatrical fruit. It was Joe and Fred's grandfather, Frederick William Evans (1842–1909) who had set his descendants on their show business path in the early 1850s. At the age of 11 he had persuaded his father, a Covent Garden baker, to allow him to take lessons from "Monsieur Chapino," who was well-known as a dance master and pantomime Harlequin. As one of an extensive juvenile troupe Frederick appeared at enormous proletarian theaters such as the Victoria (later familiarly known as "The Old Vic"), in Waterloo Road; the Royal Surrey, Blackfriars Road; and Sadlers' Wells, Clerkenwell. The pantomimes in which "Chapino's Talented Pupils" featured were stupendous productions which provided an intense theatrical experience by mixing drama, song, dance, comedy, and spectacular effects. Fairy tales were amalgamated with mythology; contemporary society was caricatured; and elements of shock and surprise were always present. But at the height of its popularity pantomime was already tinged with an air of nostalgia. Successive generations of jaundiced writers and critics drew unfavorable comparisons between the pantomimes of their childhood and the form's modern incarnation. Even the most hilarious of contemporary clowns were described as miserable substitutes for the late, lamented Joseph "Joey" Grimaldi (1782–1836).

By 1860 Frederick had made rapid strides, or leaps, in his profession appearing as Harlequin in the Victoria pantomime *The Enchanted House; or, Harlequin and the Fire King, and the Fairies of the Frozen Dell*. Although individually talented he preferred to work with others and for a time he and Clara King appeared as a music-hall double act, billed as "Operatic and Characteristic Dancers." In 1862 Frederick entered another partnership by marrying a young performer, Harriet Honor Penn (1842–1885). During her pregnancy with their first child in 1863 the couple spent several months at her father's music hall in Military Road, Chatham.

The process by which the "Two Brewers" tavern became transformed into the Royal Alhambra Music Hall was typical of the foundation of many early variety theaters, with its proprietor seeking to capitalize on a large potential audience by demolishing the adjoining stable and erecting a hall for the purposes of entertainment. Harriet's father, Thomas Penn Simpson, claimed to be a descendant of the Quaker founder of Pennsylvania, William Penn, but those attending "Old Simpson's" were far removed from the "Society of Friends." Alcohol was purchased from the bar of the public house and carried through into the hall. Unruly soldiers and sailors from local bases provided a high proportion of the audience, while children and young persons were also in evidence. In 1870 an application to transfer the Alhambra's license was opposed by a local police officer:

Fig. 42.—FRED. EVANS.   (Wig made by C. H. FOX.)

The founder of a popular entertainment dynasty, the famous Victorian Clown, Fred Evans (1843–1909) (author's collection).

> Supt. Merritt remarked that no notice had been given him about the application; he further said the place was the greatest sink of iniquity in Chatham; he hoped it would continue closed, as it was at present, for he found that juvenile thieving had greatly diminished since it was closed. He had known instances of boys robbing their employers, and also their fathers and mothers, to get the means to go this place of amusement.[1]

Forty years later exactly the same accusations were made about the first cinemas.

Adopting the stage name Amy Rosalind, Harriet joined her husband in a song-and-dance act and in the traditional Harlequinades that were appended to Christmas pantomimes. On December 31, 1865, *The Era* reviewed a production at the Effingham Theatre, East London, in which Fred first appeared in the role that he was quickly to make his own:

> Among the comic scenes are two rival Barbers' Shops, a Telegraph-office, a Loan-office, and a street of shops, and the business is of the customary nature. Some of the tricks and changes are very rapid, and Mr. Fred. Evans makes a capital Clown. He will be remembered as Harlequin last year at the old Surrey, and we can hardly call to mind one that has come into such prominent notice in the meantime. His talking is quite on a par with his dancing and tumbling, and that is saying a great deal, while his Music Hall experience serves him well. With Miss Amy Rosalind, who makes, as usual, a very graceful Columbine, he sang a comic duet, "Dandy Jake," and though it is rather a novelty for a lady to sing during the Harlequinade, it is a matter that cannot be said much against in these days of change and variety.

"Change and variety" were to bring about the curtailment of the Harlequinade during the 1890s, but during the 1860s and 1870s Frederick and Harriet were major players in a form of entertainment which had reached its technical and intellectual zenith. It was a hugely disruptive process in which an imaginary storybook land (the Opening) gave way, via the Transformation Scene, to the Harlequinade, a world of familiar people, shops, and streets which in turn were devastated as Pantaloon and his servant Clown pursued the runaway lovers Columbine and Harlequin. In a succession of cartoon-like tricks, crying babies were squashed, pursuing policemen decapitated, and shopkeepers battered as they tried to protect their vulnerable merchandise.

Along with those who relished such remarkable and ridiculous acts of violence, the Harlequinade also appealed to a public who reveled in the ability to detect hidden meanings and secret messages. Allegories, puns, and riddles were visually interpreted by instantly changing scenery, disappearances, sudden manifestations, and everyday items put to strange and unexpected uses. Sometimes such everyday items included human beings, as in Fred's Harlequinade scene "Furnished Apartments" in which the performers were converted into pieces of furniture. Between the years 1871–1881 Frederick became England's top clown, chaotically cutting his capers at the country's home of pantomime, the Theatre Royal, London, often known simply as Drury Lane.

Frederick's commanding stage presence relied as much on physical dexterity as comic byplay. Like all pantomime clowns he had devised a unique make-up—in his case, a matching pair of crescent moon shaped designs on his cheek bones and jagged marks of surprise above each eye. A tall strand of hair sprung like an exclamation from his whitened scalp, while thickly painted red lips attempted to obscure a flourishing mustache. When he was not hurling himself through trapdoors and belaboring his fellow performers in Christmas pantomimes, he was doing very much the same in music halls throughout Britain and Europe. After choreographing and appearing in several ballets at the Alhambra, Leicester Square, in the late 1860s and early 1870s, he toured widely with his own company of dancers and pantomimists. It was a golden age for mime, with English performers achieving notable successes in continental Europe.

Relying heavily on the size of stages to achieve the full impact of his troupe's acrobatic tricks and trap work, Frederick was drawn to major European locations where theaters rivaled or even exceed the capacity of Drury Lane. In 1872 the company made the short journey to Brussels, followed by engagements in Berlin, St. Petersburg, Könisberg, Paris and Brussels in 1875; a three-month engagement at the Folies Bergère, Paris, in 1876; and by many subsequent European appearances. Downplaying the visual puns that were a feature of their English pantomime performances, they utilized skillful mime, astounding acrobatic feats, spectacular stage effects and an amazing degree of precision to entertain foreign audiences. In 1875 a *Figaro* reviewer observed:

In passing I went into the Gaité Theatre, where they have just brought in a new Pantomime, in the spectacle "Chatte Blanche," the *troupe* of Fred Evans. Its folly is deliciously ruled by a piece of delicious mechanism; the falls, tumbling, dancing, &c. are all counted, studied and dosed. A prodigious order reigns in the production of the disorder; in fact, it is the most piquant and striking of these sorts of Pantomime that I have seen.[2]

Frederick Evans' "comic ballets" presented simple narratives that could be appreciated by any audience. In their wordlessness and strong visual impact such productions as *The Witch! The Fiend! And the Fat 'Un*; *Quicksilver Dick*; *Here, There, and Everywhere*; and *Oscillation versus Elongation; or, The Topers Three* anticipated many aspects of early cinema. In 1879 a rival troupe, the Hanlon-Lees, created a three-scene ballet which might easily have supplied the plot for one of the first fiction films. *Le Voyage en Suisse* (*A Trip to Switzerland*) featured a frantic chase, exciting fights and an exploding carriage and locomotive. By the 1890s Charles Chaplin's future employer Fred Karno had begun to stage a series of large-scale comedy sketches performed by a company of "speechless comedians" including Frederick's son, Harry Evans.

The cast of Frederick's troupes frequently varied but were usually drawn from a small circle of family and acquaintances. For a time, he ran a company with Harriet's brother Will Simpson. Later he joined Ted Towers (the son of the lessee of the Victoria when he had appeared there as Harlequin) to present "variety in all its branches. Ballet, Farcical Sketches, Entrees Eccentrique, Aesthetic Quadrilles, etc."[3] Given the close-knit nature of such troupes and their need for strict discipline it was helpful to include family members, particularly those whose youthfulness rendered them susceptible to tight control. Gradually, Frederick's children were introduced into the troupe. Will, billed as "Master Willie," joined his father in 1881, later followed by Fred and Harry. A daughter, May Evans (1874–1911) had a separate music-hall career as a singer of comic and sentimental songs such as "He Takes Me Up in the Gallery"; "'E Means No 'Arm"; and the heart-rending ballad "The Sweetest Flower Dies."

Life in the world of Victorian popular entertainment was seldom trouble free. In 1880, Frederick lost his entire savings after a short period running the Star Music Hall in Bermondsey, South East London. In a relentlessly active profession, serious injuries were common, and on occasion engagements were arbitrarily cancelled creating an urgent requirement to find fresh work for the troupe. Harriett died suddenly in 1885, aged 42, while Frederick was absent in Europe. At the time their youngest child, Maud Lily, was only two years old. Three years later, in 1889, he married another *danseuse*, 24-year-old Marie Matthews who gave birth to Winifred Evans in 1890.

By the final decade of the 19th century changes in public taste had caused an abridgement of the role of the clown in pantomimes, reducing his appearances to a sentimental acknowledgment of the "good old days" of popular entertainment. Even had the Harlequinade not fallen out of favor, Frederick's diminishing physical prowess would still have meant that he was unable to continue with his particularly athletic form of clowning. For a time, he drew a veil over increasing age by leading his troupe in short "shadow pantomimes," performed before a bright light and behind a canvas screen. At the end of his long career, he became a member of dramatic companies run by such celebrated Victorian actors as Johnston Forbes-Robertson, Frank Benson, and Sir Henry Irving. One of his final performances took place in 1903 when he reprised his famous skit *A Clown in the Kitchen; or, Love in Many Forms* at a special benefit performance organized to raise funds to assist him in his declining years. Frederick died at his lodgings in Bristol on October 31, 1909. For one of the most famous performers of his times, the final audience was disappointing. Only three people attended the funeral.

Alfresco Entertainments

Two episodes occurring in the streets of South East London marked the grand opening and dismal closure of Frederick Evans' career. Late in the evening on January 30, 1865, Frederick was playing Harlequin to the Clown of the Great Little Rowella at the Royal Surrey Theatre, Blackfriars Road. As the pantomime *Harlequin King Pumpkin; or, Richard ye Lion Hearte* ended, flames were seen licking around the central gas chandelier. Following the evacuation of the audience the fire spread rapidly, progressing from the painted canvas ceiling, down hanging drapes to the stage area. Panic broke out among the children portraying sprites and the female dancers whose gauze and muslin fairy costumes were potential death traps. It was then that Rowella and Frederick took firm control of the situation, hurrying the frightened performers through smoke and flames to the stage door. In the street outside, the pantomime's transformation scene, "The Volcanic Caverns of Crystal and Streams of Liquid Lava," was re-enacted. An immense crowd were held in check by a cordon of police, illuminated by the glow from the blazing theater and in constant danger from falling embers and ashes. Watching the spectacle stood Clown and Harlequin, grimy from the conflagration, but heroes for the night.

About thirty-five years later Edgar Bateman (author of "If It Wasn't for the 'Ouses in Between" and many other celebrated comic songs) was passing an imposing new variety theater, the New Cross Empire. Music hall had changed radically since the days of "Old Simpson's," with small independent concerns giving way to networks of theaters run by large, well-financed public companies. The 2,000 seat Empire (opened in 1899) was part of the Moss-Stoll syndicate whose Matcham-designed "theatres of variety" offered comfort, safety, and a well-regulated standard of entertainment. While looking at the imposing building, Bateman noticed the name of Frederick's son, Will Evans, prominently displayed on the posters outside. Casting his mind back, he recalled Will as a child playing the bar of *The Craven's Head*, a Drury Lane pub run by Frederick and

Harriett. Suddenly, his memory of the pleasant domestic scene was broken by the sight of an old busker plucking a banjo in the street. It was Frederick Evans.[4]

Frederick the Second

Born at Chatham on June 6, 1863, Frederick's first child, also named Frederick William Evans, was the wandering father that Joe and Fred had gone to seek. Unlike *his* father, Fred Junior did not take to the stage until his late teens, being cared for by his grandparents, Frederick and Maria Evans, and receiving a boarding-school education before joining the famous Lauri troupe of pantomimists. In April 1883, he traveled to Paris with Charles Lauri Senior (who had partnered his father at Drury Lane) and with Charles Lauri Junior and the Italian dancer Francesca Zanfretta to appear at the Folies Bergère in *Puss, Puss, Puss* and *La Maison Tranquille* (*The Quiet House*) and, later in the year, in *Peau D'Ane* (*Donkey Skin*), a spectacular production at the 3,500 seat Théâtre du Châtelet.

The frenetic nature of such entertainments was demonstrated in a subsequent sketch *La Poule aux oeufs d'or* (*The Hen with the Golden Eggs*) presented at the Châtelet in 1884 in which the company managed 45 appearances and disappearances though various trapdoors in a 3-minute sequence. One of the most frequently used devices for projecting performers into public view was the "star trap," a counter-balanced mechanism known in France as the "trappe Anglaise." After a year with the Lauris, Fred Junior joined Fred Senior in *Puss's Holiday*, a comic ballet that toured Britain and Europe. For the latter half of the 1880s Fred, and sometimes Fredrick, formed part of a troupe that usually included Will Evans, Ted Towers (1842–1918), Ada Luxmore and her sister Carrie Newcombe.

In the second half of 1889 Fred appeared with his father for one final, triumphant engagement. As members of Charles Lauri Junior's troupe in the musical extravaganza *Le Prince Soleil* (*The Sun Prince*) at the Châtelet they attracted not only Parisians, but an audience from around the world. In the year of the Paris Exposition Universelle their visual humor, with an added dash of nonsense language, had a cosmopolitan appeal:

> Such a motley audience I have never seen in a Paris theatre. All the nations of the earth sent representatives to it, but the French peasant ruled the roost. I was seated in the front row of the stalls, between a Dutch and a Spanish family, and behind me were six hardy natives of Brittany, who took me into their confidence early in the evening, informing me that they had paid 54f. for their places, and during the entr'acte offering me a share of the cold roasted potatoes with which they regaled themselves, the first time I had seen potatoes in a theatre, where they are to be preferred as neighbours to garlic sausages. The Spaniards laughed heartily at the *battatas*, sucking huge oranges themselves, and the Dutch ladies munched sweetmeats with Batavian composure. In the boxes and first circle were dusky Orientals, noble Britons in correct evening dress, spectacled Germans, swarthy Portuguese, white-turbaned Arabs, a couple of young Egyptian Princes, but, outnumbering all other spectators, French peasants in muslin caps and characteristic blue blouses. The picture was curious, and a better public than this heterogeneous assembly

Hengler's Circus water pantomime, from *The Graphic* January 10, 1891. Slapstick comedy elements in Victorian stage entertainments anticipated many elements of early film comedy (author's collection).

could scarcely be imagined. So hearty was the hilarity that naturally it proved contagious, and although close to the band I could hardly hear its music at times, so loud and general was the laughter ringing through the house.

Despite the diversity of its audience the comedy was crude and racist:

> This gaiety is altogether due to the English pantomimists. I have already stated that they carry the piece on their backs, but their antiques have become more developed since the first night, and now monopolise all the amusing elements. From the moment when in the *pasada* near Lisbon, the nimble Hottentots, Quouaquoua, with his wife, Anaquoua, and their Chinese, Tzigane, and Highland companions give a taste of their quality, they are the favourites of the house. The scene is now one of the best in which the Lauri-Lauris have yet shown themselves here. They fight and scramble for the bed, jump through walls and doors, and chase each other on the roof with surprising agility.[5]

The Lauri troupe was a tight-knit group of performers who shared a long communal history. Charles Lauri Junior (1860–1903) had appeared with Frederick Evans since childhood. Francesca Zanfretta (1861–1952) married Lauri in 1882, subsequently featuring alongside him in many pantomimes and other spectacular productions. John D'Auban (1842–1922)—famous as a choreographer for many Gaiety Theatre burlesques and Gilbert and Sullivan operettas—had been married for 18 years to his dance partner Emma D'Auban (1842–1910). The only newcomer to the group was Fred's 21-year-old wife Jane Adelaide, known to all as Minnie.

CHAPTER 2

Minnie Jee, the Fair Equestrian

FRED'S AND JOE'S MOTHER was a courageous and resilient woman. The boys might have been forgiven for thinking that she was indestructible as they listened to her stories of being rescued from a raging fire, surviving the wreck of the Channel steamer *Victoria* and escaping from a band of marauding "Red Indians." While performing as an equestrian bareback rider and an acrobat she had suffered many accidents, but always recovered quickly. "On the stage," according to *The Era* "she was irresistible."[1] In his old age, Joe noted that she "was well loved in [her] profession."[2] But a larger-than-life personality offers no protection against every-day ailments. The short illness and sudden death of such a dynamic mother at the early age of 34, followed by the immediate re-marriage of their father to a dancer many years his junior, must have been gravely disturbing for the boys.

Fred Evans Junior had married Jane Adelaide Jee at St. Paul's, Westminster Bridge Road, Southwark, on March 8, 1888. The church was situated in music-hall and circus heartland, the area's transpontine location close to the center of London making it a popular base for performers of all descriptions and degrees. With its terraces of crowded lodging houses, busy street markets and inviting public houses the district exuded a village atmosphere, but one in which the villagers came, went, and then came back again with confusing frequency. It was a pulsating and precarious world whose inhabitants lived constantly on the edge of success or failure. Close to St. Paul's were such famous entertainment venues as the "Old Vic"; the Canterbury, South London Palace and Gatti's music halls; and the Surrey Theatre. At the northern end of Westminster Bridge Road, on a site close to St. Thomas's Hospital, stood Sanger's National Amphitheater, previously celebrated as Astley's Amphitheater. As the national home of equestrian drama since the 1770s Astley's-cum-Sanger's would have held a special significance for Minnie. Her maternal grandfather, Burnell Runnells (1826–1908), had been one of America's greatest bareback riders and her own father, Joseph Jee (1841–1890), was similarly famous in Europe for his horse-riding skills.

If the extended Evans family came to permeate music hall and pantomime, the Jees were even more widely and deeply imbedded in the circus world. Minnie was born in Edinburgh in 1868 where her parents were appearing with Quaglieni's Grand Italian Cirque. Three years later, in 1871, she traveled with her family to the United States as part of a circus managed by an American uncle, Egbert C. Howes (1831–1892). For the next seven years, the Jees settled into a regime of touring with American circuses in the summer and appearing in music halls, usually in New York, during the winter months. Minnie made her theatrical debut at the age of three, appearing at Tony Pastor's Music Hall in a hat-spinning and musical performance with her four-year-old brother Joe. For a time, she performed in a "swinging aerial and perch act," but it was inevitable that she would quickly follow in her grandfather's and father's hoof-prints. She became a "fair equestrian," leaping through hoops of flame and balancing on the back of a galloping horse.

Images of daring tricks performed on the backs of dashing steeds, whether witnessed live or viewed in the form of paintings and illustrations, captivated the Victorian public. Male equestrians were popularly portrayed as heroic and imperious figures, costumed as Ancient Greeks, Cossacks, or Native Americans. Female riders, even those as young as Minnie, were highly sexualized and were normally seen wearing tights and short skirts. Minnie's professional association with horses seems to have ended at an early age, following a tragic fire in Derby in 1879. On returning from the United States the previous year her father had become equestrian director of Charlie Keith's Circus, only to suffer the crushing blow of seeing the entire stud of horses burned to death when the wooden theater and stables went up in flames.

An Addition to the Jee Family

Minnie had no less than ten brothers and sisters, most of whom became entertainers.[3] Often the siblings married other performers, with their children also becoming members of "The Profession." While retaining close links with the circus, the Jees increasingly sought their living on the music-hall stage, and it was presumably there that Minnie met Fred. Early in the 1880s she had played with her brothers Fred and Joe in a musical act "The Three G's" followed later in the decade by appearances with her father and Uncle Harry as "The Musical Jees." A common theme, later to be carried over into her performances with her future husband, was the ability to produce music from unlikely objects.

Following their marriage Minnie joined Fred in the Towers and Evans combination touring Europe. It does not seem to have been a happy arrangement for, after a tetchy exchange of announcements in the theatrical newspaper *The Era* in December 1888, Minnie and Fred reported that they had left the troupe and were to appear in the pantomime *Robinson Crusoe* at Sanger's Amphitheater. Since taking over the theater 17 years earlier "Lord" George Sanger had used its large stage and arena to present spectacular entertainments, water shows and giant panoramas. In keeping with Astley's hundred-year history of equestrian performance Sanger used many animals in his productions, combining them with actors and clowns to create an exciting fusion of circus and drama. The self-styled "Lord" came to feature extensively in the life of the younger members of the Jee and Evans family. The son of a peep-show exhibitor, Sanger (1825–1911) had traveled the United Kingdom with several side-shows before launching his first circus in 1857. By the 1880s his entertainment empire included a circus that toured Europe for eight months of the year; an English Circus; a winter show at London's Agricultural Hall; and the famous Westminster Bridge Road establishment. Sanger's various shows were the closest thing to an academy of clowning that Britain possessed. At various times, four of Minnie's brothers were apprenticed to the "Lord," their extended training encompassing many aspects of circus work.

Pregnancy may have prevented Minnie from appearing in the 1888–9 production of *Robinson Crusoe* at Sanger's, but her family were well represented. Her husband played the shipwrecked mariner's monkey, while two of her brothers featured as a cat and a goat. A "Mr. Jee" who had the challenging task of representing a parrot may have been another brother or her father. The arrival of the latest member of the Jee-Evans clan, yet another Frederick William Evans, took place at 81 York Road, Southwark. It was a street well known to performers for at one end was an area miserably referred to as "Poverty Corner." At the junction with Waterloo Road, the York Hotel and its immediate surroundings provided a meeting place for out of work artists looking for engagements and variety agents seeking to secure cut price acts. Like his contemporary, Charles Chaplin, Fred's birth was announced in the entertainment periodical *The Era*: "On Monday 25 February, wife of Fred Evans Jr. (Miss Minnie Jee), of a fine boy. Both doing well."[4]

The presence of her first child did not keep Minnie off the stage for long. Days after baby Fred's baptism at St. Paul's Church on March 20, 1889, mother and father were appearing at the Washington Music Hall, South London, billed as "Musical Grotesques."[5] Another engagement at the end of March and in early April took place at the Royal Victoria Hall, Waterloo Road, then being run by Emma Cons as a temperance music hall and educational institution. At the end of April Fred and Minnie traveled to Paris where they started to rehearse for *Le Prince Soleil*.

The Florador Quartette

Over the next two years Minnie, Fred and their young son saw little of England. After two months of rehearsals, *Le Prince Soleil* opened at the Théâtre du Châtelet on July 11, 1889. It was a colossal production in four acts and 22 scenes, with hundreds of performers, exotic animals, and a series of spectacular effects which often anticipated cinema. One slightly dazed reviewer commented that "all these wonders, and many more, are presented one after the other with the rapidity of kaleidoscopic pictures."[6] Following on from the theater's famous dramatization of Jules Verne's *Around the World in 80 Days*, *Le Prince Soleil* also adopted an excursive storyline, illustrating the numerous sensational and comic events that took place on a journey from Stockholm to Tokyo. Full use was made of the height of the proscenium, with immense panoramic backdrops and the graceful aerial gyrations of Miss Aenea, one of Lauri's troupe. Beneath the stage an array of traps and machinery provided countless opportunities for astonishing and mystifying the audience. Although too young to appreciate the wonders of the Châtelet, Fred would soon become familiar with the various technical means by which theaters enhanced their productions. From his earliest years he would have found little, or no magic in stage illusion.

Fred's brother, Joe, was born at 54 rue d'Orsel, Paris, at 11 o'clock on the morning of May 21, 1891. The Evans' new child was given the middle name "Burnell" in honor of his celebrated equestrian great grandfather, Burnell Runnells. The following month Minnie and Fred returned to England, announcing that in future they and Fred and Bert Jee, were to be known as the "Jee Evans Musical Quartette." With a plethora of Jees and Evans appearing on the music-hall stage, the troupe quickly decided to distinguish themselves from similar sounding acts by changing their billing to "The Florador Quartette." It was a name of uncertain origin under which they were to achieve undoubted fame.

The Florador Quartette, photograph reproduced in *The Encore*, February 1, 1895. Back: Fred "Pimple" Evans' mother, Minnie. Front, left to right: father Fred, and uncles Albert and Seth (courtesy of Tony Barker).

Infant Fred's earliest theatrical memory was one of abject terror. Interviewed in 1915 he claimed that his debut had been made at the age of two years nine months in the pantomime *Little Bo Peep*: "the sheep used for the pantomime came running towards me in a dimly-lit passage one night, and I thought they were lions, and screamed my hardest. I shall never forget that night, baby as I was."[7] His recollections of childhood appear to have been confused, for at Christmas 1891–2 the family troupe were appearing at the Grand Theatre, Plymouth, not in *Bo Peep* but *Aladdin*. Fred stated elsewhere that his first appearance *had* been at the Grand Theatre, Plymouth, so Bo Peep's sheep either rampaged on another occasion or made a guest appearance in an otherwise orientally themed production. Following their Plymouth pantomime, the Floradors appeared at the Surrey Theatre in *Puss in Boots* at Christmas 1892–3 and in sketches at the Palace Theatre of Varieties, London, in 1892–3 and 1893–4.

Although his earliest appearances probably seemed like a game, three-year-old Fred was soon confronted with the harsh realities of stage life when he was placed as an apprentice with Sanger's Circus. It is possible that he was not completely abandoned to the care of strangers for his uncles Seth and Albert Jee were with Sanger for seven and nine years, respectively. In later life Fred was philosophical about his childhood experiences:

> During my boyhood's days I learnt bareback riding, trapeze work, wire walking, clowning and acrobatics and had to fill in the day by grooming horses and other stable work fixing and taking down tents, etc. In those days one had to learn every branch of circus life and I believe it was this early training that gave me a fair start when I grew up and accounts for what success has come my way.[8]

While Fred learned his craft in the circus, the Floradors became a major act on the music-hall circuits. Initially the performances drew heavily on their circus and pantomime backgrounds, with visual effects and slapstick antics taking precedence over plots. Such an approach was well suited to a burgeoning music-hall industry that was intent on distancing itself from its tavern entertainment origins. To maximize profits auditoriums were being constructed on a larger scale, with non-controversial acts increasingly preferred to attract new, middle-class audiences. In April 1892, *The Era* reported on their performance at the Middlesex Music Hall in Drury Lane:

> The Florador Musical Quartette consists of three gentlemen and a lady. The former are distinguished by a very grotesque make-up which enhances the effect of their amusing antiques as acrobatic clowns. They and the young lady also display musical ability as manipulators of bells and various other instruments.[9]

One of their most famous sketches, *The Musical Garden*, relied largely on novelty for its success. Joe remembered: "the scene was in a lovely old world garden and everything was played upon—two garden seats were xylophones, the apple trees were bells on branches, the water cans and rake were musical instruments."[10]

Increasingly, a degree of narrative was introduced into their sketches.

Written, in 1896, as a vehicle for Minnie, *Naughty Nin*, was set in the Rev. John
Daw's drawing room at "Lundberry." Following the departure of the vicar (played
by Fred Evans) his children ran amok, staging a mock drama and putting on their
own circus show. As the leader of the revels Minnie was so energetic that she once
fell across the gas footlights, briefly setting herself alight. Other musical playlets included a fire-station comedy called *Off to the Fire* and a military burlesque
Company "B." Many of the sketches, like the productions of the Hanlon Lees and
Fred Evans Senior, contained a chase element that was to become a stable ingredient of silent film comedy. *The Era* noted of their appearance in the pantomime
Robinson Crusoe at the Princess's Theatre, Glasgow, that "the Floradors introduce
their four wheel cab act, trap chase and arial flight...."[11]

"The Boy Wonder, or the Star of the Circus" (Aldine "O'er
Land and Sea Library," c. 1890). Paper cover of a juvenile
novelette providing an idealized view of a young bareback rider (author's collection).

By October 1894
Fred and Bert Jee had
been replaced in the act
by their younger brothers
Seth and Albert. In turn
Seth left to become part
of the double act Beatty
and Bentley in 1896 and
Albert followed to pur-
sue his own career in
1899. After a short period
working with non-family
members Fred and Min-
nie decided that their
sons were experienced
enough to become fully
fledged Floradors. Christmas 1898/9 saw both Fred
and Joe appearing with
their parents at the Grand
Theatre, Birmingham, in
Robinson Crusoe, subti-
tled *Funny Friday's Fool-
ish Freaks and Famous
Flighty Family*. In 1902
the boys were singled out
for praise in a review of
the Florador's new sketch.
The Professor, at Collins'
Music Hall, Islington:
"a most elaborate scene

lends itself to the many eccentric tricks of the quartet, which includes a couple of smart youngsters—one of whom is already a smart acrobat [Fred], and the other a promising step dancer [Joe]."[12]

A unique glimpse into the childhood of the two boys was provided in a letter sent by 75-year-old Marius Leopold to Joe Evans in 1965. As a member of the celebrated Leopold troupe of acrobats he had lived close to the Evans during the late 1890s. He recalled that Fred was a high-spirited lad:

> Do you remember the tricks you and Fred and us The Original Leopold's used to get up to when you and your father and mother lived just across from us in Cranmer Rd Brixton. Your Mum and Dad were dear friends of my Mother and Dad Ted Leopold and my Sisters Jessie Mamie Katie also your Uncle Will Evans and the Egberts and Daisy Dormer. In those days we were Right at the Top in the Music Hall and Circus Business. Do you recall us all one day Fred got a Crocodile Skin out of your Father's props and we put a boy called Tregley [?] in it and led him up the Brixton Rd. until a Cop spied us. I don't remember what happened after that but I guess your dad and mine paid a fine. 30/-. Also do you remember when we—you and Fred, Myself and my Brothers Albert and Walter went up to Epsom Derby Day Buskin [*sic*]. We did some acrobatic tricks and you joined in and Fred did the Bottling. I think he had a barrel organ. We got a lot of money. That same night we were working the Alhambra Leicester Square. What a contrast. We kept it very dark. If both our fathers had found out we would have got a proper walloping. Fred and my Brother Walter were a couple of terrors.[13]

A boyhood friend whose early life paralleled Fred's to an uncanny extent was the future film star Charles Chaplin. Born a short distance apart and within a few days of each other, both Fred and Charlie had performer parents who were well-known in "The Profession." The names "Fred Evans" and "Charles Chaplin" had featured on theater bills for some years before the boys inherited them. They were each to lose a parent under tragic circumstances at an early age and both had the lonely experience of touring as a child entertainer separated from their family. Joe's taped reminiscences contain an account of visiting Charlie in about 1904, soon after he had achieved his first theatrical success in a stage version of Sherlock Holmes. Charlie's role as Billy the page boy at 221B Baker Street was essentially comic, but he harbored loftier ambitions. Striding around his lodgings, Charlie played both hero and villain of the play, his portrayal of Holmes and Moriarty prompting Fred to declare "You're going to be a great dramatic actor."

A Hard Act to Follow

Fred and Joe were surrounded by skillful and talented performers, but there can have been few with greater all-round abilities than their mother. In 1893 Minnie was pictured on the front page of the *Music Hall and Theatre Review*, with an accompanying feature listing her many accomplishments:

> As an instrumentalist she possesses undoubted gifts, being able to play the piano, mandolin, guitar, xylophone, and dulcimer, and also possesses a fine voice. She is a talented

linguist, and during her artistic life she has appeared as an equestrienne, a trapeze performer, lady clown, female jester, vocalist and instrumentalist. She takes an active interest in all things convivial and likely to advance the profession, and has the honour of being elected an honorary "J."[14]

Fred Evans Senior gave a glowing account of his family to a reporter from *The Encore* in September 1902. His children were "exceptionally clever ... very good boys in every way" and, despite the many near disasters in her life, his wife was "alive and well and as hearty as ever."[15] Just a few days later Minnie became ill while performing in *The Professor* at the New Empire, Swansea. She was treated for dropsy, jaundice, and other complications, but lapsed into unconsciousness. The remaining Floradors moved on to appear at the Newport Empire with Fred fitting in journeys to visit his wife in hospital. She died on Monday, September 19, and was buried at Danygraig Cemetery, Swansea, the following Sunday. Three horse-drawn carriages followed the hearse, with Minnie's coffin heaped with floral tributes from her many friends and relatives in the variety profession.

In keeping with show business tradition, the Floradors' show was not interrupted by Minnie's death. Her place was immediately taken by "Beattie" Anthony (Maud Beatrice Anthony, 1882–1952), a young singer and dancer who had previously appeared with the "Nine Rosebuds" and the "Eight Eldorado Girls."[16] In October 1902 Beattie changed her stage name to Beattie Trixie and on the 21st of the same month she became Mrs. Fred Evans, the ceremony taking place at St. Paul's church where Minnie and Fred had married fourteen years earlier. Having been present at his mother's funeral a few weeks earlier, young Fred was now a witness to his father's remarriage.

CHAPTER 3

Uncle Will,
the Musical Eccentric

TWO "LOAFERS" WERE EJECTED from Southampton Docks with an obscene admonition to leave immediately and not to return. The police who guarded the gates had seen their sort many times before—shifty-eyed young men who, like their stories, did not wash. They were clearly a couple of cheeky tearaways, impudent cockneys whose ragged asses richly deserved the sudden and forceful application of a hob-nailed boot. Joe recalled Fred and himself receiving a cuff around the ears, a painful and humiliating experience for a young adult. In his later description of the episode Joe downplayed their ages. Perhaps, abandoned by their father and stepmother, it felt that way.

The haste with which Fred and Beattie married suggests that a relationship had existed prior to Minnie's death. Certainly, Fred's comment made to an American reporter that he had bought Beattie songs and dresses to follow a career as a solo artist seems to indicate that he knew her before she became part of the troupe. Within a short time, Fred and Joe were joined by a half-sister, Beatrice Frederica, born in Swansea in October 1903. Contrary to Joe's later version of events, the Floradors continued to perform together for some time, appearing in at least two traveling pantomimes. A review of *Little Bo-Peep* at the Queen's Theatre, Swindon, in January 1903 noted:

> Mr. F. Florador, jun., appears as Simon, Dame Durden's son, and provides much mirth by his very funny get-up in "balloon" costume, which leads to the production of many amusing situations. Another very clever youth, full of promise, is Master Joey Florador, who is got up as a fancy dog, and indulges in all sorts of antics.[1]

In the following year's *Robinson Crusoe* both boys were cast as animals, the *Falkirk Herald* commenting: "Master F. Florador as a particularly agile dog, and Master Joey Evans Florador as an equally active monkey."[2] Despite the continuing popularity of the family troupe, Fred and Beattie began to make other plans. Shortly after the death of their daughter from pneumonia, aged less than a year, they launched themselves as "Trick and Trixie, Song and Dance Duettists." With the birth of a second child, Francis, in February 1906, the brothers became excluded not only from the family act but from the family. With a chilling degree of understatement Fred Evans told the American interviewer that, following his marriage, he "gave up his troupe."[3]

Fred was packed off to his great-uncle Harry Jee to join a long-running sketch called *The Musical Smithy*. As blacksmiths, the performers produced melodious pieces of music from such normally discordant objects as anvils and iron-working tools. Being the younger of the brothers Joe was allocated to a juvenile troupe, "The New York Nippers." The action of the troupe's main sketch, *Bedtime*, took place in a school dormitory, a setting not dissimilar to the crowded lodging-house bedrooms that Joe and the other nippers occupied while touring. The limited contact that Fred and Joe had with their father disappeared completely in July 1908 when he and Beattie left for the United States. Trick and Trixie had been spotted in England by the manager and entrepreneur Michael Bennett Leavitt, who promptly booked them for his famous Rentz-Santley Company touring American vaudeville theaters. Although Fred and Joe's half-brother, Francis, was also left with relatives, he was reunited with his parents after only five months. At the age of 2 years and 9 months he was entrusted to the captain of the "Saint Paul" proving himself to be a "good sailor" before he arrived in New York shortly before Christmas 1908.[4]

A Walk to Southampton

Unfortunately, Joe had become a "New York Nipper" at a relatively mature age, and he was soon dropped from the troupe. In sympathy, Fred downed his melodious tools in *The Musical Smithy*, suggesting that they should make their way to America in search of their father. In late 1908 or 1909 Fred and Joe set off to walk to Southampton in the hope of finding an U.S. bound ship. Joe left his own account of the long and ultimately futile march:

> Fred and I set out for Southampton, if you remember, to try to get taken on as cabin boys or help in the galley and work our passage to the U.S. When we started out we had exactly 2/- and 4d. I had 4d. and Fred had a two shilling piece. Well after we had walked 7 or 8 miles we bought 4d. worth of bread and cheese. In those days bread was 2d. and cheese 6d. a pound, so we got a good amount of bread and cheese for 4d. I used my 4d. on this and the next day after another advance of 8 or 9 miles, Fred broke into his two bob piece and bought some more bread and cheese and got a shilling and 8 pennies in change. The next day we spent the 8d. and the day following we were about halfway to Southampton and Fred went into a shop and asked for 4d, worth of bread and cheese and put down the shilling and the woman threw it back and said "don't come those tricks with me" and when Fred examined the shilling he found it was a dud—a foreign coin, probably a nickel, so we now were broke—the last shop ... and given that dud coin in change, whether by accident or design we shall never know.
> That night we came across a small workman's hut at the side of the road. Being about 9 p.m. no one was there, the hut was empty, so we went in and lay down on a form each and went to sleep intending to get out very early in the morning before the workmen arrived. But we overslept and the next thing we knew we were being dragged out into the road by

an irate workman shouting "there's a couple of tramps in here" but when they saw us in the daylight they said "why, they are only kids." They questioned us as to who we were and what we were doing sleeping in the hut. When we told them our story they were very kind and after lighting the brazier fire they cooked bacon and fried some eggs and gave us a meal and some hot tea. When we left they all gave us some money which came to about two or three shillings.[5]

In the absence of any collaborating evidence Joe's account, written fifty years later, stands without qualification. Why two young adults should have embarked on such a challenging expedition with so little preparation is difficult to comprehend. It was as if life had imitated allegory, with Joe sensing a deeper significance in their unworldly setting forth and in the manifestations of good and evil that they encountered on their way. Unlike Christian in *The Pilgrim's Progress* and Dorothy in *The Wizard of Oz* the boys did not finally arrive at their desired destination. Although they failed to reach New York City, their immediate problems were solved by a remarkable intervention. After they had been turned away from several ships and escorted from the docks by the police, they threw themselves onto the mercy of a "Pro's Landlady" named Mrs. Nicholls. Recognizing the boys from previous visits, she provided them with meals and the free use of a small spare room. When Mrs. Nichols informed them that the famous comedienne Marie Kendall was appearing at the local Palace of Varieties Fred and Joe paid a visit to the stage door. Like their kind-hearted landlady, Marie knew Fred and Joe and, more significantly, was well acquainted with their families. Marie was a formidable and forceful woman. Phoning uncles Will Evans and Seth and Albert Jee, she demanded "that they must do something." Then she presented the brothers with £5 collected from performers appearing at the theater and dispatched them back to London on a distinctly non-allegorical train.

The Scent of Lavender

On their return Fred and Joe made straight for the familiar streets of Kennington. With their lodgings established they set off for the semi-rural district of Mitcham in Surrey where Uncle Will Evans had recently bought a large house with extensive grounds. Of all the Jees and Evans who had become well-known in the music-hall profession, Will was the most successful. When his brother Fred and sister-in-law Minnie left the Towers Evans combination in 1888, he had remained with Ted Towers and Ada Luxmore. From 1890 Ada and Will appeared in their own act "Evans and Luxmore—Musical Grotesques" and in 1893 the pair were married (Ada had previously been described as "Mrs. Edward Towers," although the title appears to have been purely honorary). Following Ada's untimely death from cancer in 1897, Will married Evelyn Poole, a young singer whose family were to become intricately linked to the Evans.

In a varied music-hall career Will started as an acrobat and musician, graduated to comic singing and finally featured in a series of highly popular slapstick comedy sketches. For his earlier performances as "The Musical Eccentric" he wore clownish make-up consisting of a close-fitting black wig; emphatic, dark strokes above the eyes; vivid red nose; and a pale area around the mouth that gave him a monkey-like appearance. A common feature in all Will's variety manifestations was a strident and, allegedly, infectious laugh, used to reinforce his jokes and "funny business." This prolonged simulation of merriment, preserved on many vintage recordings, was not

Will Evans (1866–1931) (courtesy of Tony Barker).

achieved without a degree of personal discomfort. When defending his decision to pull out of his music-hall contracts in 1914 Will explained "when you come to your fifth turn and you have to shriek with laughter it's a strain on the general constitution."[6] After 40 years entertaining the public Will did not find the music hall environment conducive to health or well-being:

> When you are jumping about for twenty minutes you naturally get hot, and you have to have a rub down and a change before you go out into the air. After the fifth turn I was absolutely exhausted. You have to give the public the same for the fifth turn, and I don't know sometimes how I did it. I was in a state of collapse at the finish.[7]

Passive smoking was also a major problem, particularly in suburban halls where Will found the fumes from countless pipes, cigars and cigarettes to be of a distinctly inferior quality: "People don't smoke good tobacco. The twopenny gallery people don't."

The pinnacle of Will's career occurred in 1911 when he was engaged for the pantomime *Hop o' My Thumb* at the Theatre Royal, Drury Lane. Like his father before him, Will became a fixture in the theater's famous pantomimes, appearing in both male and female roles in ten consecutive productions. His portrayal of such characters as Pompos in *The Sleeping Beauty* (1912–13) and two subsequent sequels, and Flossie in *The Babes in the Wood* (1918–1919) exposed him to a wider and more diverse public than he encountered in even the highest class of music-halls.

Unlike many of his contemporaries Will was not content to remain in the variety profession until fitness, fame and fortune passed him by. Before temporarily quitting the music-hall stage to appear in musical comedy in 1914, he had become involved with new entertainment technologies and property development. Several early screen appearances were followed by a period when he ran his own film company. From 1903 he became one of the early gramophone industry's most prolific recording artists, often making multiple versions of the same title. After purchasing a holiday bungalow at Shoreham by Sea, in East Sussex, he acquired four more similar properties for their rental potential. His move to "Greylands," Sutton Lane, Mitcham, was ostensibly for health reasons, but along with the powerful scent of the lavender fields that flourished in the area, Will was attracted by a 20-acre field that lay at the back of the house. When his plans to establish a golf and racquets club failed to materialize, he turned the pastures into a small farm.

Despite his growing aversion to music halls, Will suggested that Fred and Joe should form their own act. He agreed that when they came up with a viable idea, he would provide financial backing and help them secure bookings. What eventually provided the inspiration for their new routine was not drawn from theatrical antecedents, but from the rapidly expanding world of cinema. Fred and Joe would have seen many films presented as part of the music-hall entertainments in which they appeared, witnessing the transition from extremely short actuality shots and simple staged scenes to longer fiction movies with relatively complex plots. As American and even English-produced "Westerns" exercised such a powerful hold over the movie-going public, Fred and Joe decided to become stage cowboys, enlisting a friend, Bob Morgan, to join them in an all singing and dancing turn. Joe gave an account of the act's short existence:

> Well, we called ourselves "U.S.A. Boys" and we were a great success. But an Agent got hold of us and exploited us only giving £4 for the act and kept promising better money later. Well, in those days we could all live for 16/- each board and lodgings so we were just able to keep ourselves on the £4 and what was over paid our expenses. But when we got to Rotherhithe Hippodrome this agent had booked, we found we were bottom of the bill, in big letters. So we all thought, ah! Now we will get a good salary, but at the end of the week we still only got £4, so we refused any further contacts and went to see Uncle Will.[8]

The failure of the "U.S.A. Boys" proved to be only a temporary set-back, for Fred and Joe were immediately able to join Uncle Will's act as auxiliary performers. Will's most enduring productions were knockabout scenes occurring in a domestic setting, but others were broad burlesques of contemporary subjects. It is likely that Fred and Joe appeared in *Chanticleer*, a 1910 send-up of Edmund Rostand's play in which actor's portrayed farmyard animals. Joe reminisced:

Uncle kept us both on board and lodging and gave us 30/- each. As we had nothing to pay in rent and food we were well off—as 30/- was then comparable to £5 or £6 today [1965]. We worked for a year or so with Uncle Will, sometimes working "turns" which meant doing two or three Music Halls in a night. I remember one week we did "Building a Chicken House" at the Tivoli in the Strand and "Harnessing a Horse" at the Canterbury and "The Gambler" at the London Music Hall, Shoreditch.[9]

In 1910 Joe left one uncle to join two others. After their departure from the Floradors, Seth and Albert Jee had formed part of several variety acts before they became established as "The Brothers Egbert" in 1901. Their first routine, "The Happy Dustmen," was to prove so successful that it ran virtually unchanged throughout the first decade of the century. The comedy, which greatly amused King Edward VII on a visit to the Alhambra in 1902, was simple, but was backed up by extraordinary acrobatic skills. Opening with "Bill" and "Walter" entering a backyard, the sketch continued with them sifting through the contents of a dustbin and separating "the dead cats from other articles more fitted for further use."[10] Tiring of such demanding work, Walter decided to play a joke on his workmate by hiding in an old sack. The highlight of the act was supplied by Bill's growing horror as the sack performed a series of curious gyrations.

The Brothers Egbert in their famous "Happy Dustmen" music-hall act (author's collection).

In shriller and shriller tones, Bill called for the assistance of his apparently missing partner. Rich with the banality of all great catchphrases, his anguished cry was famously "Hurry up, Walter."

The world of variety rolled on, but things were about to change. Sometime in late 1909 or early 1910 a significant meeting took place at Uncle Will's country residence. His nephew Fred was introduced to two businessmen, well-known in Mitcham and the wider world as producers of motion pictures.

CHAPTER 4

An American Interlude

FRED AND BEATTIE ARRIVED in the United States on August 1, 1908. They were accompanied on the crossing by several other performers, including a beautiful singer and dancer named Julia Lascelles. In private life "Miss Lascelles" was Beattie's older sister, Julia Anne Anthony. Beattie had similarly striking looks and it was probably an appreciation of her physical appearance, rather than enthusiasm for the musical antics of Trick and Trixie, that persuaded Leavitt to engage the act for America. In joining the Rentz-Santley troupe Fred and Beattie were launching themselves into a world far different from their own familiar working environment. Sex had always been present in British music-hall performance but purveyed in a random fashion by saucy comediennes or uninhibited dancers. In American Burlesque, sexually orientated material and the display of female physique were systematically exploited. Once Beattie stepped out in her brightly colored tights, Fred's theatrical talents rapidly faded into the background.

The Rentz-Santley company occupied a historic position in American entertainment history, having created the institution which became known as "Burlesque." During the 1870s Michael Leavitt (1843–1935) had devised a new form of show by pairing "Madame Rentz's Female Minstrels" (a blackface combination) with "Mabel Santley's London Burlesque Troupe." "Madame Rentz" was an invention calculated to invest a degree of European *chic*, but Mabel Santley was very much alive and, lucratively, kicking. In March 1879, her dancing of the "Can Can" resulted in a conviction for misdemeanor and indecent exposure, the $250 fine representing an extremely sound investment in the company's future. Mabel's offense was largely that of flouting conventional morality by the action of lifting her skirts in public, for her legs, seen in stage costume of fringed doublet and tights, had received far greater exposure in live performances and many thousands of magazine illustrations, cigarette cards and cabinet photographs. Writing in 1879 a hard-headed editor of the *Sacramento Bee* admonished a section of his readership for bemoaning the deterioration of theatrical values: "If they [the public] bring more cash to see Mabel Santley than Edwin Booth, why then the leg show has to make its appearance."[1]

While evolving into a completely different form of entertainment, American Burlesque retained a suggestion of its London inspiration. With the Rentz-Santley company, as it became known, Leavitt established a formula that consisted of songs and dances by an ensemble of chorus girls; specialty acts provided in an "olio" section; and a final musical playlet which often burlesqued contemporary events or theatrical productions. When *Variety* reviewed the show at the Murray Hill Theatre in October 1909 the format had been modernized but retained many of the earlier elements:

> In the closing of the first part the sixteen girls perform a "Marathon" in tights, running to the rear of the house from the stage, down an aisle to the orchestra and returning. It made a lively finish. At the opening of the burlesque the girls are dressed as English soldiers, and from the costumes they must have been in the Soudan at the time, but they looked good, better than any bunch of choristers so far this season.
>
> Matt Woodward wrote the pieces. The first is "Gay Monte Carlo," with a toy roulette wheel as the only gambling prop in the exterior setting. The burlesque is "Teddy in the Jungle" with about the same stuff that everyone has on the theme....
>
> There is also a table scene between Moore and Beattie Evans, the leading woman. In this there is a suggestion of spice, nicely taken care of, and made funny instead of smutty by Moore [Snitz Moore was the company's lead comedian].
>
> Miss Evans is the woman of Trick and Trixie. The man of that act is also a principal. In the opener Miss Evans is allotted three characters on the program. By the time she reaches the third and sings the "Japanese Maid" song, the principal woman has not changed her costumes, originally built for the "Anna Held" role. Miss Evans has a fairly pleasing voice. Almost any voice in burlesque is pleasing which doesn't displease.[2]

Beattie was singled out for further praise in the same issue:

> Beattie Evans of the "Rentz Santley" show is a pretty girl and dresses with very good taste. The first costume is a blue satin made princess with which is worn a white hat with not over abundant willow plumes. In red tights Miss Evans looks very well.

In contrast, the performance of Trick and Trixie received only grudging approval:

> The musical number of Trick and Trixie could be shortened. It is a foreign turn, and seems to have been improved during the opening, where it moves along quite well, but goes to pieces as usual when the "Continental" comedy and grotesqueness are brought in.[3]

Three months later, in Washington, Beattie was again favorably reviewed although the joint appearance of Trick and Trixie failed to receive a mention:

> With a bevy of pretty girls and many new and catchy songs, the Rentz-Santley company played to a full house at the Gayety yesterday. The opening comedy act, entitled "Gay Monte Carlo," proved to be one of the most pleasing burlesques seen here for some time. Miss Beattie Evans, as "Anna Held, her own sweet self" proved to be a favorite and was encored several times. She tended her songs "Are You Out for a Ramble" and "Carry Marry Harry" in a manner that made her instantly popular.[4]

Joe is Summoned

Back in England in the early summer of 1910, Joe received an unexpected letter. Recollecting the event to Denis Gifford he explained that Beattie had fallen ill, and his father needed his support in America. Immigration records show that

Beattie was well enough to travel to the United Kingdom with Francis and Julia, arriving on June 26, 1910, and returning from Southampton on July 9. While in England, on what she later described as a "vacation," she encountered R.J. Cuninghame, a famous guide and big game hunter who had led Theodore Roosevelt's much-publicized safari to British East Africa in 1909. Perhaps Dick told Beattie the story of how he had saved the former president's life by shooting a rampaging bull elephant. In turn she may have described the hilarity provoked by the Rentz-Santley company when they satirized the expedition in "Teddy in the Jungle." Whatever occurred between the couple, Cuninghame was sufficiently amused to present Beattie with a rare trophy, the skin of an enormous African leopard. She had it made into a coat and wore it on stage when she returned to the United States.

Following his humiliation at the gates of Southampton docks just a few months earlier, Joe suddenly found a ticket for the States waiting for him at Cunard's London offices. He arrived in New York on May 15, 1910, and, for about a year, he toured the United States and Canada, apparently appearing with Fred while Beattie pursued her own career. During June, Fred and Joe were appearing on a vaudeville program presented at the Atlantic Garden, at the New Jersey coastal resort of Atlantic City. They were joined briefly by Beattie at the same venue when she returned from her UK trip at the end of July.[5]

After Beattie left the Rentz-Santley company she continued to tour the Columbia Circuit (also known as the "Eastern Wheel"), a federation of around forty theaters that stretched from New York to Kansas City. Although their shows still relied on showgirls and risqué comedy, the theaters in the circuit, many of which were newly built, offered the most "respectable" form of burlesque. The Columbia circuit was pre-eminent during the 1900s but collapsed in the 1920s years in the face (probably not the right word) of competition from the nude shows and blue humor provided by "dirty" establishments.

In September 1910 Beattie made her debut with another top burlesque company, the "Robie Knickerbockers." Two suggestively titled playlets were presented, *Reno, or Racing for a Divorce* and *The Love Kiss*, with Beattie playing the leading roles of "Miss Delmonico" and "Mrs. Armstrong." By now photographs of her were beginning to appear in the popular press. Although her strong features and curvaceous build were very much in line with Edwardian popular taste, American reviewers, often more critical than their British counterparts, also praised her singing, dancing, and acting abilities. When Fred Evans made it into the shows, he was only mentioned as an "also appeared."

The following year Beattie participated in something new in burlesque—something new. Joining the "The Ginger Girls" company in September 1911 she played in a large-scale, musical mini melodrama entitled *The Futurity Winner*. With a storyline dealing with dubious doings on the Sheepshead Racecourse at Coney Island, the piece mixed several theatrical genres. A cast of 60 actors, comedians, singers, and dancers were involved, and a team of technicians created a treadmill and a moving panoramic backcloth to create the illusion of a race between three thoroughbred horses. Despite its dramatic theme of a wicked trainer, disgraced jockey and long-lost son, *The Futurity Winner* was embellished with many burlesque set-pieces. *Variety* wrote:

> Eighteen chorus girls are nicely dressed, with more than average comeliness distributed among them. They were best in action in the "Jockey" number, led by Beattie Evans. Each girl had an opportunity to dance individually. This should work into a big hit after awhile. Miss Evans looked real fetching in tights here, and did the leading prettily, as she did in one number just before. Evans is buried in the first part, under a married woman's role, though playing that well.[6]

The Futurity Winner was a runaway success and Beattie remained a "Ginger Girl" until the close of 1912. At Christmas 1912-1913 she and Fred were back together, performing in a burlesque company called "The Merry-Go-Rounders."

Joe is Dismissed

Although providing his father with valuable support, Joe was under no illusions regarding a permanent relocation with Fred and Beattie. Father was a "hard case," he confided to Denis. Hard as nails it seems for when Joe's services were no longer required, he was unceremoniously dumped. Deserted in Brooklyn, Joe was left to fend for himself and to find his own way home.

Fortunately, he received support from an American friend of Beattie's sister. James Calhoun Sheldon was a wealthy lawyer who had served three terms on the New York State assembly. He and Julia eventually married in 1915, a partnership which lasted until his death at the age of 59 in 1931. Sheldon loaned Joe $50 to help establish him as a solo turn on the vaudeville stage. He should have saved his money. After securing an engagement at a music hall in Columbus Circle, New York, Joe performed George Robey's 1908 music-hall success "Archibald, Certainly Not!" With a verse relating how a hen-pecked husband prepared to dive into the sea to save an attractive young woman, the song was replete with Robey's "honest vulgarity":

> Archibald, certainly not!
> Desist at once disrobing on the spot.
> You may show your pluck and save Miss Hewitt
> But if you have to strip to do it,
> Archibald, certainly not!

The New York audience was unimpressed by Joe's performance, and it conveyed its dissatisfaction in a vociferous and vigorous fashion. With hopes of an American career comprehensively dashed, Joe headed for the docks where he enlisted for menial duties on a cattle boat bound for the United Kingdom. On landing at the Port of Tilbury in Essex he went directly to London. Rather than returning to the familiar territories of Brixton or Kennington he spent his first night in a doss-shouse in neighboring Southwark. From comments made to Denis it appears that he was embarrassed about the American fiasco and did not want to admit to his brother, and presumably other variety performers, that he had been a "flop." Next day he stepped out of his cheap lodgings in the Borough, wearing the sharp silver-grey suit presented to him by James Sheldon and nursing three gold sovereigns which represented his entire fortune. It was time to start rebuilding his career.

CHAPTER 5

Living Pictures

HAVING FEATURED ON the same music-hall bills as the earliest "animated pic-ture" shows, Fred had had been in a prime position to monitor the rapid prog-ress of cinema. Like his friend Charles Chaplin he would also have known variety performers who had appeared in films, and he could not have failed to notice the recent proliferation of cinemas. Perhaps he even considered that a career in films might offer a quicker route to celebrity status than the overcrowded and ultra-competitive variety profession.

When he made his first film in 1910 the industry was still in the process of formation. Purpose-built "Picture Palaces" had started to provide a new form of entertainment but one which drew heavily on show business precedents. The first films exhibited in the United Kingdom had not been projected but were made in the United States for Thomas Edison's Kinetoscope peepshow. Follow-ing the device's London launch in 1894, Robert Paul, an electrical engineer, and Birt Acres, a photographer, broke Edison's film production monopoly by devis-ing their own camera and making the earliest British movies. Their partnership foundered in 1895 (before films were first projected in 1896) but both men went on to become leading exponents of the new medium. During the late 1890s and early 1900s Paul was the leading producer of fiction films, ably assisted by George Howard Cricks and John Howard Martin. After leaving Paul's employment Cricks and Martin ran their own company, recruiting many stage comedians including twenty-year-old Fred Evans.

Projected films were first exhibited as "turns" at variety theaters, in traveling fairground shows and at exhibitions in public halls. By the early 1900s extended seasons of films at large venues were being presented in the UK, a new form of entertainment typified by Sydney Carter's "New Century Pictures" at the 2,000 seat St. George's Hall, Bradford. In the United States, Edison's attachment to the single-viewer Kinetoscope meant that he did not give his first exhibition of pro-jected films until April 1896, by which time similar shows had been running in Europe for some time. Making up for the delayed start, the Edison Manufactur-ing Company soon became a major producer, shooting many news subjects in the late 1890s and, in 1901, building a roof-top studio for filming fiction subjects. They were soon joined by powerful competitors; the American Mutoscope and

Biograph Company from 1896, Vitagraph from 1899, and later by Lubin, Essany and Selig. Similarly, Pathé-Frère and Gaumont began to dominate the European market during the late 1890s and early 1900s, introducing mass production techniques and establishing an extensive distribution system. In comparison British companies failed to expand their activities, leading to a situation where most of the films exhibited in the United Kingdom were made in other countries.

Until the early 1900s films were usually restricted to extremely short actuality subjects and acted scenes (mainly of a comic nature) whose brevity reduced plot development to a basic demonstration of cause and effect. Although some primitive attempts were made to synchronize gramophone recordings with motion picture subjects, proper sound films were many years in the future. Following isolated examples of multiple-scene narrative productions such as *Cedrillon/Cinderella* (Méliès, 1899), *Attack on a Chinese Mission* (Charles Williamson, 1900) and *L'Histore d'un Crime/The Story of a Crime* (Gaumont, 1900), a proliferation of longer fiction films occurred in the watershed year 1903. Amongst several extended British productions were the Sheffield Photo Company's 9-scene crime drama *A Daring Daylight Burglary* and Cecil Hepworth's 16-scene version of the children's classic *Alice in Wonderland*. In the United States Edwin S. Porter directed a nail-biting rescue in *The Life of an American Fireman* and a proto–Western, *The Great Train Robbery*. The British arm of Gaumont made a specialty of fast-paced, longer films with *Welshed—A Derby Day Incident*, *The Pickpocket—A Chase Through London* and *The Runaway Match*, all directed by the music-hall and pantomime performer Alf Collins.

The ground was prepared for the cinema not only by the public's growing familiarity with films, but by the increasing length of productions. Up until the early 1900s films had lasted, at the most, just a few minutes. As such they were easily combined to provide a varied compilation in a 10–15-minute slot on a music-hall bill. But, by the mid–1900s with fiction films beginning to extend to a whole reel (1,000 feet lasting for about 15 minutes), a selection of subjects occupied a far greater amount of time than the variety theater allowed. In an establishment exclusively dedicated to films, a series of balanced programs could be run throughout the day.

The Cinema Boom

To accommodate longer productions and more intensive exhibition practices, buildings devoted entirely to showing films began to appear in the United States from the summer of 1905. One of the first, opening in Pittsburgh in June of that year, was called "The Nickelodeon," a title that was soon applied to many other storefront theaters in large metropolitan centers such as New York, Philadelphia, Cleveland, New Orleans, and Chicago. By December 1906, *Billboard*

Close to Cricks and Martin's Mitcham studios, the Broadway Cinematograph Palace, Tooting, was typical of the first great wave of cinema building. The Broadway offered its 800-member audience a "Half a Guinea Entertainment for 3d., 6d. and 1s." (*Daily Mirror*, April 27, 1912). The sender of the postcard has written "The picture palace on the left is one of the best and most comfortable in London. You would not hardly know Mitcham Rd now, all new buildings, you know" (author's collection).

listed 313 nickelodeons in 35 states. The United Kingdom's first cinema was probably the Daily Bioscope which opened in Bishopsgate, London, on May 23, 1906, with a program of fiction and news films. Children's matinees took place on Saturday afternoons and the admission charges of 2d and 4d were pitched low enough to make the establishment widely accessible (cheapest seats at good quality London music halls were set at 6d or 1s). From anecdotal evidence, it appears that around 50 percent of early cinema audiences consisted of children. At the Picture Palace, Tooting, in 1909 it was alleged that "boys and girls sat on windows smoking, and if people standing in front of them were not alert they got the ash down their necks."[1]

Potential audiences were sometimes confused and even annoyed by the earliest cinemas. Edward Laurillard, the head of the Electric Theatres Ltd. circuit, opened his first cinema in a converted shop at Shepherd's Bush, West London, in 1907. Six years later, his recollection of the event was reported by *The Cinema News and Property Gazette*:

> When they first opened, people stood outside and stares, wondering what this new kind of "penny-peepshow" was. After a few days a few boys and girls came in, but chiefly to giggle. He [Laurillard] said to Mr Sedger [his business partner Horace Sedger], "This is no good; we had better give up and go home," until one Saturday night the business went up with a jump. They took 6s. 1¼d. On his asking the cashier how the farthing came there, she

replied that a little girl offered it for admission, saying that she hadn't any more, and she (the cashier) did not like to turn away money. They commenced to lose heart, but kept pegging away, the takings gradually creeping up, until they were making £50 to £60 per week profit.... They afterwards went to Walworth Road, and took over a chapel, much to the disgust of some of the residents, who called them Americans. Walworth was at once a success. Marble Arch followed, and immediately they initiated the West-End Cinema Theatre. Others quickly followed, and grew like plants in a hot house.[2]

The number of cinemas operated by Electric Theatres Ltd. reflected the extraordinary growth of the wider industry. By 1909 the chain had increased to 12 and by 1910 to 23. In 1910 the company employed 168 staff, which by 1911 had grown to 333.

Fred's First Films

With increasing demands for motion pictures, studios began to be established on the outskirts of London, where access to the amenities of the capital was enhanced by the possibilities for alfresco filming. Britain's leading producer during the period, Cecil Hepworth, based himself in the tranquil village of Walton on Thames, while Gaumont constructed an open-air studio on the gentle slopes of Dog Kennel Hill, East Dulwich. On leaving his post as Robert Paul's sales manager George Cricks opened a studio at Mitcham with Henry Martin Sharp in 1904 and, when Sharp left in 1908, he was joined by John Martin, formerly supervisor of Paul's darkroom facilities. The Cricks and Martin studio, with its Lion's Head logo, was located at Ravensbury Lodge on farmland alongside Mitcham railway station, London Road. Amongst its most popular films were a series of short comedies which made full use of the area's ponds, streams, and other hazardous features. Some years later Fred remembered his early days with the firm:

> I started as a super at 6 and 6d a day—but I kept my eyes open and determined to reach better things. To this end I did everything I could to gain knowledge. In addition to acting I helped to develop and cut the films, assisting with the sets, and painting the scenery, while if there happened to be anything out of the way to done, such as falling into a river, or taking a crack over the head—all for the sake of art, you know—why, everybody would say: "Oh Fred'll do it!"[3]

The studio and its surroundings were rustically ramshackle. Twenty-five acres of grounds and a stretch of the River Wandle provided the natural background for many movies. A small cottage was pressed into service as offices and dressing rooms, while greenhouses were converted into darkrooms for developing and printing purposes. A former orangery was used as a store, accommodating a selection of scenery which largely consisted of painted "flats" used as backgrounds. Filming was conducted on two open air stages in an orchard, the only protection against inclement weather being canvas awnings. Amused by the naivety of the finished product compared to the height of 1947 "realism," Leslie

Wood wrote in *The Miracle of the Movies* that "a high wind would snatch the coverings from a dying child's cradle and the sun might burst into beaming motes in a coal mine, but no one seemed to mind."[4]

Production was relentless. Plots were frequently prepared one day and filmed the next, with a trade showing at Wardour Street, Soho, taking place on the third. Extensive files were kept which listed available performers, recording their professional experience and special skills such as the ability to ride a horse, drive a car, or, crucially, to swim. Helpings of bread and cheese was supplied for lunch, with an allowance of beer to fortify the cast in their exertions. Amongst Fred's fellow performers were many local people and the variety comedians Bob Reed, Johnny Butt, Ernie Westo and a famous pantomime clown Harry Paulo. Two actors, A.E. Coleby and Dave Aylott, were also the company's principal directors.

The Thrill of the Chase

Although screen comedies had moved on from the single or two shot productions of the 1890s, films remained of limited duration. Restricted by time and by the uncritical acceptance of audiences, plots were usually variations on a few hackneyed themes. With fiction films present from the very birth of cinema the requirement to create a concise narrative based around movement led naturally to the chase movie. The earliest British fiction film *The Arrest of a Pickpocket* made by Paul and Acres in April 1895 shows a police constable pursuing a lawbreaker from right to left, then back again into the captive grasp of a helpful sailor. During the early 1900s Alf Collins drew heavily on the traditions of the Harlequinade and comic sketch in a series of chase movies which were influential in both Britain and the United States. Collins, who may well have known Fred and Joe, frequently pitted the underdog against the forces of law and order. In true pantomime tradition, his film policemen were constantly outwitted and outrun. As the years passed chases became longer and more complex, drawing in a wider range of pursuers and a greater variety of locations through which the action unfolded. But despite the chase being established as the principal form of film comedy, its constant repetition resulted in an unimaginative and stereotyped product.

Dandies, Dudes and Duckings

Fred's first traceable film *The Last of the Dandy* was a 450-foot production released on April 8, 1910.[5] Although it no longer survives, a detailed description was provided by the *Kinematograph and Lantern News*:

A young fellow strolling along, supremely conscious of his own attractions, and possessed of a bad memory, sees a lady drop her handkerchief, and hastens to restore it. Rewarded with a smile, he replies with gallant remarks, and ends by making an appointment for the evening. Further along he is so clumsy as to collide with another young lady. Another appointment is made, in forgetfulness of the first. Taking off his hat in a parting salute. The dandy falls into an inconveniently-placed dustbin, while a boy runs off with his hat, which he drops when pursued by the hero. The latter has the hat returned to him by yet another pretty maid, to whom he again appoints a time and place, and a similar procedure is followed with a barmaid, a nursemaid whom he encounters in the park, and the waitress at his favourite restaurant. In the evening, the lady killer approaches a young lady seated on the appointed spot, but he has barely greeted her when the others appear in rapid succession, and angry reproaches are poured upon him, followed by more vigorous action, the unfortunate fellow at last being chased by the angry crowd of aggrieved ladies, who run him down at last on the banks of a river and hurl him into the water.[6]

It was the simplest of plots, but the familiarity of its title added humor to the production. Often *what* films were called was their most distinctive feature, with jokey references to contemporary fashions or events being employed to attract audiences. Since Clyde Fitch's elegantly mannered play about the Count D'Orsay, *The Last of the Dandies*, had been presented by Herbert Beerbohm Tree in 1901, the phrase had quickly passed into popular usage. Fancy dress competitions were flooded with "Last of the Dandies"; a racehorse ran under the name; and music-hall comedian George Robey fed off the production with a "number" whose humor would not have been out of place in a Cricks and Martin production:

Me, Clarence, the Last of the Dandies, the society lion. I sometimes wish I were a mere mortal. These daily functions are becoming a bally nuisance. Here's tomorrow's programme: Bath at 8, breakfast at 9, ride in Rotten-row 10, interview by the "Rotten Review" 11, dog-fight at 12, a reception at 3, and then I have to find time to wash the children and clean the windows.[7]

A Punishing Routine

Dave Aylott recorded his vivid, though sometimes faltering, memories of the period in *From Flicker Alley to Wardour Street*, an unpublished biography from 1949:

Mitcham in those days was a very pretty place, but there was a very slummy patch where the rent-collector was greeted with abuse and sometimes a shower of something more solid. It was a terrible district. The houses were in a deplorable condition. Hardly any of them had cupboard doors or bannister rails, which were used as fuel.

I wanted a crowd of tough women for one picture, and went to this district to recruit some. What a reception! I thought at first they were going to lynch me, but when they found out I was from Cricks and Martin and wanted some of them for a film they volunteered in a body. I only wanted about ten, and picked out the ones I wanted and told them to be at the studio at nine the next morning. But in the morning there were about thirty hovering around the gates, all saying they had been fixed, and as I had taken no names and was not certain who I had picked, I agreed to take the lot, in order to prevent them from declaring war and wrecking the place, as they were quite capable of doing.

What a riot they were, and they did not need much direction. I had only to tell them what I wanted and they did it, and when it came to the final scene, where they had to mob Fred Evans, who had swindled them, they almost tore him to pieces. Coleby and I came to the rescue. The scene was really a "ripping" success. His clothes were practically in ribbons, and his nose was bleeding where some dame, carried away in the excitement, had punched him. I think Fred got ten shillings extra as a "salve."

Fred's talents as a comedian—and his ability to soak up punishment—were quickly realized and he was put on a weekly salary of £2. In an early role, he exploited the comic potential of the cane, a prop later employed to such humorous effect by Charles Chaplin. *A Costly Gift* (August 1910) opened with "Dandy Jones" receiving the present of a 2s 6d cane in from his "latest flame Miss Brown."[8] Soon, swinging his new stick, he set of to meet his generous lady friend. The by-play with the cane was an obvious piece of innuendo that was easily recognizable to music-hall audiences, particularly those who had recently heard Fred Earle sing:

> It's the little wigger-wagger in my hand
> That makes me such a dandy,
> It's not my strut, nor my face tut-tut,
> Not the brand new cady like a pimple on my nut.
> Maidies and ladies I meet when I'm walking in the Strand,
> They admire my togs and I keep away the dogs
> With my little wigger-wagger in my hand.

Overenthusiastic use of his own "little wigger-wagger" resulted in Jones being forced to make a series of repayments as he broke a display case in a flower shop, smashed a hanging lamp and upended a couple of waiters. Costs spiraled even further when he was forced to repurchase the stick after it had been stolen by a tramp and sold to a second-hand dealer. In a final act of gallantry, the dandy attempted to rescue Miss Brown's hat which had been blown into a pond. Over extension of the "costly gift" resulted in a sudden but not unexpected immersion.

Topicality

The fast-moving schedule followed by Cricks and Martin provided opportunities for topicality of content. When Home Secretary Winston Churchill delivered a speech on the need for prison reform, Aylott and Coleby were quick to respond with a vision of what such changes might involve. Writing of *Prison Reform* (October 1910). Aylott recalled:

The convicts were seated in the prison hall facing the stage. In front of them at various intervals were very attractive wardresses who had replaced the warders. On the stage was a collection of Black-Faced Minstrels, headed by Fred Percy who had his own sketch company with a sketch based on "Uncle Tom's Cabin." There was also Johnny Butt, Bob Read,

Fred Evans, and several other really funny comedians. They put on a real good show. The wardresses were supposed to keep perfectly straight faces, especially as they were facing the camera, but really it was a very difficult job in view of the remarks from the audience of convicts, who were mainly recruited from the district at five shillings a time. The climax came when I, as the prison governor, came on to sing "Oh, dry those tears." It was quite impossible for the girls to keep straight faces, and instead of drying those tears, their eyes were streaming as the scene finished in an uproar.[9]

Later, Fred's abilities were further rewarded when he received £5 for providing the script of an 800-foot-long film *Prescribed by the Doctor* (November 1910). Once again, he played a dude character involved in a series of comic episodes:

A very week jointed swell young man consults his doctor about his health, and is told that all he wants is vigorous exercise and plenty of it. He leaves with the firm resolve to become a vigorous participant in manly sports of all kinds and in the next scene is seen taking "Dose 1"—on the cricket field, where his antics at the wicket puzzle the fielders and will convulse audiences. Beginning by facing the wicket, he proceeds by knocking down the wicket keeper in attempting to slog the first ball, then falls on his own wicket and, refusing to accept the umpire's "out" is carried off the field by force. A brief trial of fishing cures him of any love for that sport. A Japanese ju jitsu professor soon convinces him that his *forte* does not lie in that direction, and, as soon as his bruises are a little less painful, we find him in the role of a Territorial officer. His attempts to mount are amongst the funniest things in the film. At first he faces the horse's tail, and on being reversed sets off at such a pace that his men have to follow at the double. On the way he collides with a coster's cart, and what the coster does cures him of his love of soldiering. At golf he hits his opponent oftener than the ball, and a cycling excursion ends in a ducking in the river. He is no more fortunate at shooting, peppering a countryman, who has to be compensated, but all his other troubles sink to nothing compared to those which await him when he dons boxing gloves. Even the teacher's small boy gets the best of him, and he is finally knocked through the window into the street, where, encountering his doctor, he assaults him angrily, both eventually being taken away by the police.[10]

Unlike his later films in which he became famous for instigating subversive and anti-social behavior, Fred's standard role for Cricks and Martin was that of a victim. Because of his willingness to perform uncomfortable, even dangerous, stunts he was often depicted being beaten and physically abused. In the extant *How Puny Peter Became Strong* (June 1911) Fred plays a weakling whose strength is insufficient for him to lift a blacksmith's hammer, carry a lady's bag or to shift the needle on a test-your-strength machine—until he eats a loaf of "Standard Bread." In an early scene Fred, as Puny Peter, becomes the butt of cruel fun as a group of workmen, one played by Coleby, striking him vigorously about the backside.

A few years later Fred proudly revealed the injuries he had sustained "all for the sake of art":

Look at this leg…. More like a switchback, isn't it? And every scar tells a story. *That* was the pedal of a bike; *that* was a kick from a horse; *that* was a super's hob-nail boot; *that* was a fall from—Oh yes, the other leg's just as pretty. I have over a hundred scars. Yes, they all made someone laugh.[11]

Charlie Smiler

In the early part of 1911 Cricks and Martin invented a new character in which Fred was to make his first major, though uncredited, success. Dave Aylott remembered:

> I had written a comic called "Charlie Smiler joins the Scouts" casting Fred as Charlie Smiler, a gawky loutish looking lad who joins the scouts and gets into all sorts of comedy situations. I well remember the finale of the film. "Charlie Smiler" has borrowed penny-farthing cycle to make a quick getaway from trouble. He loses control of the machine and after careering around country roads at a terrific speed runs into a high fence and disappears over the top. We had intended to show him coming over the fence into a pond at another spot and, and had not taken too much notice of what was on the other side of this particular fence. Consequently, when we heard yells coming from the other side we rushed to look over, and there was Fred seated in a three-parts dry pool of very stagnant water, simply covered with mud and filth, so instead of moving on to the other pond location, we took a shot of Fred climbing back onto the road and slinking off. He was in a deplorable condition, and we had to get a hose to wash off the mud and filth before he could change.

Graphic memories indeed, and richly evocative of Fred's role in the early days of filmmaking. They were misplaced, however, and related to *Charlie Smiler Competes in a Cycle Race* (July 1911). Aylott was correct in placing *Charlie Smiler Joins the Boy Scouts* (May 1911) at the beginning of the series, but the surviving film held by the British Film Institute shows Fred on foot and not on wheels. Carried away by the romance of scouting, Charlie enlists and sets out on a hike, only to resign after falling foul of puddles, ponds, patches of stinging nettles, pugnacious farmers, and gun-toting sportsmen. Fred may have left the boy scouts, but the boy scouts did not leave Fred. They were to reappear in many of his later productions.

Other Charlie Smiler films were *Charlie Smiler Takes Brain Food* (June 1911) in which Charlie's repeated attempts to carry eggs home resulted in messy failure; the extant *Charlie Smiler is Robbed* (August 1911) featuring an unsuccessful chase to recover a stolen watch and chain; and *Charlie Smiler is Stage Struck* (November 1911) where a series of acrobatic stunts resulted in disastrous consequences. Three surviving scenes from *Charlie Smiler Takes Up Ju-Jitsu* (August 1911) show strong similarities with Fred Karno's music-hall sketch *Mumming Birds* (1909) and its subsequent recreation on screen by Charles Chaplin in *A Night at the Show* (1915). Smiler's chaotic intervention in a fairground wresting exhibition echoes Karno's drunken dude (a role played by both Billie Ritchie and Charlie Chaplin) taking on "The Terrible Turk," while the unexpected involvement of a member of the audience in a staged performance is reminiscent of Chaplin's film character "Mr. Pest."

There was no consistency in the spelling of Charlie Smiler's name in publicity and film reviews, with "Charley Smiler" frequently being employed even by Cricks and Martin. Similarly, his appearance altered drastically during the series.

Aylott's "gawky loutish looking lad" (confirmed by the BFI copy) became, according to *The Bioscope*, "a fashionable man about town."[12] Joe remembered his outfit as being "Max Linder style: a silk hat, frock coat, fancy waistcoat, spats, a little moustache and a walking stick,"[13] a costume seen in the two other surviving "Smiler" films. In whatever guise he was presented the character continued to be popular with filmgoers into 1912. Fred, however, no longer played him. Towards the end of 1911 Cricks and Martin refused to increase his salary to £5 a week[14] causing him to transfer his newly acquired talents to another company. In private life, other skills needed to be developed. Fred had become a family man.

CHAPTER 6

The Pooles as Partners

A surviving program for the South London Palace of Varieties, dated January 17, 1896, is typical of the schedules of entertainments produced on a weekly basis for the convenience of Victorian and Edwardian audiences. It is dog-eared now and splitting along its folds, but still decorative with cover images depicting dancers, musical instruments and the overlapping masks of tragedy and comedy. Inside are adverts for local pubs and such useful products as embrocation and whiskey. A precisely timed list of "turns" promises a mirth-provoking evening. But the presence of "Violet and Evelyn Poole, Variety Duettists" early on the bill may have evinced sympathy more than merriment. Just a few weeks earlier they had lost their mother, Ellen Poole, a hard-working and charismatic woman whose thirteen-year tenancy of the South London Palace had ended in bankruptcy. Ellen's premature death, attributed largely to being forced to give up the theater, was one of a series of tragedies which afflicted the Pooles over a period of many years. It was a protracted ordeal in which they were often supported by two other show-business families, the Evans and the Hughes (known professionally as the Alberts). By his early twenties Fred had formed a relationship with another of Ellen's daughters which, although unconventional, was to last a lifetime.

John Joshua Poole ran the South London Palace, at first in partnership and subsequently alone, from 1873 until 1882. Following his death his widow took over the lease and continued to control the fortunes of what was one of London's premier variety theaters. It was an extremely unusual move for a woman to undertake music-hall management, particularly as she had been left almost £16,000 and had the responsibility for six young children aged between one and nine years. But she and her family had the theater in their blood. Situated at 92 London Road, in the Elephant and Castle district of South London, the theater had a 4,000-seat capacity and a large stage which was famously employed for presenting ballets and spectacular sketches. All the leading performers of the time (including Charlie Chaplin's mother and father) appeared at the hall and several of Ellen's children had featured on its bills. Despite her commitment to the theater Ellen ran into financial difficulties and was forced to transfer its ownership to a large and powerful syndicate. Her death at the age of 49 left the family totally unprovided for, causing the profession to set up a testimonial fund to assist the younger Pooles.

Ellen's death in November 1895 was quickly followed by those of her son, Josh Poole, aged 22, in December 1895; her stepson, Sivori Poole, aged 44, in March 1896; and her youngest daughter Clara, described as the "Tiny Tim of the Family," aged 14, in January 1897. Following this grim chain of events, two happy occasions brought some relief to the family. On December 2, 1897, at the church of St. John the Evangelist, Drury Lane, Evelyn married Fred's uncle Will Evans. Four months later, on April 11, 1898, Violet, wed Edmund Miller Hughes (1858–1949) at a ceremony at St. Giles Parish Church, Camberwell. The best man was Edmund's father, James John Hughes, who as "Frank Albert" was the founder of the famous Alberts and Edmunds comedy troupe and one of the most successful music-hall agents in the country. Bridesmaids were Edmund's sister Blanche Albert and Violet's 17-year-old sister Lily May Poole. Another of Ellen's children, Harry Poole, became Will Evans' manager and subsequently his brother-in-law when he married Maud Evans (Fred's aunt) in 1904. The Pooles were not yet free from their collective ordeal, for Harry died suddenly at the age of 25 in 1905.

Lily Poole

On April 2, 1900, Lily May Poole married a 26-year-old stable and horse-drawn cab owner named Harry Viscount Hughes. Although his profession seemed only to have a peripheral connection to the variety theater, Harry had extremely close associations with the entertainment world, being another son of Frank Albert. While Lily May, like all the surviving Poole sisters, lived into old age, she did not grow old and grey alongside her husband. In fact, their own personal crisis occurred long before mid-life. Sometime during the 1900s Lily left her Kennington home, perhaps to stay with Maud or Violet. At the many social gatherings Lily must have been aware of young Fred Evans, an "aunt" and "nephew" relationship that was soon to take on an entirely different character. The April 1911 census records Fred as "Head of Household," living with Maud Poole and Lily Huges [*sic*] at 41 Ashen Road in the London suburb of Wimbledon Park. It was an unremarkable road of Edwardian houses later celebrated in several works by the illustrator artist Raymond Briggs who had spent his childhood there. The location of Fred's home, convenient for the Cricks and Martin studio at nearby Mitcham, helped to shelter Lily from the unwelcome attention she might have received in her native Lambeth. She and Fred were expecting their first child. When Harry Hughes died in 1946, Lily May Hughes was named as his widow, inheriting £250. By this time, she had lived with Fred for many years and had given birth to Jose Lilian on September 21, 1911, to Betty May in 1913 and to Peggy Adelaide in 1915.

Precision Film Company

As Jose Lilian was about to make her debut, Joe made an unexpected come-back. After his return to England, he had spent time in Dover, appearing with a Pierrot troupe and playing in traditional melodramas at the Palace Theatre. Once the brothers were reunited, a new project soon materialized. Across town in Walthamstow, East London, the Precision Film Company had constructed a large glass-roofed studio which possessed some of the most up to date facilities in the country. Despite this studio, Precision do not appear to have been particularly active, their most significant production being a 1,500 feet production of the Victorian tear-jerking melodrama *East Lynne* (November 1910).

In quest of lighter material, a director working for the company, A.E. Radcliffe, recruited Fred and Joe to make comedies. Radcliffe was also involved in running cinemas and it is probable that he and Fred had met while he was managing the King's Hall Picture Palace, in Tooting High Street—the establishment where boys and girls sat smoking at the windows. By the time Fred and Joe started to work for Precision, Radcliffe managed the New King's Hall, situated on the busy "Baker's Arms" junction of the High Road, Leyton, in East London. Opened in March 1910, it was a 1,000-seat cinema, giving two shows an evening. Although Fred's reason for leaving Cricks and Martin was a dispute over money, the new financial arrangement with Precision was hardly an improvement. With a joint salary of £5. 10s. Fred and Joe were required to write and appear in films, recruit actors, paint scenery and act as ushers in the Leyton cinema.

The films that Fred and Joe made for Precision did not share a common Charlie Smiler–like character. *Fred's Police Force* (February 1912), in which a self-appointed PC became drunk and stole money and alcohol from a gambling den, was typical of the comic reversal found in Cricks and Martin's *Prison Reform* (1910) and in many of Fred's later films. Other productions were little more than animated jokes. In *Stop the Fight* (December 1911) a pacifist was subjected to a violent assault; in *Cowboy Mad* (February 1912) an over-enthusiastic youth emulated his comic-book heroes; and in *Fifty Years After* (May 1912) a man was arrested half a century after stealing a bicycle. By the spring or summer of 1912 Fred and Joe had decided to escape the hard labor of Precision by concentrating on their own filmmaking ambitions. Joe had developed a business plan which he floated to family members and several performer friends at a meeting held in a Buffaloes Hall, over a pub. As with many small film companies the set-up requirements were simple. Joe later explained:

> Film costs three-ha'pence a foot raw, that's for your taking, and a good comedy film shouldn't run to more than five hundred foot. Now you've got to make your positive, and that film costs you the same, so that's a thousand foot at three-ha'pence. Then there's the cost of your chemicals, which I forget now. Then there's your studio, the rental of a building which must contain a bit of ground at the back, and some flats which your carpenter can knock up very easily: some battens two-by-one, and some scenic canvas.[1]

CHAPTER 7

Ec-Ko and Co

A SIX-MINUTE SILENT FILM viewable on YouTube features the "Famous Kellinos" in their music-hall act *A Fete in Venice*. Released by Pathé in 1909, it is a remarkably complete record of a top Edwardian acrobatic troupe, showing a complicated sequence of gymnastic tricks performed before an ornate stage setting. The movie, rescued by the Scarlet Pimpernel of nitrate film John Huntley, had an indirect influence on the career of Fred Evans. A leading member of the troupe was soon to transfer his talents to the film industry and to help establish the company which launched "Pimple" on his comic career.

Having been a performer since his childhood in the 1870s, Will Kellino was becoming too old for such extended acrobatic routines. Comedy films, with their slapstick stunts and need for precise timing, provided an attractive alternative to stage-work. It was no surprise, therefore, that he was enthusiastic about Joe's plan to set up a new film company in collaboration with Seth Egbert. Ec-Ko was officially incorporated on July 26, 1912, with "Kellino" providing one of the capital letters and "Egbert" being represented by the other. The nine company directors were all listed as "actors": Peter Cannon (stage name Pete Bijou); J.H. Gislingham (Jim Kellino); W.H. Gislingham (Will Kellino); W. Baird Lang (Will Hanvaar); Arthur Carlton Philps (Carlton); Seth Egbert Jee (Seth Egbert); F.B. Jee (Fred Maple); G.T. Goodfellow; and Fred Evans. All were well-known in the variety profession. "Carlton, the Human Hairpin" was a highly paid clown magician; Will Hanvaar, a skillful comedy juggler who appeared in sketches with his partner Anna Lee; and Peter Cannon, represented one half of the song and sketch act "Bella and Bijou" (the other half being Will Kellino's wife, Blanche).

Although Kellino became the company's principal film director, Fred Evans' previous experience was reflected in a memorandum of agreement dated July 29, 1912, which specified that he would "become and continue to be the managing operator and producer for the said company in the said business for the term of five years."[1] Will remained with Ec-Ko throughout its existence, later directing many productions for what appears to have been a reincarnation of the company named Homeland Pictures. Fred, however, served a considerably shorter term of office. Despite £50 in shares, a five-year contract, and the inducement of a £3 weekly salary, he soon left to start his own company.

High Street, Teddington, Middlesex, in about 1910. The offices of the Ec-Ko Film Company were located at St. Alban's Yard, situated on the far side of the road, to the extreme left (author's collection).

Ec-Ko's offices were established in St. Alban's Yard, a narrow passage leading off a slightly less narrow suburban high street. In 1912 Teddington was a rapidly expanding Middlesex township which combined proximity to parklands and riverside with good train and tram links to central London. Although quaint Thames-side pubs and nearby market gardens created a semi-rural atmosphere, rows of regulation-built semi-detached houses spread out from the High Street. Conveniently close to Ec-Ko's premises was a 17th-century tavern, The Royal Oak, while, a little farther along the High Street, the unfinished bulk of St. Alban's church provided a passable imitation of Notre Dame cathedral. Music-hall performers were well acquainted with Teddington, having frequently visited its attractions individually or as members of organized professional excursions.

Professional Associations

The profession was naturally gregarious, with constantly changing variety "bills" resulting in the formation of close friendships and extended family networks. Such clannishness was dictated not only by familiarity, but by the need to create security in an often-precarious working (and sometimes not working) environment. Several organizations were created to bring about better employment conditions, legal and financial assistance and to support theatrical charities. Self-help was combined with recreation by several convivial societies that flourished during the 1890s and 1900s, one of the most extensive being the "J's" which provided an organized framework for Jee family activities. Travel, an intrinsic part of the performer's life, was similarly divided between work and play. In 1897 a proto-trade union, The Music Hall Artistes' Railway Association, campaigned to achieve reduced fares for its members traveling between engagements. When not on their way to fulfill theatrical commitments, performers often arranged large group outings to local beauty spots. During the summer months, the London public would be treated to a free show as trains, horse-drawn coaches and steam launches made their way to attractive locations such as Box Hill, Sunbury on Thames, Windsor, and Teddington Weir where picnics, partying and practical jokes were the order of the day.

The highlights of the "pro's" outings were events staged not only for personal amusement, but for the benefit of bystanders, journalists, and photographers. In June 1894, soon after the inauguration of the "J's" Fred and Minnie Evans and Seth Egbert were part of a large group who enjoyed a boozy river outing. A trade paper, *The Encore*, reported:

> Waterloo station. Nine. Cold and wet. Sundry arrivals. And departures. Of whiskey. Down throat. Quarter to ten. Left. Saloon carriages. Sixty souls. Mostly thirsty. During journey. Programmes distributed. New fashion. Reached Windsor. Eleven fifteen. Still wet. Had more wet. Met Leybourne. Not crabb-ed or Surley. See steam launch.... We thereupon started. Ate and drank. Particularly the latter. First halting place. Surley Hall Hotel. Albert Boissett. Fished in punt. With butterfly net. No salmon caught. Game with dogs. Shooting biscuits. Dog fell in water. Gallant rescue. By Sam Jones. He was presented. Amid ringing cheers. With handsome medal. Penny with a hole in it. For the brave act. Another launch past. How lovely! Then hie for Monkey Island. Stopped mid-stream. To be photoed. By Mr. Slater, of the Wiltons.... Still drinking and smoking. First one, then the other. The "J's" splendid band. Discoursed music. Much enjoyed. Arrived at woods. Turned homewards. Songs charmingly rendered. By Mrs. Bentley and Miss Hettie Monaghan. At one of locks. Gymnastic display. On iron bar. Big crowd gathered. At locks. To hear singing. Much curiosity displayed. Weather lovely. All in good spirits. Also more in cabin. Back to Monkey Island. "Man overboard." Another Gallant rescue.[2]

Films had been associated with the music hall since the variety performer "Viscount" Hinton had managed the very first public exhibition of Acres and Paul's Kinetoscope subjects in May 1895. Thereafter, most music-hall programs included a "Cinematograph," "Bioscope" or "Animatograph" display, showing news, actuality, and brief fictional scenes. Given their familiarity with moving pictures it was hardly surprising that many performers made screen appearances. Fred and Joe's uncle, Will Evans, provides examples of the various type of films in which an "artiste" might feature. In 1899 the Warwick Trading Company released *Interrupted Courtship*, *"Let 'Em All Come"* and *Will Evans—The Musical Eccentric*, one-minute extracts depicting the visual side of his stage act. In the same year A.D. Thomas was present at the Grand Order of Walter Rat's summer outing, filming

Will and several other music-hall stars fooling around at a picnic. Eight years later the vocal part of Will's performance was utilized when Gaumont produced three "Chronophone" films of the comedian synchronized with disc recordings.

A Music-Hall Co-Operative

Although members of the profession had frequently worked in motion pictures, Ec-Ko became the first film company to be entirely owned and operated by music-hall performers. Of the 14 shareholders listed on July 31, 1913, all, but one, were variety artists. In 1914 *The Bioscope* reported:

> We hear that Ec-Ko Film Company, Limited, are very busy producing their well-known "Nobby" Series (played by Sam T. Poluski) and other films to cope with the demand for this brand. They have enrolled the services of many famous music-hall stars, and even small parts are played by well-known artistes. Among some of the stars are the Brothers Egbert, the Kellinos, Bella (of Bella and Bijou), Goodfellow and Grigson, Hanvaar and Lee, the Maples, Fred Russell (of "Coster Joe" fame), Sam T. Poluski, Lottie Bellman, Phillipi ("Bumbles"), Winifred Ward, etc.[3]

Given the background of the filmmakers and the nature of the locations that were available it is not surprising that Ec-Ko comedies embodied the knockabout humor of music-hall outings. The extensive riverside grounds and outbuildings of Weir House in Broom Road were utilized, but comedies were just as often filmed in the streets of Teddington. Children and housewives stood on doorsteps and at garden gates to watch the chaotic chases and collisions, their interest resulting in them later appearing as background figures on screen. Sometimes, bystanders featured more prominently, either by invitation or through a misunderstanding of the nature of the unfolding events.

The Genesis of Pimple

As Cricks and Martin owned "Charlie Smiler," Fred was compelled to develop a fresh figure of fun for his Ec-Ko appearances. Unlike his predecessor the new creation was not christened from the extensive collection of names considered to possess amusing social connotations or onomatopoeic qualities. The obscure title "Pimple" was eventually chosen for the comic persona that Fred was to inhabit throughout his career in films—and sometime after that. Comedy film historian John Montgomery repeated (or invented) a piece of cinema mythology by suggesting that "Pimple" had been shouted out by children on first seeing the comedian's little cap. It is true that "pimple" was slang for the head and was also often applied to hats, but Fred claimed that he had been known as "Little Pimple" when appearing as a boy clown in the 1890s (from the 1900s and possibly earlier Herbert Sanger and subsequently James Freeman had appeared in Sanger's circuses as "Pimpo," an equestrian and acrobatic clown). It is just as likely that the name was dredged from the dark and unkind depths of Victorian humor. A pimple was an ugly blemish, a spot that marred beauty and spoiled symmetry. It was small, but not insignificant—a sign of potential disorder in a well-regulated system. At the beginning of his career, in 1891, George Robey sang of an attractive, well-dressed woman whose pimple provoked a series of embarrassing episodes:

> I courted once a pretty girl dressed in the smartest clothes,
> She'd only one defect which was a pimple on her nose.
> I thought I was her first love, but my pals said "Well, what cheek,
> Old Man, that girl of yours went out with three of us last week."
> They knew her by the pimple, simple pimple
> And some one's sure to know her, no matter where she goes.
> Said one, "You court her Sunday, some other cove on Monday!"
> They knew her by the pimple, the pimple on her nose.[4]

Another comedian had a far more legitimate claim to the name. In about 1890 the comedian Tom White (1858–1900) had formed a troupe of juvenile performers which created a prototype for such later acts as Casey's Circus and Will Hay's scholars. The most talented of the young singers, dancers and comedians was a child whose disproportionately large head resulted in the stage name "Pimple." Throughout the 1890s "Tom White's Arabs," featuring "Pimple," were a major music-hall turn, appearing in sketches set in a schoolroom, a police station, and a naval vessel. A large part of the humor was to see children burlesquing adult behavior, with "Pimple" excelling in imitations of performers like the dramatic and patriotic singer Charles Godfrey. After White's early death "Pimple" ran the act for several years, but the troupe disbanded shortly before Fred started his movie career. Fred and Joe would have been well-aware of "Pimple," having featured on the same bill on several occasions. An appearance at the Paragon Theatre of Varieties was advertised in the *East London Observer* in 1901:

> TOM WHITE'S ARABS
> Including the famous PIMPLE
>
> —
>
> WILL EVANS
>
> —
>
> THE FLORADORS[5]

The "famous Pimple" continued to appear as a solo act into the 1930s. Each year he remembered his old employer in an entry placed in *The Era's* "In Memoriam" section. The last appeared on August 16, 1933:

> In Loving Memory of Tom White (Founder of Famous Tom White's "Arabs"), who died Aug 17, 1900. Gone, but never forgotten. Thirty-third year of insertion by "Pimple" (the original) Tom White's "Arabs."

New Costume—Old Clothes

For his new character's costume Fred was largely indebted to a category of comedians generally referred to as "red-nosed." Generations of such music-hall

performers had balanced attraction and repulsion by dressing
in ill-fitting clothes and singing
songs which placed them in ridiculously inappropriate situations.
Although aiming to establish a
rapport with their audiences, they
presented themselves as society's
outcasts wearing a haphazard
selection of society's cast-offs.
Their material might place them
on the outer fringes of a working-
class environment where disregard
for authority and acts of criminality were commonplace, but
they also made disorderly excursions into high society, throwing events such as banquets, balls,
and exhibitions into a ridiculous
perspective.

The seedy costumes adopted
by both Charles Chaplin and Fred
Evans were similar because they
emerged from the same background. Legend has it that Charlie threw his tramp outfit together

The tradition of juvenile behavior portrayed by
adult performers. A song about a greedy schoolboy presented by music-hall star "The Great
Vance" in 1865 (author's collection).

from the random collection of garments available in the studio's property depart-
ment, but if this was the case his choice was informed by the stage outfits worn
by Dan Leno, T.E. Dunville and, above all, George Robey. Joe recollected Fred's
clothing as being: "a little cricket cap on his head, long hair down the sides of his
face, parted in the center, and a cricket blazer. I always remember the green and
yellow stripes, muffler round his neck, big baggy trousers, and big boots."[6]

Different roles meant that Pimple's costume sometimes varied, although
whether portraying a policeman, naval officer or fireman, the jacket was invariably worn very tight and the trousers inevitably loose.

As Fred's facial make-up was the major factor defining him as "Pimple," it
remained largely unchanged throughout his film career. Given his background it
is tempting to describe the unusual application of greasepaint as clown-like, but
the features were less obvious and, once again, owed more to music-hall antecedents. The greatest influence was clearly that of Uncle Will whose make-up consisted of a light area stretching over the lower part of his face, emphasized by
reddened lips, rosy cheeks and, of course, a crimson nose or "boko." Fred largely

Left: **A "Silly Billy" clown from about 1900.** *Right:* **Pimple in cap and blazer (both photographs author's collection).**

replicated the arrangement, but in place of Will's close-cut wig, wore his hair in long strands framing his painted features.

Adopting an extended historical perspective, Pimple's appearance would have marked him out as a traditional "fool," a comic character with license to behave inappropriately and to extract humor from normally sacrosanct areas of everyday life. An infantile predisposition to reckless acts and unrestrained cheekiness was indicated by the little cap that perched so precariously on his head. Such destabilizing comedy linked to such unstable costume, particularly head gear, had characterized "Tom Fools," "Lords of Misrule" and "Silly Billy" clowns for hundreds of years. In the 16th century the master of extempore humor and the dramatic "jig" Richard Tarlton uniformed himself in a rough suit and buttoned cap for his comic assaults on all ranks of Elizabethan society. During the 1860s a "Silly Billy" interviewed for Henry Mayhew's *London Labour and the London Poor* described his traditional costume:

> Short white trousers and shoes, with a strap round the ankle, long white pinafore with a frill round the neck, and red sleeves, and a boy's cap. We dress the head with hair behind the ears, and a dab of red on the nose and two patches of black over the eyebrows.

The performer explained that "a good Silly had to imitate all the ways of a little boy," which apparently included acts of violence, theft and flirting with female spectators. A satirical element was present in the "scenes" or sketches performed with a clown partner. Mayhew's "Silly Billy" mentioned skits on hypnotism, church sermons and temperance lectures. In an echo of Elizabethan jigs, the performer would enliven his show with a comic dance—"what we call a 'roley polely'" he added.[7]

Pimple's First Films

Appropriately, Pimple's cinema debut took the form of a frenetic dance. The Selsior company had recently devised a system of films synchronized to cinema orchestras by the presence of an on-screen conductor. Widely advertised as being performed by America's foremost Ragtime dancers, Joe Bissett and Enid Sellers, *The Turkey Trot* (September 1912) utilized the music of Irving Berlin's "Alexander's Ragtime Band" and "Everybody's Doing It."[8] In *Pimple Does the Turkey Trot* (November 1912) Fred became infected with rag-time mania by seeing a couple performing on a platform in a local park. In search of partners, he attempted to dance with a washer woman balancing a heavy load on her head, a worker carrying a tray and a shop man outside a crockery shop. All three reacted violently to his unwelcome attention, forcing him to engage a more compliant companion in the form of a tailor's dummy. Chased by the police for stealing the mannequin, the newly created Pimple was arrested and escorted away. But, as with many of his later comedies, Pimple shared a final joke with his cinema audience by slipping out of his jacket and watching the forces of law and order solemnly marching away with an empty garment.[9]

November 1912 also saw the release of *Pimple and the Snake*, the earliest Pimple comedy known to have survived. The film starts with Pimple inspecting a poster advertising a reward of £500 for the recapture of an escaped "African Black Snake." A sudden gust of wind blows a dark feather boa from a lady's shoulders and Pimple, judgment clouded by the enormity of the zoo's offer, thinks that the garment is the missing snake. A chase ensues with the wind providing the boa with its motive power. In his efforts to catch the supposed reptile, Pimple crashes into a butcher outside his shop, scrambles between the legs of a policeman, and interrupts the courtship of a soldier and nursemaid. Further collisions occur with a costermonger, an invalid in a wheelchair, a street musician, and an angler. As Pimple finally realizes his mistake, he is caught and mobbed by the people that he has, literally, upset.[10]

An argument with Seth Egbert's solicitor, who was acting as studio manager, resulted in Fred and Joe leaving Ec-Ko after only a few months. Of the small number of films that they made for the company in the summer and autumn of

1912 not all featured the new character. *The Taming of Big Ben* (October 1912) was a cautionary tale showing how a bully was taught a salutary lesson, while *Grand Harlequinade* (November 1912) gave Fred a chance to emulate his illustrious grandfather by playing "Clown." In *The Whistling Bet* (December 1912) Fred and Joe merely played Fred and Joe, rivals for the affections of a young woman named Nellie. Fred proved to be successful suitor until he entered a £5 wager which meant that he had to dance whenever Joe played a penny whistle. Such behavior did not endear him to Nellie—particularly when it resulted in them both falling out of a boat—and consequently she transferred her favors to Joe.

The final two Pimple comedies made for Ec-Ko were based on the less than reputable acquisition of money—a recurring theme in Fred's films. In *Pimple Gets a Quid* (January 1913) Pimple was the driver of a horse drawn cab who raced off when he realized that he had been overpaid—only to find that an elderly passenger remained on board. A circular chain of events was represented in *Pimple Wins a Bet* (January 1913) with Pimple initiating the sequence by betting a friend that he could not pick up a cork from the pavement, only to kick him on the backside and steal the sixpenny wager. The trick was repeated by the friend, and then by subsequent victims until Pimple himself was challenged to retrieve the cork. By now the bet had swollen to £5, which Pimple was able to pocket by the simple expedient of hiding a spiked board inside the seat of his trousers. It was one of the few occasions when a kick to the backside ended more favorably for Pimple than his assailant.

In November 1912, the Cosmopolitan Film Agency (who handled Ec-Ko films) announced that from January 1913 they would be releasing Pimple comedies made by a new company, "Follies."[11] A key figure in the move appears to have been Cosmopolitan's general manager E.T. Williams, who was to become strongly associated with the brothers for several years. With the economic necessity for an uninterrupted supply of films, Williams persuaded Fred and Joe to set up a temporary base in a cottage close to Ec-Ko's premises. Upstairs was designated as a ladies' dressing room, with an office and props room on the ground floor. Films were either made in the small back garden or in the neighboring streets.

When Fred, Joe and "Pimple" made the move to their new company (now named Folly Films) Ec-Ko were obliged to create a new comic character, "Nobby," who was played by another young music-hall comedian, Sam T. Poluski. Seth and Albert Egbert continued to make comedies for several years (including a "talkie" of their act made at Warner Brothers First National's Teddington studio in 1935), while Will Kellino's non-acrobatic career flourished to such an extent that he became one of the country's most prolific directors during the next two decades. His wife also had a successful cinema career, writing scenarios and featuring in films as Blanche Bella or Blanche Kellino.

CHAPTER 8

Folly and Phoenix

THE PAST CAN SEEM eerily close at Twickenham riverside. There are sleepy bow-fronted houses with cast-iron verandas; an ancient tavern approached by a flight of well-worn steps; and a canopy of mature trees reaching down to the water's edge. Across the gently flowing river are the grassy banks of Eel Pie Island. The poet Alexander Pope's 18th-century Arcadia on Thames is only a blink away. But in 1913 things were quite different. Crowds of pleasure seekers jostled on board ferries bound for the entertainment complex on the island; perspiring movie technicians hauled their equipment on to barges; and film actors joked raucously as they set off for Folly's newly created studio.

There had been a tavern on Eel Pie Island for several hundred years and, in 1820, its bucolic delights had been portrayed by England's master of artistic caricature Thomas Rowlandson. Boatbuilding also took place, an activity that increased in scale when "Thames Launches" occupied a boatyard there in the early 1900s. The company was taken over in 1907 by Joseph Mears, an entrepreneur who ran river excursions from his pub, "The Old Ship," in Richmond, Surrey. Mears had extensive interests in the leisure industry and alongside his fleet of launches and paddle steamers he was co-founder of Chelsea Football Club, as well as creating a small chain of cinemas during the 1920s. In 1913 he found himself with enough spare capacity on Eel Pie Island to rent a boathouse and outbuildings to Fred, Joe and their partner, E.T. Williams.

Much of the island was occupied by a large public house, "The Island Hotel," and its extensive grounds. Joe remembered:

> The pleasure part of the Island was rented by a man called Stevens, who ran a nice hotel for food and had the grounds all cultivated with flowers and bushes and paths with rows of electric lamps lining the paths and in the bushes which looked very nice at night, and people flocked there mostly weekends.[1]

A high fence ran across the island, shielding Folly's studio from the pleasure grounds. Two long, single story huts served as an office and dressing rooms, while the boathouse had workshops on the ground floor and an upstairs studio, illuminated by "Kleig" electric carbon lamps. There was also an outdoor stage, with photography in the hands of E.T. Williams.

At first Folly comedies were marketed by Cosmopolitan and, like Ec-Ko

Eel Pie Island, Twickenham, Middlesex. Photograph, c. 1900, showing the popular tavern and the adjoining boathouses and industrial buildings which later became the Folly Films studio (author's collection).

productions, they remained basic in style and content. Plots usually consisted of a series of episodes which allowed Fred to indulge in athletic comedy stunts. In *Pimple Becomes an Acrobat* (January 1913) a street performer sold Pimple a 1d booklet. After studying "How to Become an Acrobat" Pimple contrived to dive through a large painting being carried by removal men; smash a pile of china plates by attempting to balance them on his chin; and land in a basket of clean washing after leaping over a small boy's back. A final disastrous attempt to perform a handstand on a chair led to a trouncing by an angry shop-owner.

Pimple as a Ballet Dancer (February 1913) followed the same pattern:

> Watching a ballet dancer perform, and with a graceful kick reach a tambourine she holds above her head, Pimple is seized with the desire to do likewise. He begins to practice, and kicks a tray out of a waiter's hands. He gets flung out of the show. He goes dancing through the streets. And lifts the tray off a muffin-man's head. When the muffin-man has done with him he goes on his way, and this time kicks a satchel out of a young lady's hand. He creates a disturbance at the pot-shop, upsets a street-seller of "Wait-and-See" Pills, and waltzes into a circle of, where some street minstrels are passing round the hat. His flying foot catches the hat, and scrambles the cash amongst the crowd. There is a rush for it on the part of the spectators, and a rush for Pimple on the part of the minstrels. They turn him upside-down, shake his pockets out, gather up the spoil, and leave him weeping in the roadway.[2]

Occasional variations were attempted with one experiment inverting the popular chase format to make Pimple the pursuer rather than the pursued. Fred's earliest surviving Folly film, *Pimple's Motor Bike* (May 1913), lacks the opening section where the comedian finds a wallet stuffed with money but preserves the disastrous consequences of his purchase of a motor bike. Pimple is seen ploughing into the inevitable policeman, and then a bricklayer, a suffragette, a gardener, a fence painter, a group at a garden party, and finally three people whose location in a boat might have invested them with a false sense of security.

Burlesque Battles

In April 1913 Williams announced that his newly founded Phoenix Film Agency would take over the distribution of Folly Films. It was not long before his understandable dissatisfaction with the repetitive nature of plots led to a fresh approach that was to become closely identified with Pimple films. In search of novelty the brothers looked to the wider film market for inspiration, homing in on the recently introduced "feature" film. Originating in Europe and the United States, longer fiction films, extending over several reels, had started to be produced in the UK. With their more complex, often implausible, plots and sometimes superfluous content such productions provided an open invitation for comic parody. Like the familiarity-based

Top: **One of the most popular published images of "Pimple." A cheeky Fred Evans resplendent in striped blazer and schoolboy cap (author's collection).** *Above:* **Main title for a Folly film, decorated with an image of a jester, the traditional instigator of chaotic but meaningful disorder (courtesy of Bob Geoghegan, Archive Film Agency).**

titles of *The Last of the Dandy* and *Pimple Does the Turkey Trot*, the widespread publicity that distributors provided for their films could be exploited merely by tacking the name "Pimple" onto the latest release. Consequently, the red nosed recipient of various duckings, scraggings, and backside beatings was soon to find himself presiding over the nine circles of hell in *Pimple's Inferno*, representing the flower of Anglo-Saxon chivalry in *Pimple's Ivanhoe* and commanding the Imperial French Army in *Pimple's Battle of Waterloo*. With a pedigree steeped in the art of satire and burlesque, Fred and Joe found it an easy task to produce their own humorous take on cinema's most recent innovations.

Folly had already produced a simple skit on a 1912 American film *The Indian Massacre* (*The Adventures of Pimple—The Indian Massacre*, May 1913) but in July 1913 the brothers saw the potential of producing a more extended send-up of one of the year's most successful British films. In *The Battle of Waterloo* the American director Charles Weston was exploring the possibilities of the feature film format, concentrating its 4,500 feet and 75 minute duration on spectacular action rather than narrative development. Although it represented a new type of entertainment, the British and Colonial production accorded with a long tradition of theatrical portrayal of Europe's most famous military engagement. Throughout the 19th century the immense scale and significance of the battle had formed the basis for many dramatic presentations, ranging from basic peepshows to elaborate panoramas, and from music-hall songs backed by a few extras to massive re-enactments presented at Astley's Amphitheater.

By the 1880s the event had become sufficiently distant in time for it to treated humorously, as in the monologue "How Bill Adams Won the Battle of Waterloo" in which the up-market entertainer G.H. Snazelle portrayed a cockney veteran reminiscing about his conversation with the "Dook" of Wellington: "Bill, I won't deceive yer, I'm in a bit of an 'ole. I've only got about a 'undred and fifty men available, and 'ere's Bonyparty a coming over the 'ill with a million o' men—picked men most of 'em." Bill's version of his crucial role in the battle became one of the most popular recitations of the late 19th and early 20th century, disseminated to mass audiences not only by direct performance, but by several gramophone recordings (by Snazelle himself) and a set of lantern slides (including an anachronistic view of Bill Adams and the "Dook" talking on the telephone).

While capitalizing on the success of spectacular American productions such as D.W. Griffith's *The Battle* (1911), Thomas H. Ince's *The Battle of Gettysburg* (1912) and Hal Reid's *The Victoria Cross: or, The Charge of the Light Brigade* (1912), *The Battle of Waterloo* drew heavily on the traditional and romanticized images created by Victorian artists specializing in war paintings. Although historical accuracy was a major selling point of the film, there remained an impetus to illustrate key events as they had been traditionally portrayed, leading *The Bioscope* to observe that "the present production aims not so much as giving us a 'war drama' as at offering a vivid series of battle pictures."[3] As a consequence, the British cavalry were depicted charging head-on *a la* Lady's Butler's *Scotland Forever* and Napoleon was shown posing glumly before his carriage, as in Ernest Croft's *On the Evening of the Battle of Waterloo.*

Such instantly recognizable vignettes were set within battle scenes enacted by extras whose numbers were variously estimated from a plausible 400 to an unbelievable 4,000. The filming, which took place at Irthlingborough, Northamptonshire, over three days early in June, provided an entertainment in itself, with schools and local businesses closing as hundreds flocked to watch the proceedings. An added attraction was the behavior of the film's diminutive director who played to a popular stereotype by striding back and forth, barking instructions through an oversized megaphone. Coincidentally, the theme of a film company descending on a country village to make a movie about Napoleon was central to *The Girl on the Film*, a musical comedy that had opened at the Gaiety Theatre in London a month previously.

Fred and Joe may have been prompted to produce their burlesque after seeing a preview of Weston's film or having read some of the extravagant publicity that preceded it. It was claimed that the 116-scene production had featured 1,000 horses and 50 cannons. Amused by such grandiosity and self-importance, the brothers set to work to cut the film down to size with their own low-budget version. They worked with such enthusiasm that their film was released at the end August, apparently a few days before the original. Joe remembered that there had been a brief discussion with Williams about the legality of burlesquing the production, but they had decided to risk British and Colonial's annoyance.

Based on what appears to have been copy supplied by Fred and Joe, *The Cinema* review of *Pimple's Battle of Waterloo* made fun of Weston's claim to have spent much time studying a collection of books about the subject:

> War, war, and rumors of war. The war fever has invaded the "cine" business, and Pimple's caught it bad. Stirred to the very bottom of his boots by the tremendous advertisements in the trade papers, Pimple was seized with the spirit of emulation, and nothing short of the great and historic Battle of Waterloo would satisfy him. For nights and days he sat with ice packing around him, reading history, and evolving the picture we now present you.[4]

Whereas only about 20 minutes of the British and Colonial production survives, Pimple's film exists in most of its chaotic, 587-feet entirety. The comedy starts with Pimple/Napoleon leading his army across the Alps—a mountain range constructed from plywood with the convenient signpost "To Alps." In place of the rearing steed immortalized by Jacques-Louis David in several heroic versions of "Napoleon Crossing the Alps" he is mounted on a cavorting pantomime horse. On his way to "Gay Paree-e-e" he survives an assassination attempt by a banner wielding suffragette—the first of several humorous anachronisms. Next Napoleon and his army arrive at Waterloo Station, a scene which appears to have been filmed at a local railway station. A sentimentally apocryphal episode is then revisited and revised. On the night before the battle Napoleon finds a sentry asleep at his post. British and Colonial perpetuated the traditional story by showing the emperor taking the soldier's musket and mounting guard himself, but the humanity of Pimple's Napoleon is rewarded only by a sharp blow when the sentry thinks that he is attempting to steal his weapon. Arriving at the field of battle Napoleon meets the Duke of Wellington and, in sporting fashion, they toss a coin for first shot. Unfortunately, the French forces have forgotten to bring ammunition and a soldier is sent to a local teashop advertising cannon balls at "3 a 1d." The battle rages and becomes so frantic that the combatants break into a rag-time dance—including Napoleon's horse which has previously been killed. At the crucial moment, the British unleash their elite force. A troop of Baden Powell's Boy Scouts, 90 years before the movement was created, sweep over the horizon, and put the French to flight. Napoleon begs his army to save the cannons, but when they desert him, he is compelled to lift a piece of heavy artillery onto his shoulder and stagger from the battlefield. The final scene depicts Napoleon in captivity, not on H.M.S. "*Bellerophon*," but H.M.S. "*Ballyruffian*," bidding farewell to the shores of France (labeled "France") which look suspiciously likes the Thames riverbank at Twickenham.

Folly burlesques were almost invariably targeted at current films. Such a parasitical process, irritating perhaps to the original producer, created a symbiotic relationship which amused cinema audiences and was readily exploited by exhibitors. Unlike *The Battle of Waterloo*, most of the films burlesqued were themselves

Extravagant claims for the importance and authenticity of the film *The Battle of Waterloo* made in an advert published in *The Daily Express* on September 2, 1913 (author's collection).

Pimple's Battle of Waterloo (1913). Fred Evans, as Napoleon, at Waterloo ? mainline station (courtesy BFI National Archive).

based on novels, plays and poetry, sometimes blurring the line as to which form was being sent up. A review of *Pimple's Ivanhoe* (December 1913) approached the film as if it were a direct burlesque of Scott's novel rather than of Imperial's 1913 epic version the work: "the burlesque of Scott's 'Ivanhoe' is really fine. Sherwood Forest is pictured just off Twickenham where Pimple finds Robin Hood with his boy scouts. Telephones and taxicabs also add to the absurdity."[5]

A classic piece of Victorian doggerel verse, "Kissing Cup's Race," provided the title if not the plot for another English feature film of 1913. Cecil Hepworth's 3,500-foot racing drama *Kissing Cup* owed substantially more to the 1909 Drury Lane melodrama *The Whip* than to Campbell Rae-Brown's famous poem. But as the *Kinematograph Weekly* noted "issued, as it is, under a title which is known to everybody—there are few people, we imagine, who have not heard the recitation in which the old jockey tells how the mare 'Kissing Cup' won Lord Hilloxton his bride—it will in all probability be circulated over a wide area."[6] Always keen to pursue an equine subject, Fred and Joe responded with *Pimple's "Kissing Cup"* (595 ft.), a surviving fragment showing that their version replaced the kidnapped jockey with his mount. Pimple is seen breaking into the villain's lair and rescuing

"Kissing Cup," a pantomime horse tied to a chair and gagged to prevent it neighing for help.

Sometimes Fred and Joe did not parody an entire film but merely used its title as a starting point for their own comedy. Although the lancers in *Pimple's Charge of the Light Brigade* (October 1914) were dressed in uniforms appropriate to the Crimean War, the "Valley of Death" into which they bravely rushed was an inviting local tavern rather than the grim battlefield commemorated in the poem. By parodying the words of Tennyson which had been used as intertitles in the 1912 Vitagraph film, the Pimple film once more subverted a romanticized approach to British history:

> Theirs not to reason why,
> Theirs but to do and die,
> And as their throats were dry
> Into the Valley of Death flew the six hundred.

CHAPTER 9

A Cast of Thousands, More or Less

FOLLY BURLESQUES CAME INTO BEING because films had become longer. In the whole of 1912 only four British films exceeding 3,000 feet were released, followed by two more during the first half of 1913. By the end of that year production had mushroomed, with a further 37 feature-length films appearing.[1] Driven by a desire to legitimize their industry and to dispel its music-hall and penny-gaff origins, those making feature films frequently turned to literary classics for their subject matter. Such seriousness of purpose, coupled with the narrative constraints of silent film, provided Fred and Joe with rich and regular targets.

Burlesque had occupied a central position in the entertainment world long before Fred and Joe started to make films. The theater-historian George Speaight wrote of early Victorian theater:

> Nothing was safe, nothing was too sacred for the burlesque writers to fasten upon, and turn into a grotesque mockery of the original. Every popular success was burlesqued before it was many months old; *Black Eyed Susan* became *Black Eyed Sukey*, *The Sorrows of Werther* was guyed as *The Sorrows of Water; or Love, Liquor and Lunacy*. Even, or rather, especially Shakespeare was exposed to the indignity of *King Lear and His Daughters Queer* or Romeo and Juliet dressed up as costermongers.[2]

Later in the century, London's Gaiety and Strand theaters became the twin homes of burlesque with a string of productions such as *Ivanhoe in Accordance with the Spirit of the Times; Bluebeard, or the Hazard of the Dye*; and *Faust Up-to-Date*, ridiculing literary targets. Male and female roles were swapped; ludicrous situations introduced; and intricate comic wordplay employed. Following its demise during the 1890s, burlesque was reincarnated in the early 20th century in the form of revue. Usually occupying the second half of a music-hall program, revues were presented by a company of performers who often impersonated well-known entertainers and provided pastiches of current theatrical productions. The most sophisticated satires were those supplied by the Follies, a close-knit troupe of comedians and singers put together by H.G. Pelissier in 1901. Like Pimple's film burlesques, "Pelissier's Potted Plays" presented versions of *Raffles*, *Hamlet* and *The Whip*. And, as with Fred and Joe, the Follies made use of supplementary printed material—such as their spoof music-hall program which advertised "Boss Empires, Ltd. Registered Capital £000000000."

To adequately burlesque feature films, Folly productions had to increase in length. Within eight months of *Pimple's Battle of Waterloo*, the company had produced a string of extended send ups of the latest cinema successes. At 686 feet *Dicke Turpin's Ride to Yorke* was a burlesque of British and Colonial's *Dick Turpin's Ride to York* (1737 ft.); *Pimple's Ivanhoe*, was a 980 feet version of *Ivanhoe* (3500 ft.); and the 990 feet *The House of Distemperley* lampooned an adaption of Arthur Conan Doyle's novel *The House of Temperley* (4500 ft.).

Pimple's Purgatory

The more spectacular or sensational a subject was, the more humor was to be extracted by Pimple's incongruous presence. When an Italian version of the First Canticle of Dante Alighieri's *Divine Comedy* was released in the United Kingdom in the autumn of 1912, its cavernous Hell, complete with thrashing semi-naked bodies, flesh-eating monsters, and hideous demons, was a region to which Fred was irresistibly drawn. The equivocal nature of the film's promotion was also a source for amusement as the distributor and exhibitors alternated between emphasizing its high moral tone and seeking to exploit its more shocking and salacious aspects. With its title changed from *L'Inferno* to *Dante's Inferno* the production was stated to be 5,000 feet long, taking 2½ years to make and costing £50,000. A full-page advert in the trade press ran:

> GO as far as you want. There is nothing TO beat it. A most remarkable scene takes place as Virgil takes Dante through the gates of HELL.[3]

Audiences across the country decided to go to Hell in their thousands. Their approach to the visualization of Dante's "Divine Comedy" was frequently to treat it as a divine comedy. At the Pavilion Picture House, Hunslet, Yorkshire, long queues waited to see the film. A reviewer commented:

> It is difficult to understand the peculiar sort of narrow-minded or grandmotherly administration that has led to the film being banned in certain towns, but it is easy to realize that the naked horrors of the scenes portrayed are such as many refined and sensitive people would shrink from witnessing.
>
> Hunslet, however, is saved by its sense of humour. The audience laughed at all the most horrible parts. Pictures of tortured souls being hurled into flaming pits or lakes by flying fiends roused a chorus of merriment. Even the picture of Count Ugolino's tortured shade embedded in ice chewing the scull of Archbishop Rugieri, and the horrid face of the arch-fiend himself, with the body of a writhing victim in his arms, hardly succeeded in chilling their sense of comedy.[4]

Following the film's exhibition at the Hanwell Grand Theatre, Middlesex, in August 1913, an indignant letter writer complained:

> The suggested contortions projected on to the screen travestied rather than portrayed the spirit of Dante's poetry, and must have sickened all normally-constituted persons, who

saw them. But there could have been but few normally-constituted persons present on the occasion of which I write, for during the exhibition of the purgatory scenes the place rang with indecorous laughter and vulgar comments were given loud expression.[5]

It seems that when the comic character Pimple arrived at the entrance of Hell he was pushing on an open door.

Pimple's Inferno was released on October 27, 1913, and was 720 feet in length. Unlike Dante, Pimple's excursion into the underworld was preceded by a crab supper. In his subsequent nightmare he was dragged by a robed figure into the depths of hell where amongst the tormented souls encountered were suffragettes, politicians, and some old friends in the form of film comedians. They arrived at a particularly barren spot which was "guarded" by sleeping imps. A notice proclaimed, "Reserved for Pimple." His guide asked him, via an intertitle "Come, and I will introduce thee to the famous Mr. Nick." The devil politely offered Pimple a seat, which proved too hot to sit on, and then sent for the books detailing "the records of his deeds." Another subtitle conveyed Mr. Nick's plans for Pimple's future—"Pimple, if thy good deeds doth not outweigh the bad, then thou art mine." Unfortunately, Pimple's bad deeds were recorded in several impressively large volumes, while his good deeds were limited to once giving a blind beggar a "bad halfpenny." Pimple was seized by the imps and during a terrible struggle he woke up. "By George" he exclaimed "that was a narrow escape."[6]

Titillating Titles

The complexity of burlesques necessitated a greater use of intertitles (known as subtitles at the time) than was normal for film comedies. Explanation of plot, however, was not the only reason for their extensive use. Fred and Joe were addicted to written as well as visual humor, loading their titles with jocular slang, puns, and the occasional innuendo. Although the limited number of surviving films provides relatively few examples, it appears that Pimple intertitles drew heavily on music-hall sketch dialogue and cartoons and comic strips. Even allowing for changing taste, some of the humor seems to have been calculated to provoke more groans than guffaws, its lameness, perhaps, intended to poke fun at the general artificiality of intertitles. For the burlesque of the film of George Du Maurier's *Trilby* the humor started with the title itself. The credits for the 1914 London Film Company's production announcing "Sir Herbert Tree and this Haymarket Theatre Company in Trilby" were sent up as "Trilby. By Pimple and Company." *The Bioscope* commented: "the film is cleverly played, and owes not a little of its interest to the very numerous subtitles, all, as in Pimple productions, destined to point a more or less obvious moral."[7]

The beguiling artist's-model Trilby O'Ferrell was played by Fred, but in *Pimple's Royal Divorce* (May 1915) Joe took the female lead, appearing as the Empress Josephine to his brother's "Boneypart." Once again, written humor was much in evidence:

As Josephine refuses to oblige, the county court judge is called upon to declare the marriage null and void, which he proceeds to do, at the same time interjecting a pun in true judicial style.

The producers of the "Pimple" films evidently make a great feature of puns, and realizing that their plays would be better for a little patter, the latter is introduced through the medium of subtitles. Thus, sometimes, there is quite a duologue flashed up on the screen.[8]

In conjunction with intertitles, the Evans' often accelerated their plots by including written material within the action of the film. Close-ups of explanatory letters are seen in *Pimple and the Stolen Submarine* and *Pimple's Uncle*. Comic signs and notices were regularly included, as in *Pimple and the Snake* where the action is initiated by Pimple reading a reward notice. The comedy in *Pimple's Complaint* (incomplete copy held by BFI) depends entirely on a piece of writing. Two naughty but clearly literate boys compose and surreptitiously attach a warning note to Pimples back. Its message "I have got the smallpox. Please keep away" is so alarming that a passer-by drops some money in his attempt to avoid infection. Pimple uses the cash to stop at a café and to attend a music hall but is confused when people hurry away from him. Finally, alerted by the notice, two doctors arrive.

Fred and Joe would frequently satirize the publicity that accompanied the release of new films. In the summer of 1913, the trade press carried verbose advertisements for the film version of John Lawsons long-running music-hall sketch *Humanity*:

The whole of the original cast, including Mr. JOHN LAWSON as "THE JEW." 3000 ft. of sensations.

Write us at once for special invitation performance this month.

"HUMANITY" has been greeted with enthusiasm everywhere, but great as the music hall sketch was produced, the film is infinitely greater, and is a miraculously stupendous production.

"HUMANITY" is full of thrills, including the greatest "Smashing" scene ever attempted, a thrilling race by motor car, a dare-devil struggle on a tottering staircase, a realistic fight for life, etc., etc., etc.

"HUMANITY" is the biggest and greatest effort of realism in Cinematography.[9]

Exciting content of a similar nature was claimed for *Pimple's Humanity* (February 1914):

PIMPLE'S POTTED PICTURE PLAYS
PIMPLE'S
HUMANITY
See Pimple as Johnny Walker, the Scotch Jew.
A study in black and white. See the great fight
on the staircase. Produced at the Enormous
Cost of **£25,000,000** –––more or less.[10]

Lieutenants Rose, Daring and Pimple

Fred and Joe did not restrict their burlesques to films of literary works, but also satirized productions with original screenplays. Two long-running series depicting the exploits of "Lieutenant Rose" (Clarendon, 1910–1915) and "Lieutenant Daring" (British and Colonial, 1911–1914) provided sitting-duck targets. Both characters were dashing naval officers, imposing order abroad in the British colonies and thwarting the machinations of foreign spies at home. The characters drew heavily on a theatrical tradition of swashbuckling sailors, augmented by the heroes of juvenile literature as portrayed in part-issue publications and cheap novelettes. Like Rose and Daring, Lieutenant Pimple was a member of the "Senior Service," but instead of their immaculate uniforms his outfit was shabby and ill-fitting. While the Clarendon/British and Colonial characters were featured sailing on real ships, leaping onto real trains and even piloting a real airplane, Pimple's adventures were enacted before crudely painted scenery and in ridiculously constructed vehicles. Eight "Lieutenant Pimple" films appeared in 1913–1914, one of the first being *Lieutenant Pimple and the Stolen Submarine* (February 1914).

In the still surviving film Pimple is ordered to inspect a newly invented submarine and to negotiate its purchase ("25/- less 5% for cash," the intertitle explains). Filmed on the banks of Eel Pie Island, the vessel is clearly a small boat onto which a flimsy and unconvincing superstructure has been built. In a studio shot, the

Underwater scene from *Pimple and the Stolen Submarine* (1914). Pimple pauses to scratch his head through a convenient opening in his helmet (courtesy BFI National Archive).

interior of the craft is portrayed by a badly painted backcloth with two up and down levers which Pimple seems to find confusing. Having foolishly accepted a badly disguised agent's offer to mind the submarine, the lieutenant returns to find that it has disappeared. He dons a diving costume and is lowered to the bottom of the sea/ River Thames. There then occurs a comic juxtaposition between the actual water on the surface and the imaginary water in the undersea scene. Becoming overheated beneath the waves, Pimple removes his helmet and mops his brow, while the studio lighting casts his shadow onto a backcloth depicting seaweed and submerged debris. He soon locates the stolen submarine and, disregarding the difficulties of underwater communication, expresses his pleasure to the cinema audience. A "thrilling" combat with one of the spies ensues. Pimple is victorious but is then overwhelmed by other members of the gang who leave him to perish inside the craft. With time running out our hero pulls off a stroke of imaginative genius. He pens a missive, breaks open a window and quickly locates a fish (perhaps the most realistic prop in the entire film). The rescue note is attached to the creature, which obligingly delivers both itself and the message to an angler. On escaping from the submarine, Pimple joins a party of Jack Tars on board H.M.S. "*Horrible,*" a diminutive warship of dubious design. Their pursuit and eventual capture of the spies is watched by many interested spectators lining the Twickenham riverside.

Audience Participation

The appearance of members of the public, either seen in the background or as active participants in filmmaking, was a feature of many Pimple productions. As with music-hall outings, Fred, Joe, and their fellow actors delivered a free show while filming, their efforts being rewarded by the ad-hoc audience who also acted as unpaid extras. Rather than representing a distraction to cinema-audiences, the presence of "ordinary" people on-screen appears to have acted as a visual endorsement of the films.

While Fred was filming at Newhaven, East Sussex, during the summer of 1914, residents supplied the audience for a comedy boxing contest:

> In one of the pictures which were taken, viz., "Pimple beats Jack Johnson," a crowd was required for the scene depicting the match, and a crowd was obtained, too, in a manner unexpected and unexplained. The local carpenter was requisitioned to put up the seats round the ring. He asked what match was to be fought and was duly enlightened that Pimple was to fight Jack Johnson. Tongues will wag, and the old "worker with wood" was no exception to the rule. He informed one or two friends as to his "job" for the next day. Imagine the surprise of the picture-makers on going to the ground to find about 300 people waiting to see the fun—and wasn't the producer pleased to see his "supers" already waiting for him—ready to do their part without fee or payment.[11]

Similarly, the inhabitants of Twickenham turned out in force to watch proceedings and to represent on screen what they were in reality—a crowd:

"H.M.S. *Horrible*" pursues a group of foreign spies in *Lieutenant Pimple and the Stolen Submarine*. Interested spectators watch from the Twickenham riverside (courtesy BFI National Archive).

Recently the pedestrians of Twickenham had a little excitement all to themselves when, with bell a-clanging, the prehistoric vehicle, drawn by a real live horse, went rambling down King-street. "Fire! Fire! Fire!" yelled the driver, on whose head was poised a tiny gilded helmet. "Fire!" screamed the half-dozen firemen, their heads also carrying tiny helmets. Smoke belched from the broken funnel of this weird "engine," the boiler of which looked like nothing so much as a dustbin. Tramcars were held up, shopkeepers rushed to the doors, and all Twickenham wondered. Then someone spotted the painted legend "Pimple's Fire Brigade." Onward came the fiery steed and the still less fiery engine—on, and on, and again on, never halting it its mad career until it finally dashed into the—camera, or rather missed it by a few inches, and the scene was taken. Loud were the cheers a little later when the valiant "Pimple" failed again and again to affect a "rescue" from the first floor of a burning mansion, and many were the sorrowing hearts when it was announced that the remaining scenes would be taken across the water in the Phoenix Studios on Eel Pie Island, to which there is "no admittance except on business."[12]

Pimple's popularity with the Twickenham public was reinforced on at least one occasion by a full-scale theatrical performance. In March 1914, the Twickenham Town Hall was rented for a variety show featuring Fred, Joe, and Lily Poole. The series of sketches that were presented closely resembled Pimple films, with an emphasis on visual comedy as in Fred and Joe's boxing contest in "The Tenderfoot" and Fred's animal impersonation in "The Gorilla's Revenge." A comic allusion to the company's reason for being in Twickenham was given in "Taking a Cinema Picture," while its connection with the area was further emphasized by the presence on stage of a fifteen-year-old local boy, Tommie Collett. Of the many children who were "persuaded" to perform in Folly films, only Tommie seems to have drawn a salary. Born the son of a bricklayer's laborer in Twickenham in 1899, he was spotted by Fred and E.T. Williams delivering newspapers. His "jolly countenance"[13] immediately persuaded them to offer him the role of "Young Pimple," a part he played in several films.

Adult actors in Folly productions were usually drawn from the inter-related worlds of sport and entertainment. Boxers, including the well-known professionals Joe Beckett and Billy Wells, and jockeys such as Will Asher played alongside minor variety performers. Joe remembered that the comedian Gus Garrick (who, at the time, was presenting a troupe of burlesque ragtime Russian dancers) also appeared. A young music-hall artist, James Reed, was paid £2 a week for acting as Joe's assistant, devising plots, and playing in films.

An actress who did not survive long in the Folly fold was Emma Maude, whose attempt to retrieve an alleged debt resulted in a violent and embarrassing altercation. At Brentford Police Court on May 16, 1914, she alleged that Joe had assaulted her after she demanded to see Fred, who owed her a guinea. Her sister claimed that after Maude had threatened to obtain a summons, Joe had used bad language, struck her, and enlisted the aid of eight or nine workmen to push her into a boat. Under oath, Joe denied that he had struck her and claimed that she had become excited, slapping his face after he asked her to leave the island.[14]

CHAPTER 10

Uncles on Screen

FOLLOWING THE RAPID DEPARTURE of Joe and Fred from Ec-Ko, uncles Seth and Albert Jee continued to make films with the company, sometimes supporting their "Pimple" substitute, Sam T. Poluski. Despite the rift, the Evans brothers were happy to form a loose partnership with another uncle, Will Evans. Having provided them with employment and support for their earlier music-hall efforts, Will probably helped to finance Folly Films. In turn, the brothers assisted Will when he established his own film company with Fred co-starring in at least two of its productions. Just as Will's status as the principal comedian in the nation's leading pantomimes assured the success of moving picture versions of his variety sketches, Seth and Albert also capitalized on their stage celebrity by issuing a series of "Happy Dustman" films. Although Fred had carved out his own career as "Pimple," he was more than happy to promote his films by frequently invoking the names of his well-known uncles.

The Egbert Brothers

Although Seth and Albert, as the Egbert Brothers, were universally identified with their Happy Dustmen act, they did not feature "Bill" and "Walter" in their earliest Ec-Ko films. Following *The Coster's Wedding* and *Yiddle on My Fiddle* (both released December 1912), they appeared in several productions as "Inkey and Co." It hardly mattered which of them played "Inkey" for the two tramp characters were identical in their intense dislike of work, love of alcohol and generally criminal disposition. It was not until the end of 1913 that the Egberts reverted to their celebrated stage personas in a "comical and elaborated version of the funny antics which constitute the famous variety act."[1] *The Happy Dustmen* (December 1913) was followed by *The Dustmen's Holiday* (December 1913); *The Dustman's Nightmare* (April 1914); *The Happy Dustmen Play Golf* (August 1914); *The Happy Dustmen's Christmas* (December 1914); *The Dustman's Wedding* (September 1916); and *The Dustmen's Outing* (December 1916). Seldom diverting from the knockabout nature of their music-hall routine, the humor in the films was robust. In *The Dustman's Wedding* the pair won a huge hamper at their local pub, immediately consuming its alcoholic contents. Waking with hangovers on

Christmas morning they proceeded to make a complete hash of cooking dinner and to flood their cellar while tapping a barrel of beer. A *Bioscope* review of the film commented, "The issue is of a broadly humorous character, and will especially appeal, from the nature of its fun, to audiences in the middle or working class districts."[2]

Film making continued to be supplementary to their music-hall appearances, although the two were occasionally linked. In September 1913, the brothers combined an engagement at the Swansea Empire with the production of *The Dustmen's Holiday*. Their public antics as they were filmed riding on donkeys, playing on swings and roundabouts and finally walking through the town in their bathing costumes would certainly have acted as an advertisement for the Empire show.

Left to right: Albert and Seth Egbert as "The Robbers" in the Drury Lane pantomime *Babes in the Wood* of 1918–1919 (author's collection).

Will Evans

Will Evans also started to transfer his famous sketches to film in 1913. He and the Brothers Egbert joined a growing number of music-hall performers who realized that the increased length of films provided a golden opportunity to create fresh interest in their stage acts. Filmed sketches could capitalize on the familiarity of productions that had exhausted their stage life, bringing them to a wider cinema audience and allowing the introduction of revitalizing elements such as close-ups and real locations. In the case of a sketch that was still being performed, a filmed version possessed current interest and helped promote the original act.

The issue of whether the filmed music-hall sketch acted as an incentive to attend a theater and view the live performance proved contentious when Will filmed versions of *Harnessing a Horse* (May 1913) and *Whitewashing a Ceiling* (December 1913). In January 1914, a major music-hall syndicate, London Theatres of Variety, Ltd., made a legal attempt to stop the exhibition of Evans' filmed sketches in the metropolitan area by invoking a clause in his contract which prevented him giving "any colorable imitation, representation, or version of his performance," other than at their 22 theaters. Such a prohibitive course of action reflected concern among music-hall proprietors about growing competition from cinemas and fears that, boosted by film-fueled popularity, performers would demand higher salaries. The combine sought an injunction, claiming that the local exhibition of the filmed sketches *Harnessing a Horse* and *Building a Chicken House* undermined profits when Will was appearing at their theaters. Will's counterargument was that the clause related to live performances of his material by "second-string" troupes, added to which films acted as an advertisement for stage performances. He must also have noticed a crucial error relating to one aspect of their case.

Justice Bailhache pondered over the meaning of "colorable imitation." "What was the nature of the defendant's performance" he asked, "and what was the nature of the cinema film?" He went on to argue that:

> The two sketches referred to were alike in that a great deal of their effectiveness depended upon the action, facial expressions, gestures, etc., of the defendant. But in addition to these physical outward and visible acts, which could be reproduced on cinema films, the defendant interlarded his performances with what was known as "patter" or "gag."[3]

Having accepted that there was a material difference between the sketch *Harnessing a Horse* and its film counterpart, he moved on to examine *Building a Chicken House*, which he considered to be an exact reproduction of the stage performance. Despite the latter film being declared a breach of contract, the plaintiffs abandoned their claims for damages and an injunction. It had been discovered that *Building a Chicken House* did not, in fact, feature Will Evans but was a Hepworth "Vivaphone" production in which studio performers synchronized their performance to a commercial recording. An appeal court judge found there had been a "miscarriage of facts" and that it would be unfair to retry the defendant.[4]

The Sunny South

A more substantial venture into filmmaking involved Will with a remarkable theatrical colony that had established itself on the Sussex coast, at Shoreham by Sea. Like Ec-Ko, the Sunny South Film Company combined commercial enterprise with a holiday-outing demeanor. In the late 1880s a local entrepreneur began to exploit the picturesque appeal of a row of fisherman's huts on Shoreham Beech, by selling plots of land (or sand) where summer holiday homes might be erected. Initially, buildings were constructed from redundant railway carriages, but soon an eclectic conglomeration of single-story houses, each given its own name, had arisen. By the 1900s "Bungalow Town" had become the occasional home for many actors and variety performers, attracted by the fresh sea air, proximity to the recreational facilities of Brighton and by a clannish disposition that had long been evident in London areas such as Kennington and Brixton. Will, who was eventually to own at least five bungalows in the settlement, spent much of his spare time at "Hop o' My Thumb," named after the 1911 Drury Lane pantomime. It was there that an old theatrical colleague, Albert Le Fre, introduced him to another neighbor, the scenic artist F.L. Lyndhurst.

Film poster Will Evans showing his distinctive stage make-up (courtesy of Glenn Mitchell).

In September 1914 Evans and Lyndhurst announced the creation of the Sunny South Film Company, issuing a prospectus that stated that the concern was to have a capital of £5000, made up of one-pound shares. An unlikely assertion that *Harnessing a Horse* had made a profit of £10,000 was sufficient inducement to persuade Le Fre to hand over £64 for a stake in the new enterprise. Film making started immediately with Will, as leading performer, joined by two other well-known pantomime comedians, Arthur Conquest (1875–1945) and George Graves (1876–1949). Prior to the first trade show in December 1914, it was announced that further music-hall performers were to appear, including Albert Le Fre, Fred Earle (another Bungalow Town resident), R.G. Knowles and G.P. Huntley.[5]

The courtyard of a 19th-century coastal defense, Palmerston Fort, was used as an open-air studio, with location filming taking place in the streets of Shoreham and on the Sussex Downs. Like Cricks and Martin, Sunny South recruited their extras from the local community, advertising their requirements by attaching a notice to the front of Lyndhurst's bungalow: "People wishing to appear in a film will be allowed to do so free of charge if they present themselves at the Old Fort at 10 o'clock on...."[6]

Such an approach was not uncommon. The novelty benefits of individual members of the public being able to see themselves in motion had been exploited by showman since the earliest days of filmmaking. During the early 1900s Mitchell and Kenyon supplied hundreds of "local" films depicting crowds staring into the camera at factory gates, sporting events, pageants, processions, and parades. A handbill for a show given by A.D. Thomas at the Curzon Hall, Birmingham in 1900, offered an invitation to: "COME AND SEE YOURSELVES REPRODUCED ON THE SCREEN IN ANIMATED PHOTOGRAPHY. EVERY FACE A POR-TAIT!" By 1912 "locals" were still proving a powerful draw, with the author of *How to Run a Picture Theatre* advising:

> There can be no two opinions as to the value of the local topical film as a means of fill-ing your theatre. Everyone loves to see himself, or herself, or friends, or children, on the screen, and the local topical is the best means of gratifying this desire.[7]

Although less overt in offering members of the audience the chance to appear on screen, fiction productions often provided a similar incentive for the participation of non-actors. One of those drawn to the old fort was Norman Wolters, the nine-year-old son of a theatrical manager. In his account of film-ing activities, published 70 years later, he recalled taking part in *The Showman's Dream*, being "rescued" from a fire created by several smoke bombs. "NEB" Wolt-ers also described the action of the film after "Professor Evanso" had fallen asleep and dreamed that his circus was in flames. A tiger (played by Arthur Conquest) escaped and was pursued to the thatched post office in Old Shoreham, where it ran into adjacent cottage and leapt into bed with an elderly woman (probably played by Joe Evans). While chasing the "senior citizen" through the village, the animal encountered a man taking his leave of the "Red Lion" tavern. The tipsy local's fright and flight along the Steyning Road was apparently so amusing that it was retained for the film's final version. Whether "NEB" Wolters was witness to the events or whether they were part of Bungalow Town folklore is not clear. However, photographs from the production show the ornately painted entrance to "Evanso's Circus and Menagerie," and a cage containing a fierce "lion" accom-panied by a considerably less intimidating looking "tiger."[8]

For those members of the public not concerned with their own screen glory, the greatest incentive for attending a Sunny South production was to see the famous stage performer Will Evans. Promotional material for his films empha-sized Will's reputation as a comedian and the previous success of his sketches. In December 1913, *The Cinema* reported:

> Will Evans, one of the greatest successes of modern times in his own particular line, the favorite of the music-halls, and the star of Drury Lane's pantomime, might aptly be described as an unequalled mirth provoker. The witnessing of a performance by him pro-vides the best known antidote for a fit of the blues, and Mr Will Day is, therefore, to be congratulated upon having secured his services and those of his company for a cine-matograph reproduction of his great rib-ticker, "Whitewashing the Ceiling," which has amused countless thousands during successful runs at all the principal variety halls in this country.[9]

A year later the same magazine reported on a "good start by the Sunny South Co.":

The personality of a famous variety artist is made up of many tricks of manner, dress, and voice, which, taken as a whole, constitute the hall-mark by which we know his merits as an entertainer. Mr. Will Evans, the celebrated comedian, is a typical example. One can appreciate his quaint and whimsical brand of humor to the full without realizing, or even caring, how he arrives at his mirth-provoking results. At first blush it would appear impossible that the full effect of such a rich and many-sided personality as that of Mr Evans could be transferred, without loss, from the footlights to the screen. Yet in the three films which we laughed over at the trade show held by the Sunny South Co., in which Mr. Evans is chief partner, at the Shaftesbury Pavilion, on Monday last, it was clear that we had the familiar personality of the great comedian before us in all its rare and resourceful eccentricity. Of course, we missed the voice, but on the other hand, we got more of the inimitable detail which Mr. Evans gets into his sketches, and we saw it against many and varied backgrounds. Even the absence of the voice was counter-balanced to a large extent by the introduction of a singularly ingenious method of "sub-titling," in which the words "spoken" were made to appear as coming from the mouths of the actors and animals—the latter such creatures as Hagenbeck never knew!—who took part in the productions. The conversation between Mr. Evans and the horse, in a film entitled "The Jockey," was extremely funny, and seems to open up a vista of fresh fields for film comedy, but Mr. Evans is careful to point out that he has already copyrighted the idea and that he intends to exploit it further.[10]

Five films were made during the autumn of 1914: *Building a Chicken House, The Jockey, Moving a Piano, The Showman's Dream* and *Tincture of Iron*. Some were versions of earlier sketches, but unlike *Whitewashing a Ceiling* they were not direct transcriptions of the original productions. At 1,000 feet in length, their 15-minute duration would have made them slightly shorter than their stage counterparts, while their location filming and lack of sound resulted in a stronger visual emphasis. Despite scenes filmed against a rural background they were made at a time when the Shoreham landscape was undergoing dramatic changes. With the outbreak of World War I in August 1914, Field Marshal Kitchener had headed a massive recruitment campaign and by the following month the fields close to Bungalow Town were lined with bell-tents, put up to accommodate thousands of volunteers. The Sussex Downs had become a military training ground, hardly compatible with random filmmaking.

The filming of one local scene caused Will and several members of the company to be placed in temporary detention. A haystack had been selected as a suitable feature around which Will, dressed as *The Jockey*, might chase his runaway (pantomime) horse. Despite the ludicrous nature of the proceedings a zealous sergeant-major and a troop of soldiers from Shoreham Camp were alarmed by the presence of movie camera. Will, Arthur Conquest, F.L. Lyndhurst, a camera-operator, and the front and rear ends of the horse were escorted to the camp commander who, having satisfied himself that they were not German spies, requested them to supply an impromptu concert.

With a dispute over mismanagement and financial irregularities causing the demise of the Sunny South company in 1915, only two further Will Evans

A traditional Harlequinade recreated on screen for *Some Fun* (1915) with Will Evans portraying Clown and Fred "Pimple" Evans taking the role of Pantaloon (courtesy of Glenn Mitchell).

comedies were issued.[11] *A Study in Skarlit* (December 1915) was a Sherlock Holmes spoof in which Will played "Scherlokz Momz," a comic version of Conan Doyle's famous detective, and Fred portrayed his nemesis, "Professor Moritorium." In *Some Fun* (December 1915) Will and Fred played another fictional pair who were invariably linked by intrigue, suspicion, and hostility. Will followed the distinguished footsteps of his father by featuring as Clown, while Fred upheld family tradition by appearing as Pantaloon. There was little storyline to their two-reel homage to the Harlequinade, one reviewer commenting: "it is merely sufficient to provide a peg on which to hang the usual familiar antics of clown and pantaloon, but it is all done with such a wealth of suggestion, so much humor, and such spontaneity, that one cannot refrain from laughing."[12]

Having provided several of his sketches with a film make-over, Will introduced a comic recreation of movie making on the stage. A sketch, introduced at the Shepherd's Bush Empire, West London, in July 1915, revolved around a husband, wife and friends setting up a film studio in their kitchen. An amused *Kinematograph and Lantern Weekly* reported:

> The various roles of hero, heroine, and villain are handed out with a cheerful disregard of convention, while the ancestral castle, railway lines and 9.30 express, to say nothing of the plans of the submarine, and the keys of the plans, betoken a profound regard for the elusive solidity of "make-believe," The scenario is read out and the rehearsal proceeded with in one operation, and after a few minor mishaps due to a failure to grasp the essentials of silent expression, there is an adjournment for the "chase."[13]

The theme was explored again a few months later at Drury Lane when Will introduced "a most diverting skit of a film production in a country village" into the first act of the pantomime *Puss in Boots*.[14]

Following his brief excursion into filmmaking—and satirizing the practice of filmmaking—Uncle Will continued to appear in pantomimes and at music halls. In 1922 his comedy *Tons of Money*, co-written with Arthur Valentine, proved a major success when produced at the Shaftesbury Theatre, later transferring to the Aldwych Theatre where it became the first of an extremely popular series of farces. Despite making a large amount of money from the long-running play, he was declared bankrupt in 1928. Liabilities of £8000 were attributed to an inability to find regular stage work and substantial maintenance payments made to Evelyn Poole after their bitter divorce in 1923. With his finances in a critical state, he continued to present comic sketches on stage and in early radio broadcasts, assisted by his third wife Nora Emerald. Still "Harnessing a Horse," Will died in 1931—the ups-and-downs of his career demonstrating that the life of a music-hall performer, even an outstanding one, was precarious and unpredictable. The Brothers Egbert continued to present their strenuous routines until their deaths during World War II. When they appeared in *Babes in the Wood* at the Grand Opera House, Belfast, in 1938–39, it was estimated that it was their fiftieth pantomime.

Fred's attachment to his family was of a practical nature, with relatives providing training, work opportunities and contacts. By connecting his name with other well-known members of his family, he achieved additional publicity and legitimization. There was also historical, if tongue-in-cheek, capital to be made from his ancestors. Great grandfather Burnell Runnells appears to have been invested with a new ethnic background seemingly invented in 1923 when the *Hull Daily Mail* reported:

> On his mother's side "Pimple" can trace his ancestry to his great grandfather, a Red Indian Chief, whose name in English was Burnall Reynolds [*sic*]. He was Chief of the Moscojee [Musocogee] tribe. Pimple himself, when in America some time ago was made a blood chief by virtue of his descent.[15]

CHAPTER 11

Pimple's Popularity

IN JULY 1915 *Pictures and the Picturegoer* announced the results of its poll to establish the "greatest British film player." The winner was Cecil Hepworth's twenty-year-old leading lady Alma Taylor, who received 156,000 votes, followed by stage and screen beauty Elizabeth Risdon with 145,030 and Charlie Chaplin on 142,920. Fred was ranked sixth with 122,185, behind two further Hepworth players, Stewart Rome, 133,470 votes, and Chrissie White, 122,200. The electorate was largely restricted to those film fans who could afford to purchase a copy of the magazine and a postage stamp with which to submit the voting form. If a poll had been held inside cinemas, the results would probably have been quite different, with greatly increased support for Charlie and Fred from juvenile and poorer working-class fans.

The star system that developed in cinema before World War I closely resembled the process by which leading music-hall celebrities were promoted towards the end the 19th century. Success achieved as a stage performer was amplified by regular publicity published in periodicals devoted to the variety theater and in the wider popular press. Interviews with the most popular artists frequently appeared and details of their home life, hobbies, recreations, and charitable activities became widely circulated. Personalized souvenirs in the form of photographs, cigarette cards, illustrated sheet music, ornaments and, in Dan Leno's case, a comic, were produced in large numbers. During the late 1890s and early 1900s short sequences from famous performers' acts were filmed and viewed in projected shows and on mechanical devices such as mutoscopes and flip books.

When the initial novelty of moving pictures had abated, filmmakers were still keen to announce the occasional appearance of stage stars like Dan Leno, Marie Lloyd, George H. Chirgwin and Will Evans in their productions. But when it came to the less celebrated performers who were increasingly appearing in story-telling films there was a marked reluctance to provide credits. The director Cecil Hepworth was concerned that when actors became well-known by name, they would demand increasingly larger salaries. With a degree of hindsight, he wrote in his 1951 autobiography:

> We were employing for the main part, completely unknown artists in our films and of necessity publicizing their appearance and skill. When the time came when we wanted to advertise them, both on the screen and in the press, by posters and by "stills," I foresaw

that what was beginning to happen to other firms would certainly happen to us. An actor had the value which was due to his own good work. He also had a fortuitous value, not contributed by him, and due to the money spent in advertising him. That accumulated value he was free—unless, and only for as long as, he was under contract—to sell to any rival firm for as much as he could get. His new firm would, of necessity, add to that increased value and the process would go on, higher and higher, until the producers were impoverished and the actors near millionaires. That, indeed, has largely come to pass and it is one of the reasons why the film production industry is nearly always in difficulties.[1]

Even actors playing lead roles were consigned to anonymity, and it was not until about 1910 that the names of American stars such as John Bunny, Florence Lawrence, Mary Pickford and Norma Talmadge started to become familiar to cinemagoers throughout the world. Those who had become popular as the same character in an extended series were simply advertised and known to their fans by a *nom de film*, such as "Charlie Smiler." Significantly, one of the first actors to achieve international prominence under his actual name, the American cowboy star G.M. Anderson, had also established his own film company. In France and Italy, the successful stage comedian André Deed (1879–1940) made many slapstick film comedies as "Boiteau" (from 1906) and "Cretinetti" (from 1908), changing to "Foolshead" for the British market. Deed's rival, Charles Prince (1872–1933) was known, from 1908, by a variety of names in different countries; "Rigadin" in his native France, "Moritz" in Germany, "Tartufini" in Italy, "Prenz" in Russia and "Whiffles" in Britain.

A third French comedian, Max Linder (1883–1925) was to confirm Hepworth's worst fears about spiraling wage bills. His worldwide popularity playing a disaster-prone boulevardier had made him so valuable to Charles Pathé that, by 1912, he was able to command an annual salary of one million francs. As "Max Linder" he had been projected into international fame by a massive publicity campaign in 1909/1910. Unlike comedians whose nicknames altered across geographical boundaries, Linder's film credit remained the same. By 1913 *The Sphere* could comment "the most popular man in the world is Max Linder, the hero of the gayest and merriest French cinema plays."[2] His rivals Foolshead and Wiffles were not commonly recognized as André Deed and Charles Prince until 1912–1913.

Prince's breakthrough into public recognition was symbolically enacted on the stage of the Alhambra Theatre of Varieties, Leicester Square, in July 1915. As a guest star in the revue *Eightpence an Hour* the comedian crawled from beneath a screen depicting his movie character "Foolshead" to appear "in person" as Charles Prince. A similar device had been employed by Fred earlier the same year, when he opened a tour of cinemas at Kingston upon Thames, Surrey. At the conclusion of a film depicting "Pimple" at the Phoenix Studio on Eel Pie Island, an intertitle announced, "Here he is," signaling the frantic arrival of the comedian from the back of the auditorium. For the next fifty minutes the film performers Fred Evans and Tommie Collett entertained a live audience with a "very comical burlesque drama."[3]

The identification of the music-hall comedian behind the character "Pimple" occurred with the foundation of Folly Films in late 1912. Deciding to capitalize on a family name familiar to theater goers of all ages, Fred and Joe issued a series of press releases which acknowledged their uncle and grandfather, but, perhaps significantly, did not refer to their father:

> WHO IS "PIMPLE"? Cinema goers who have seen "Pimple" in many comic films. And in his original skits on well-known plays and films, may be interested to know that in private life he is just plain Mr. Fred Evans. This laughter-maker is a nephew of Will Evans (who has appeared so extensively in London and the provinces), and is also a grandson of Fred Evans, the Drury Lane clown of some years ago.[4]

Poster advertising Pimple films (courtesy of Glenn Mitchell).

Pimple's entertainment pedigree was firmly established and was thereafter consistently reasserted in extensive advertising and publicity.

Pimple and the Picturegoer

The cult of the "star" was promoted by a proliferation of periodicals aimed at the lengthening queues of information-hungry film fans. Magazines serving the cinema trade such as *The Kinematograph and Lantern Weekly* (first published in 1907) and *The Bioscope* (1909) were later joined by *Pictures and the Picturegoer* (1913); *Pictures and Pleasure* (1913); and *The Picture World* (1914). Reviews of the latest productions were published alongside portraits of the celebrities, details of their careers and, of crucial interests to readers seeking the personality behind the face, their views about anything and everything. To create a feeling of connectivity between stars and their admirers, periodicals ran competitions, published reader's letters, and provided an enquiry service. It was a forum not previously experienced by actors from the legitimate stage, but one which was familiar to Fred and Joe and their fellow music-hall performers. The brothers made extensive use of written publicity, particularly in the pages of *Pictures and the Picturegoer*.

A week seldom went by without Pimple's activities being mentioned or the comedian writing a humorous letter to his followers. In a readers' letter competition, he offered framed portraits to the three winners. Almost 2000 entries were received with the results being published on June 19, 1915. Second prize winner Robert Dunlop wrote:

> Dear "Merry" Pimple—I do not think I am wrong when I address you thus, for it is hardly possible for any actor to play parts such as yours unless he be of a merry disposition. I have been keenly interested in your work ever since the first "Pimple" film came out, and for a good many reasons, not the least of which is a desire to see our British film makers surpass those on the Continent and in America.
>
> Few British companies have tackled comic picture-making of the "American" type; yet as a rule these get the greatest applause of any with the exception of "Pimple's," which are the most laughter-making "take-offs," showing at present. As Punch is in the newspaper world, so is "Pimple" in the universe of pictures. As I said to a friend a few nights ago, "Pimple" films stand in a place of their own on account of the originality and conception of plot, the style of acting, and the eccentric make-up; whilst the "titling" is as funny as it is forceful. I well remember enjoying your acting in Dick Turpin's Ride to York, and, being a Cockney from Bermondsey, "Saart-east," I could fully appreciate the humour in the title "Hark! Hear ye not the belles of York?" followed by a presentation of a muffin seller "doing" his round.
>
> Another I enjoyed very much was Ivanhoe. A week or two previously I saw the dramatic picture of this historical story, and not unnaturally, had to go and see yours. I consider that your version was far and away the best, because, although in humorous vein, it kept very close to the real story.
>
> Picture-going is a thing I revel in; there is nothing takes one out of one's self as a night out at the cinema; troubles and worries are, for the time being, forgotten, and one goes home to sleep in a humor that even "old King Cole" himself would envy. Therefore, seeing that people want "cheering-up" after a day spent in the factory or workshop, at the same old job hour after hour, from year's end to year's end, I trust that you will always in the future have one end in view when making the pictures, and that is to try to make

Fred Evans portrayed as "Lieutenant Pimple" on the front cover of *Pictures and the Picturegoer*, March 13, 1915 (courtesy of Glenn Mitchell).

them even better than what they were before, however high the standard, and remember that you are performing something for the public good in doing so, for "laughing citizens" are usually "contented citizens," and these are the kind we require. I wish you every success in the moving-picture business and trust that it will be many years ere you retire from picture-making, even though you have a fortune at your bank.

I have three little girls and one boy, and as they all know "Pimple," a picture of you hanging on the parlour wall would be a source of unbounded pleasure for us all.[5]

In the issue for the week ending July 31, 1915, the magazine published a letter from Pimple asking his fans to nominate a holiday venue for him and his film crew. Considering that the filming break was to start on the 31st, it seems that the destination had already been selected. A typically jokey letter confirmed the comedian's whereabouts:

MY DEAR READERS—Here I am down at Hastings. I don't know how many films I shall take, as the sea is so tempting. I think I shall go winkling to-morrow, but it is awfully hard work chasing the winkles over the rocks. I think I had better go shrimping, but it is hard to catch these little bounders unless you dive for them. I hope to do a lot of good pictures while I am down there. One of them will be called "Pimple at Hastings," so look out for it. If there are not too many girls to take out I suppose I shall get it completed. Will write more next week—Yours "Pimple."[6]

In announcing Fred's success in the Greatest British Film Actor competition *Pictures and the Picturegoer* alluded to the part it had played in promoting his universal popularity:

Fred Evans, whose picture name is "Pimple," you *all* know. He tells us something about himself in his own peculiar way in this paper every week; and in addition we frequently have more or less to tell you about him. There was more than usual in our "Pimple Past and Present" article which appeared in our issue of April 3rd last. We have long suspected that "Pimple" was an immense favorite with picturegoers, and now, we know that he is, your votes having made for this busy and versatile comedian a place in the sun—that is to say, he is one of the six greatest British film players.[7]

Pimple's Juvenile Fans

Despite (or because of) the recurring themes of criminality, sexual behavior, drunkenness and disregard for authority, Pimple comedies were popular with children as well as adults. Dr. Luke McKernan has shown that, in the inner London area in 1911, cinemas were at their highest density in working class areas, with around a quarter of a million people visiting a show daily in 1914. Those attending were heterogenous in terms of age and gender, with children (including adolescents) predominating to such extent that they probably formed half the audience.[8] A survey conducted in 1913 at a Leeds school for 7- to 14-year-olds found that of 336 children, 331 had visited a cinema on at least one occasion. Seventy attended 2 to 4 times a week, while a further 163 went once a week.[9]

That Fred and Joe appreciated the role that children played in the reception of their films was demonstrated by their frequent employment of juvenile actors.

"Welcome to Pimple." Crowds gather outside the Empire Cinema, Seaford, Sussex, to greet the arrival of Fred Evans (wearing light suit). Photograph reproduced in *The Cinema* for June 11, 1914 (courtesy of Glenn Mitchell).

"Young Pimple," as portrayed by Tommie Collett, featured in several films; troops of boy Scouts often appeared; and gangs of children were regularly depicted terrorizing the adult world. In *Big Chief Little Pimple* (July 1914) Tommie received blood-curdling support:

> The youngsters in the film capture a policeman, tie him on a line fastened to the back of a horse, and drag the arm of the law through a pond. A picnic party is surrounded and captured by the young Redskins, an elderly gentleman is scalped, and this is followed by a war dance. It is interesting to note that most of the young actors appearing in this film are Twickenham boys.[10]

A regular children's section in *Pictures and the Picturegoer* written by "Uncle Tim" referred to Pimple as a favorite of its readers. His popularity with a juvenile audience was also confirmed by the list of the runners up in the letters competition which suggests that many of his fans were adolescent and even younger. The identities and addresses of the contestants are often hard to verify, but by consulting census records it is possible to estimate that most were female, predominantly aged 18 and under. Of the 54 contestants listed, at least 36 and possibly as many as 43 were female. The age of 22 females cannot be ascertained, while

A small boy ponders the movie camera, one of a crowd following Fred Evans' car in Coventry in October 1917. From *Pimple's End of a Perfect Day* (courtesy BFI National Archive).

four women were aged over 18. At least 10 of the letter-writers were females aged under 18. Where it can be established, the social background of the letter writers was upper working class to lower middle class. Miss Florence Papworth, age 47 of Catford, South London, was a shorthand typist; Miss Kate Coleman, age 18 of Camberwell, also South London, worked with confectionary; and the father of Maria Foster, age 16 of Accrington, Lancashire, ran a gentleman's outfitter. Other fathers of younger women included two who were involved with railways, two who worked in the piano trade, one who was a shoemaker and another a warehouse clerk. The father of Gladys Tarbotton, age 17 of Pudsey, Lancashire, was a designer of fancy-dress goods.

Picture Palace Perils

The identities of some young film fans are known because of less acceptable activities than letter writing. Like the juvenile inhabitants of Chatham in 1870 who were accused of stealing money to visit the Alhambra Music Hall, many children in the 1900s aroused grave concerns because of their insatiable desire to attend cinemas. Two boys from Devon, Archibald Ford, aged 11, and Freddy Taylor, aged 10, were each given three strokes of the birch for snatching a girl's purse outside a boot shop in Barnstable. At the local Juvenile Court in January 1912 Archie stated: "When we were outside Tucker's shop. Freddy Taylor said to me 'We are burglars.' We have seen pictures like it at the Picture Palace and that is why we did it. We stole the purse to go to the Picture Palace to-night."[11]

Many other instances of the corrupting influence of the cinema on young people were reported and discussed. The early French feature film *Zigomar* (1911), depicting a master criminal and his sinister confederates, contributed to the downfall of four Scottish youths. In April 1913 two boys were sent to reformatories, one to an industrial school and another placed on probation after they had committed a string of robberies in Edinburgh. Basing themselves on the film the boys had formed the "Black Hand Gang" under the leadership of "Zigomar," a 12-year-old named William Costagliola (itself a reasonable moniker for a cinema villain). Although their haul of gas-piping, an iron fender, a few boots and shoes and an alarm clock was a poor substitute for the heaps of jewelry plundered by the original Zigomar and his black-costumed band, the boys remained true to their original inspiration, spending their ill-gotten gains on return visits to the local cinema.[12] Commenting on the case of three boys who stole flashlights from a shop at the end of 1912, the Chief Constable of Wigan, Lancashire, stated picture palaces "had a bad effect on boys of that class and they would stop at nothing to get possession of toy pistols and the like."[13] Some cases took the imitation of films to a more dangerous level. In May 1914 two boys were sentenced to 12 strokes of the birch for attempting to derail trains on the main line

"I 've seen it—'tain't no good."
"'E gets 'ung, don't 'e?"
"Yus, but they don't show yer that."

The adverse effects of films on young cinema goers depicted in a 1916 *Punch* cartoon (author's collection)

outside Falkirk High Station, Scotland. Agreeing that he had witnessed a similar scene in a film, one boy stated that "the picture showed a man putting things on the rails, and that a train came along and was thrown over a cliff."[14]

The film models for boys committing such criminal acts were usually alleged to be bandits, outlaws, cowboys, charismatic malefactors like Zigomar and uncontrollable children such as Little Pimple. As with other new forms of entertainment (before and since), films were criticized for an addictive quality that adversely affected the behavior of young people. Alongside those who condemned the cinema, there were some saw its negative influences as only the latest manifestation of an age-old situation. In 1913 a Lancashire local newspaper reported:

> During the course of the Literary Society's lecture on Monday on "The Modern Theatre," the lecturer stated that in his opinion the visiting of children to picture palaces put ideas of craft and cunning into the minds of children. He illustrated this by the fact of youthful offenders often stating in the police courts that they had "seen it done on the pictures," The point was strongly contested by Mr. W. Cross, who was of opinion that the lust for crime was in the youthful mind long before they saw the pictures and that the picture palace was only an up-to-date excuse for criminal acts which a few years ago were attributed to the evil influence of reading "penny dreadfuls." &c.[15]

Among the unruly stacks of ephemera in Denis Gifford's collection there were many examples of the publications that were claimed to have had such a baleful effect on the nation's youth. Throughout much of the 19th century and into the 20th, young people had devoured weekly serial issues that romanticized the fictitious exploits of historic criminals such as Claude Duval, Dick Turpin, and Jack Shepherd. Young "heroes" were also created who rebelled against society to embark on defiant and subversive adventures. A periodical that was also present in Gifford's archive was *Comic Life* which from October 1920–December 1921 portrayed the disreputable escapades of "Pimple." The cartons, by artist Bertie Brown, were clearly aimed at a juvenile readership, but appeared at a time when Pimple films were beginning to disappear from the cinema screen.

CHAPTER 12

The Humor of the Halls

Last Christmas Eve just for a lark
I went with a burglar after dark
We broke into a lady's salon, my,
And then I heard that burglar cry.
"Come and have a look what I've got!"[1]

REVERBERATING FROM A clockwork gramophone, the song is conjured up by the interaction of a steel needle and a rapidly-spinning shellac disc. Vibrations of the artist's voice have been cut onto a wax master—via a large horn—and then recreated as grooves on the issued recording. Analogous to light projected through celluloid film, it is a satisfyingly direct process which seems to preserve the very essence of a long-dead performer. In this case, the personality provided with mechanical resurrection is Billy Williams, a comedian described on the record's label as "The Man in the Velvet Suit." Like his friend Fred Evans, Billy was an archetypal exponent of what was condescendingly referred to as "The Humor of the Halls."

"Come and Have a Look What I've Got" describes the sort of imaginary escapade regularly embarked upon by Pimple fans after taking their seats in the darkness of the cinema. Billy's recordings and Fred's films were often set in a comically distorted working-class world where drunkenness, deception, random criminality, illicit flirtations, and violent behavior were the rule rather than the exception. Deviant and anti-social conduct had been "celebrated" by comedians on the variety stage for many years, but, through new technology, both men represented such themes to wider audiences than had previously been accessible. Billy and Fred gave extended exposure to music-hall humor, frequently exhibiting a jocular disregard for "middle-class morality" and many aspects of its unwelcome enforcement.

Historians have frequently dismissed the influence of music-hall humor on early British cinema as a short-lived phase during which comedies were cruel, vulgar and, most damning to modern eyes, primitive. But, even after the last variety theaters has succumbed to the advance of picture palaces, aspects of the cultural heritage of the earlier medium persisted. Social historian Andy Medhurst was one of the first to offer an opinion that diverged from a predominately aesthetic view of film history:

Clearly, the likes of Pimple and Old Mother Riley are less than central to film histories with commitments to privileging stylistic forms or directorial authorship. Yet any history of British cinema that realizes the need to situate the cinematic institution within its shifting webs of social relations needs to pay great attention to the legacies of music hall. British popular culture would be unrecognizable without the diffused influences of music hall modes. Film comedy, and radio and television light entertainment, can only be thoroughly understood in relation to those influences.[2]

Alf Collins

The ill-fitting costumes of red-nosed comedians and the extravagant falls and collisions of knockabout troupes are obvious areas in which cinema reflected music-hall antecedents. Less clear are the ways in which film inherited content and structure from theatrical stereotypes, multi-versed songs, and stage chases. Before the advent of the Ec-Ko company, the most significant music-hall influence on film was that exerted by the comedian and director Alf Collins (1867–1951). Many of his films made for the British Gaumont company from 1902 adopted a strongly anti-establishment approach that was consistent with his background in popular theater and music hall. Born in Brewhouse Yard in the poverty-stricken South East London district of Newington, Collins consistently sided with the alienated and downtrodden in his films, often featuring the overthrow of oppressive authority. Typically, the surviving *The Eviction* (1904) depicts a group of impoverished Irish cottagers resisting and finally routing the bailiffs who have come to eject them from their homes. Less violent, but equally subversive were productions such as *When Extremes Meet* (1904) in which Collins and his wife Maud play a costermonger couple whose uninhibited sexual behavior disgusts a middle-class couple

Pimple in the familiar role of burglar, cartoon advertising *Pimple's Good Turn* (1915) (author's collection).

and, indirectly, leads to arrest of a clergyman. The blundering "bobby" taking the unfortunate priest into custody was typical of Collins' treatment of the police who were inevitably depicted as cowardly, greedy, stupid, lazy, or lascivious.

As with other aspects of Collins' films, the negative portrayal of policemen had its origins in long-established music-hall practices. With one brother, George Collins, famous as a comedian and a sister, Nellie Cotter, a popular *soubrette*, Collins was well-versed in the humorous protocols of the variety stage. An extensive compendium of such conventions was also provided in the work of another brother Charles Collins (1874–1923), one of the most prolific and successful of music-hall songwriters. It is not difficult to detect similarities between Alf Collins' films and Charles Collins' songs. Frantic movie chases reflect such quick-fire comic numbers as "Any Old Iron" and "Cover It Over Quick, Jemima," while the working-class background of many of his films is inseparable from that of the songs "Are We to Part Like This, Bill?" and "Now I Have to Call Him Father." The output of both brothers was generated by and for the music hall, most of Alf Collins' films being originally shown on the same stages that echoed to Charles Collins' songs.

From Song to Screen

Although Fred's comedies were made for exhibition in cinemas rather than variety theaters, they shared many elements with Alf Collins' earlier productions. Like the older comedian, Fred had spent much of his time in a music-hall environment and his subjects and situations frequently echoed its songs and sketches. In Fred's first known film, *The Last of the Dandy*, his hostile reception by a party of jilted woman was a standard theme in comic-songs, exemplified in Fred Earle's hymn to profligacy "For Me":

> Down the street there's a blooming riot.
> Five-and-twenty girls are waiting there,
> And the police cannot keep them quiet,
> They won't go—for you know—ev'ry maiden fair—
> For me! For me! Is waiting there for me!
> But they'll have to wait till a man can swear,
> There's not a tart near Leicester Square,
> Ah! Ah! Eh! Eh! I'm not going back, you see,
> If anybody knows a thing worth two.
> It's me, me, me, me, me![3]

It is not difficult to find Pimple films that correspond to the episodes and imagery of comic songs. Fred pursuit of the feather boa in *Pimple and the Snake* echoes Billy Williams' "Come and Have a Look What I've Got":

> Auntie Jane's got a feather boa, came home late and left it on the floor,
> Uncle came home tight and spied that feather and loudly cried

"Come and have a look, come and have a look, come and have a look what I've got."
He cried out to Auntie Jane "Oh Good Lord, they're coming on again.
I've seen some snakes," said Uncle John "but I've never seen a snake with feather on.
Come and have a look what I've got."

The uncontrolled, and uncontrollable, use of a paste brush is central to both Billy Williams' most famous song "When Father Papered the Parlour" and the existing film *Pimple's New Job*. The protagonist of the song is an amateur paperhanger who brings chaos to his home:

> When father papered the parlour, you couldn't see pa for paste,
> Dabbing it here, dabbing it there, paste and paper everywhere,
> Mother was stuck to the ceiling; the kids were stuck to the floor
> I never knew a blooming family so stuck up before.[4]

Although employed as a bill sticker, Pimple still contrives to cause domestic disorder by pasting posters onto a man taking a bath and a woman cleaning the doorstep.

There are many further examples. A confrontation with a belligerent tenant in *Pimple as a Rent Collector* was anticipated by Harry Freeman in a song of 1900:

> I took a job as broker's man, and once I had to roam
> Up half a dozen flights of stairs to mind somebody's home.
> The husband came out with a gun, and said "Now, what's the row?"
> I answered "I'm the broker's man, but really I think now
> I'd better call again next week."[5]

A splash of music-hall vulgarity. Pimple gleefully invites the audience to join him in a gross invasion of personal space and privacy in *Pimple's New Job* (1914) (courtesy of Bob Geoghegan, Archive Film Agency).

The runaway vehicle that caused such havoc in *Pimple's Motor Bike* had a four-wheeled counterpart in Vesta Victoria's "Riding on a Motor Car":

> Off we started at a rare old speed,
> Knocked down a policeman but we took no heed,

The lackluster firefighters in *Pimples Fire Brigade* and *Pimple's Great Fire of London* were rivaled in their ineptitude by those in T.E. Dunville's "The Fire was Burning Hot":

> Our gallant lads were fast asleep
> Awaiting duty's call,
> When someone brought the fearful news
> That mesmerised us all.
> A chimney pot was smoking
> Only ten miles further on
> And if we didn't hurry up
> The beer would all be gone.[6]

Understandably, Fred and Joe sometimes appropriated comic situations and themes from their performer relatives. The Egberts' most enduring gag was introduced into *Pimple Gets the Sack* (August 1913) with Pimple frightening a burglar by hiding inside his voluminous swag bag. One of Will Evan's earliest experiments in the sketch format, "Lady Godiva" (1903) supplied a prototype for *Pimple's Lady Godiva* (c. May 1917). Will's original music-hall production also featured a pantomime horse, a comical animal that was to feature in many Pimple films.

Comic Characters

Of all the comic stereotypes shared by music hall and film, one of the most popular of the time and least palatable to modern tastes was the character of "The Suffragette." Campaigners for women's suffrage provided several immediately recognizable features (placards, sashes, and offensively deployed umbrellas) and were easy to caricature on stage and in film. But, like the similarly distinctive figure of "The Anarchist" (long cape, broad brimmed hat, and smoking bomb), the suffragette's political objectives were not examined. Often a male comedian sang about the personal inconveniences created by the women's suffrage movement, identifying its main objective as the subjection of mankind. In "The Land Where the Women Wear the Trousers" Billy Williams sang:

> The fellows all go out on Sunday dressed in petticoats,
> They're not allowed in parliament; the girls have all the votes.[7]

Fred's colleagues at Ec-Ko, Bella and Bijou produced a comic sketch, "The Suffragette," in which a shrewish wife, the president of the "Society for the Abolition of Man," confiscated her husband's door key and forced him to remain at home mending the linen. In his music-hall act Will Evans went as far as to represent the

Fred Evans follows in Will Evans' footsteps by burlesquing Lady Godiva in *Pimple's Lady Godiva* (1917). The only surviving film in which Fred Evans plays a female role (courtesy of Bob Geoghegan, Archive Film Agency).

leader of the movement Emeline Pankhurst as "Mrs. Pancake," haranguing a public meeting about "Women with a big 'W' and a small man."

When portrayed in Pimple films, suffragettes might sometimes behave in a violent manner, as in the lone woman who ambushed Napoleon in *Pimple's Battle of Waterloo*, but usually they were merely "types" such as the policeman, the shopkeeper, the muffin-man and the nursemaid, taking their place in a long line of characters to be set up and then demolished. The motives for Pimple's female impersonation in *"Miss Pimple," Suffragette* (June 1913) were inexplicable, and the film seems to have aimed at ridiculousness rather than ridicule:

> Pimple's eye alights on an advertisement in the paper: "Wanted. A strong, able, fearless woman to smash windows.—Apply Mrs. Hammer, Headquarters." With the help of the landlady, Pimple is transformed into a veritable suffragette and proceeds to headquarters. Here "Miss" Pimple is armed with a bomb, and the militants interview Mr. Asquirt. This ends disastrously for that gentleman. Mr. Geoyd Lorge, is next tackled whilst playing golf. Miss Pimple aspires to something great, nothing less than the stopping of the Boat Race. This is carried out, the crews being thrown into the water by the Suffragette launch. "Miss" Pimple soon finds "herself" in the dock, and decides to hunger-strike unless supplied with the best of everything. Afraid of the consequences, the authorities at once accede, and a little later we find "Miss" Pimple and the warder hobnobbing together in fine style.[8]

"The Suffragette" was a stereotype of recent evolution, but others went back to the early days of music-hall. Songs based around occupations had long been popular and, like generations of performers, Fred utilized the familiar appearances and

Pimple's New Job (1914). Pimple becomes a bill sticker with predictably disastrous results (courtesy of Bob Geoghegan, Archive Film Agency).

characteristics of various workers as a frame on which to hang his comedy. Pimple tried his hand, usually unsuccessfully, at many jobs including actor, ballet dancer, billsticker, boxer, busker, jockey, member of parliament (corrupt, of course) and rent collector. Despite playing policemen and detectives, he was depicted more frequently as a lawbreaker. If "criminal" could be categorized as a profession, Pimple portrayed a great many of its subdivisions. He was alternatively a burglar (on multiple occasions), bicycle-thief, child-stealer, conman, fraudster, convict, extortionist, gunrunner, highwayman, smuggler, and an anarchist. Such was the expectation that he would be engaged in illegal activities, that Folly produced one film titled *Pimple Turns Honest*. A consequence of Pimple's criminal activities was that he was often on the run, pursued from one frantic scene to the next. In his frequent use of the chase Fred was not only following earlier filmmakers, but theatrical precedents. Like Alf Collins, Fred drew heavily on the chase elements of the traditional Harlequinade, but he also took inspiration from the multiple verses of the comic song and their interpretation on stage for a flight-based, episodic narrative.

Burlesques and Parodies

One of the few crimes not committed by Pimple was stealing another person's work, a misdemeanor that might be—and once famously was—leveled against Fred. Like the efforts of many of his contemporaries, his comedy was often founded on the original productions of others. Ridicule of different forms of entertainment, both content and performance, had been an intrinsic feature of music hall since its establishment in the 1840s. Early performers such as W.G. Ross and Sam Cowell specialized in sendups of serious songs and dramas, with both achieving success in comedy versions of Shakespearean tragedies. Music hall's undisputed master of burlesque and parody, Harry Pleon (1864–1911), died at about the time of Fred's first film appearances. As both a writer for other artists and performer of his own material, Pleon's humor was by no means subtle. It was typified by gibberish versions of drawing-room ballads and dramatic recitations and by the broadest pastiches of melodrama. Among his scores of parodies of popular songs were at least eight versions of "Ta-Ra-Ra-Boom-De-Ay."

Burlesque and parody existed side-by-side on the music-hall stage and were often confused with each other. The most famous comedian of his day, Dan Leno, employed them in conjunction in his parody of the drawing-room ballad "Queen of My Heart." The original romantic words:

> For my heart is wildly beating,
> As it never beat before.
> One word! One whispered greeting
> In mercy I implore.

Became the distinctly unromantic:

> And my nose began a bleeding,
> As it never bled before
> And while his mercy I was pleading
> He rolled me up and down on the floor.

While the words that Dan sang were clearly a *parody*, his comic imitation of a serious concert singer (preserved in an early recording) was a *burlesque*. Generally, performers restricted themselves to one mode, such as Will Evans and company dressed as chickens in their 1910 burlesque of Rostand's *Chanticleer* or Billy Williams in his series of infectiously cheerful parodies of popular songs. Fred's films contain elements of both parody and burlesque and were influenced not only by his direct involvement with music hall and pantomime, but by the comedians that he appeared with or knew personally. Both Billy Williams and Fred Earle were acquainted with Will Evans, occupying neighboring residences in "Bungalow Town."

Music Hall's Reality Check

Although trading in fiction, many music-hall comedians presented a first-person account of the world around them. They might adopt the roles of serial lawbreakers or transgressors of social etiquette, but their characterizations usually possessed a veracity that established a close rapport with audiences. As Eric

Midwinter observed in *Make 'Em Laugh*: "part of being a great comedian lies, consciously or unconsciously, in being attuned to the refrains of society, in hearing its melodies, in orchestrating them, and in playing them back." Comedians, he continued, were offering escapism, but it was an "escape *into* reality" rather than *from* it.[9]

It was not Fred Evans or Billy Williams who acted as the public's guides to this humorously re-engineered reality, but "Pimple" and "The Man in the Velvet Suit." Both characterizations were easily identified by their costume and make-up. While their appearances were well-established, their behavior and psychology fluctuated wildly from one episode to the next. The dichotomy was illustrated by the artists who provided the covers for the published sheet-music versions of comedy songs. A central, static portrait of the performer in costume was detailed and precise, clearly based on an original photograph. But surrounding this image were usually a collection of vignettes which illustrated the varying verses of the song. Although the comedian was once again featured, it was as an animated, cartoon-like character. The need to establish and maintain a unique visual identity, did not bring with it the absolute necessity of maintaining a consistent narrative. On gramophone recordings and in films, "The Man in the Velvet Suit" and "Pimple" revealed a series of disparate and only loosely connected adventures. But punctuating the chaos there were moments when they asserted their central authorial presence with an apparently unscripted comment or sly gesture to the camera.

The sense of reality created by music-hall comedians was not entirely reliant on the representation of a familiar personality and reference to everyday subjects. In a fluid performing environment, topicality was easy to introduce and added immediacy to performances. Such was the popularity of songs about contemporary issues that a whole sub-category of comic singers billed as "Topical Vocalists" flourished during the second half of the 19th century. During the early 1900s such material formed a routine part of many comedian's acts. Billy Williams sang about the recently introduced taxi-meter cab; suffragettes; the new-fangled gramophone and "When Mother Backed the Winner of the Derby," all subjects covered in Fred's films.

Billy and Fred appeared together in at least one "Pimple" production although it and its title are now lost. The film, or at least a section of it, survived into the 1970s when the recorded-sound historian, Ernie Bayly, was alerted to its existence in a private collection. By the time Bayly arranged to inspect the film, its owner's grandchildren had employed it as a disposable plaything, leaving only a fragment showing the two comedians in discussion before a notice proclaiming, "Home Sweet Home." Unlike his moving image, Billy's hundreds of disc and cylinder recordings made between 1907 and 1915 insured that his name and voice were remembered for years after his premature death. He died, aged 37, in 1915, and his grave can be found in Shoreham Cemetery, alongside Fred Earle who died in the same year at the same early age.

CHAPTER 13

Pimple's Patriotism

WHEN BRITAIN DECLARED WAR against Germany on August 8, 1914, not everyone was carried away on a flood of patriotic fervor. With hostilities showing little sign of being concluded by Christmas, many potential recruits began to search for ways in they might appear to be "doing their bit" without putting themselves in harm's way. Recognizing the inevitability of conscription, many men contrived to enlist in regiments less likely to be involved in combat. There was no need for Fred to consider such a strategy for his value to the country's morale was strong enough for him to be allowed to remain at home. Over the course of one year and 113 days his performance as a private in the 1st Surrey Rifles was perhaps his finest piece of burlesque acting.

Remarkably, Fred and Joe had just made a feature-length drama that enabled them to capitalize on an initial enthusiasm for military subjects. At 3000 feet *Stolen Honours* (May 1914) was amongst their longest films and one of the few in which the brothers attempted serious roles. Joe's tale of love, heroism and betrayal set against the background of the Boer War was just the sort of overblown melodrama that the brothers would normally have subjected to ridicule. An advert for the Pavilion Cinema, Wigan, announced:

> The Most Thrilling War Drama ever filmed. STOLEN HONOURS! In the plethora of War Drama now showing, this great film stands alone. The story is one of Intense Human Interest and the very spirit of warfare permeates the atmosphere.[1]

Despite the stirring themes and exciting scenes of "military maneuvers, ambuscades, trench-fighting and gun-running" depicted in *Stolen Honours*,[2] the brothers were not moved to enlist until they were left with little choice. There was no such delay in deploying their comedy hero. In *Pimple Enlists* (October 1914) the newly recruited Pimple fell asleep at his post and dreamt about being captured by a horde of invading Germans. Such farcical antics shown alongside newsreels depicting refugees fleeing their shattered homes in Belgium do not appear to have struck a discordant note with cinema audiences. *The Bioscope* commented:

> Pimple is a wonderfully adaptable person. All is humor that comes to his net. He can make fun of people and of things, of ideas and institutions. Whatever he touches turns into laughter. And throughout his adventures he is consistently amusing.
>
> It was inevitable, of course, that Pimple should turn his attention to the great war, which seems indeed to have provided him with exceptionally favorable material. War, of course,

is not, as a whole, a laughing matter, and it should be pointed out that Pimple's skits in connection therewith are strictly confined to such aspects of the subject as lend themselves to jesting. The jokes which this talented comedian knows so well how to crack have always been in the best of taste, and never cruel or out of place. In fact, he vies with Punch in the tone of his humor, which is ever kindly, free from bitterness, and inspired by the true spirit of mirth.

"Pimple Enlists" may be described as a skit on the German Army and the Kaiser, who are unmercifully satirized in this excellent film. Every weak spot in the enemy's armor is pierced by the keen wit of Pimple, and the result is a burlesque which will make every audience that sees it fairly shout with delight. In these sad days we have quite enough of the horrors of war in our newspapers, if not in our own lives, and there is none who will not hail with pleasure the welcome relief provided by this really clever film. As we have already pointed out, it's fun is pure and legitimate fun which can be painful to no one. There are no burlesque war scenes. It is simply a merry joke at the expense of our foe. Altogether, "Pimple Enlists" is a thoroughly wholesome and delightful little entertainment.[3]

For the first year of the war hostilities only featured in a few Pimple comedies, notably *How Lieutenant Pimple Captured the Kaiser* (November 1914); *Pimple in the Kilties* (January 1915); and *Pimple's Dream of Victory* (March 1915). As might be expected, Pimple films treated the gravity of the European situation with scant respect. An earlier form of entertainment, the Harlequinade, was invoked for *The Clowns of Europe* (November 1914). After an opening in which the Kaiser and Crown Prince were transformed from their normal appearance into Clown and Pantaloon, a series of comic episodes—such as the rampaging duo attempting to "nick" the globe—paralleled the frantic comedy of the traditional Christmas pantomime. Britannia was depicted as Columbine and the Prime Minister, Herbert Asquith, as an unlikely Harlequin. Review the production *The Kinematograph and Lantern Weekly* observed that "on one hand it is seasonable—nothing could be more so—while on the other side it should appeal to the patriotic inclinations of an audience which delights in seeing the enemy trounced on the screen."[4]

For Pimple and Country

If the authenticity of letters to *Pictures and the Picturegoer* can be trusted, the armed forces were amused by Pimple's treatment of the conflict:

> I went to the Pictures the other night (a thing I never do) and saw a fine film, "The Long Way." It was splendidly put on though the subject was not quite what I like; but "Pimple" livened us up afterward in giving "his dream" of what he could do with the German Fleet and the Kaiser. His walking about on the bottom of the Kiel Canal was a scream. What a queer card he must be in real life! I simply roared with laughter, and a sailor chum who was with me—well, I have never seen him laugh so much before. This was my first to Pictures since we were brought into dry dock at Liverpool, but I assure you it will not be the last. A SAILOR OF THE KING (Liverpool).[5]

Fred was gradually drawn into the war effort, at first just lightening the national mood with his absurd comedies but subsequently making personal appearances to persuade able-bodied men to accept the "King's shilling" and to take their places in the trenches. Entertainers, particularly female performers, had been used to encourage recruitment since the earliest stages of the conflict. On the music-hall stage Vesta Tilley sang "The Army of Today's All Right" while Marie Lloyd offered "I Do Like You, Cockie, Now You've Got Yer Khaki On." The war's most famous recruiting song had originally been performed by Gwendoline Brogden in *The Passing Show* at the Palace Theatre, London, shortly before the outbreak of hostilities. The beautiful and enticing Gwendoline sung:

> The army and the navy need attention
> The outlook isn't healthy, you'll admit,
> But I've got a perfect dream
> Of a new recruiting scheme
> Which I really think is absolutely it.
> If only other girls would do as I do
> I believe that we could manage it alone
> For I turn all suitors from me
> But the sailor or the Tommy
> I've an army and a navy of my own.
> On Sunday I walk out with a soldier,
> On Monday I'm taken by a Tar.
> On Tuesday I'm out with a baby boy scout
> And on Wednesday a Hussar,
> On Thursday I gang oot wi' a Scottie,
> But on Saturday I'm willing,
> If you only take the shilling
> To make a man of anyone of you.

Many of those who serving in the armed forces were not impressed by Miss Brogden's generous offer. In a brutal parody of the song, they retorted:

> I don't want to join the army,
> I don't want to go to war.
> I'd rather hang around, Piccadilly Underground.
> Living on the earnings of a … well-bred lady.
> I don't want a bayonet up my arsehole,
> I don't want my bollocks shot away.
> I'd rather stay in Blighty, in jolly, jolly Blighty
> And fornicate my fucking life away.

Fred did not object to joining the army, but he did not want a sharpened blade anywhere near his cinematic parts. By early 1915 he and Joe had left Folly/Phoenix to start making films for the Weston-Finn Feature Film Company at studios situated in a converted ice-rink, at 225 Queen's Road, Westbourne Grove, West London. Charles Weston and Arthur Finn had founded the company when they left British and Colonial in 1914, creating three subsidiaries "Regent," "Pussyfoot" and "Piccadilly." Pimple comedies were released under the Piccadilly brand and distributed by H.A. Browne. Joe told Denis Gifford that he had never met Finn but remembered that Weston left after they had made only a few films. "He was an American" he recalled "and had a shattered leg for which he had to take doses or injections of morphine to stop pain."[6]

Charles Weston was in his movie-making element following the outbreak of war. Already a specialist in "battle films," he lost no time in directing a string of patriotic features for Regent; *Called to the Front, Saving the Colours, Through the Firing Line, For King and Country, On the Russian Frontier, Facing the Enemy, None but the Brave, The War Baby, The Bugle Boy of Lancashire* and *The Road to Calais*—all released by December 1914. He may have regarded his two new comedians with mixed feelings, for he was also the director of the film that provoked their first prolonged bout of ridicule, *The Battle of Waterloo*.

When the first three Pimple comedies were released by Piccadilly in April 1915, Weston's publicist placed special emphasis on their production values—a curious move when Pimple comedies had previously been noted for their low budget and ramshackle approach. Advertised as "Number 1," *Pimple's New Job*, attempted to show the extensive scale of Weston's activities by portraying the comedian seeking employment in three films which were being made alongside each other at the Regent Studio. Number 2, *Pimple Up the Pole* was claimed to have a cast of 500, while number 3, *Pimple's Three Weeks*, was claimed to be the "Largest and Greatest Comedy Ever Produced." The raucous send up of Elinor Glyn's scandalous novel reportedly used "twenty motor cars, a cast of 300 people, including the Regent Stock Company and entire stock of scenery."[7] It was a lavish departure from Pimple's usual humble offerings and one which soon became a cause of national debate (see following chapter).

One of Fred and Joe's first productions for the new company was a burlesque which obliquely reflected their own non-enlisted status. "Christopher Brent," the central figure in the 1914 stage drama and the 1915 Hepworth film *The Man Who Stayed at Home*, had been condemned as a coward when he ignored the call to the colors but was later revealed to be a secret service agent bravely attempting to crack an enemy spy ring. Although the Evans brothers had no such secret mission, there appears to have been little public criticism of their own stay-at-home position. As with reviews of other films, the description of *Pimple's The Man Who Stayed at Home* (June 1915) published in a provincial newspaper focused on the comic character, not the performer:

> Pimple, in the uniform of a naval lieutenant comes up to the Admiralty to begin a job. But when they see him the board decide that he would undoubtedly be better off on a less maritime mission, and he is told off to hunt down a gang of dangerous German spies, whose machinations threaten the state. When Pimple gets properly going he is not quite sure whether a fair siren wants to make love to him or to make mincemeat of him, and she alternately wheedles him and follows him with a long knife. He invites her to spend the evening with him at the café, and whilst there she drugs his champagne. Luckily, however, he sees her do it and instead of drinking the poison he throws it away. In order to deceive her he feigns death, and she returns to the secret meeting place of the spies and informs them that at last she has killed the much-to-be-feared Pimple. He has not met his end, however, and subsequent events in his career are most amusing, the picture being one continuous laugh.[8]

Fred and Joe Enlist

During the summer of 1915, every person aged between 15 and 65 was recorded under a National Registration Act and the details of men aged from 18–41 were transcribed on to pink cards, sometimes called pink forms. Informed by these colorful, but dreaded, pieces of stationery, recruiting officers began to put intense pressure on eligible men to join the armed forces. It was becoming clear that conscription was only a matter of months away. Joe explained to Denis Gifford that his brother eventually came to an arrangement with the authorities that, if he enlisted, his military duties would be confined to recruitment. Pimple would make a series of film-related personal appearances throughout the UK, dressed in khaki and encouraging adult males in his audience to join up. After enlisting in the 1st Surrey Rifles on August 5, 1915, Fred spent three weeks filming and recruiting in Hastings, on the Kent coast.[9]

The situation in British cinemas in the summer of 1915 was summarized by the *Motion Picture News* published in the neutral United States:

> Pathé is releasing a number of films showing scenes of actual trench warfare. Despite the excellence of the numerous war films I have seen, over and over again, cinema managers have said, "I don't believe in featuring too strongly war films. People come to picture houses for amusement, and it is up to us to give them a good wholesome entertainment, without recapitulating the horrors of the battlefield."

> For the benefit of American manufacturers, I give a summary of an official document issued by the Liverpool magistrates on the subject. They say that no pictures should be shown which emphasize the sadness and suffering of the war, but on the other hand pictures which act as an incentive to recruiting, and stimulate loyalty, are pictures which are acceptable and desirable. Thus cinemas will assist "to preserve a healthy public tone at a time of great national crisis."

> Trade is in a flourishing condition. New cinemas are opening every week, without affecting to any serious degree the business of the older established houses. Comedies treated in a novel way, and featuring a striking personality are in demand. A number of British firms are now specializing in this direction, particularly H.A. Browne & Company, who are handling the "Pimple" productions, which have had an extremely good run.

> Although "Pimple" has enlisted,

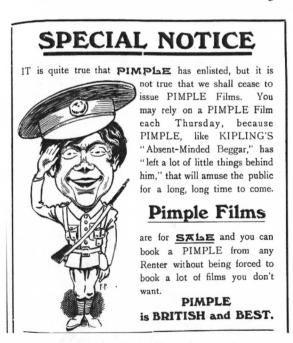

SPECIAL NOTICE

IT is quite true that **PIMPLE** has enlisted, but it is not true that we shall cease to issue PIMPLE Films. You may rely on a PIMPLE Film each Thursday, because PIMPLE, like KIPLING'S "Absent-Minded Beggar," has "left a lot of little things behind him," that will amuse the public for a long, long time to come.

Pimple Films

are for **SALE** and you can book a PIMPLE from any Renter without being forced to book a lot of films you don't want.

PIMPLE is BRITISH and BEST.

Following Fred Evans joining the armed forces in 1915, adverts assured distributors that Pimple comedies would still be available (author's collection).

Messrs. Browne hold a large number of negatives featuring him, and a new film will be released every week for the next twelve months.[10]

Preventing Pessimism

The war did not often feature in Pimple films and when it did, it was usually as the background to events on the home front. Pimple's comedy became a weapon for combatting national pessimism, as in *Rations* (March 1918), which was described as "a delightful 'all British' comic which shows how we as a nation have the knack of making fun of our troubles."[11] Divided into two parts, the film consisted of "Pimple in the Queue" and "Pimple and his Coupons." In the first reel Pimple tried a series of unsuccessful ruses to get to the front of a food queue and was later caught by a policeman hoarding supplies up his chimney (the PC confiscated them and carried them home to his wife). Pimple's problem in the second reel was his limited supply of coupons for essential commodities such as kisses—happily resolved when his numerous lady friends contributed their own coupons.

Pimple's Zeppelin Scare (April 1916) depicted a couple taking shelter after mistaking a musician for an air-raid siren, while *Pimple's Pink Forms* (April 1916) showed the comedian rejected from the army and having to deliver the unwelcome official forms. Having been captured by Lieutenant Pimple at the beginning of the war, the German emperor returned the compliment by snatching the comedian with the aid of a zeppelin in *The Kaiser Captures Pimple* (September 1915). The Western Front and its trenches were palely reflected in *Pimple's Better 'Ole* (August 1918), a burlesque of a film of a musical comedy based on a cartoon.

When Fred enlisted, comparisons were inevitably made with Charlie Chaplin's decision to remain in the United States. Chaplin's contractual arrangement with Mutual sought to avoid the danger of the star being mobilized by stipulating that he should not return to Britain for the

PICCADILLY FILMS.

The Kaiser Captures Pimple

A really funny film with a laugh in each scene.

DON'T MISS IT.

Released · *Sept. 16th, 1915*
Length · *1020 ft. approx.*

Look out for the funniest film of the year.

Pimple's Burlesque
of
'THE STILL ALARM'

Length · *1750 ft.*
Released · *Oct. 4th.*

All Open Market Films.

Pimple dreams that he has been abducted by the Kaiser operating a German sausage–shaped Zeppelin. Advert for *The Kaiser Captures Pimple* published August 26, 1915 (author's collection).

duration of the hostilities. It was a situation generally accepted by those who saw the comedian's films as boosting public morale. But criticism of Chaplin came to a head with a blistering attack in the *Weekly Dispatch* in June 1917:

> Charlie in khaki would be one of the most popular figures in the Army. He would compete in popularity even with Bairnsfather's "Old Bill." If his condition did not warrant him going into the trenches he could do admirable work by amusing troops in billets. In any case, it is Charlie's duty to offer himself as a recruit and thus show himself proud of his British origin. It is his example which will count so very much, rather than the difference to the war that his joining up will make. We shall win the war without Charlie, but (his millions of admirers will say) we would rather win with him.[12]

The 1915 Christmas issue of *Pictures and the Picturegoer* contained a two-page cartoon depicting cinema stars at a festive party. Chaplin was depicted tripping Pimple, an incident which was described in the accompanying text:

> A moment later the door crashed open, and amid cheers a waiter staggered in beneath a pyramid of plates, while a rich voice trolled gaily:—
> "When I get my civie clothes on—"
> "No more soldiering for me—
> But Rule Britannia, Brit–"
> —Crash! Bang!! Crash!!!
> A little man whose pedal extremities are the envy of every village policeman, and whose moustache has set the fashion among Army officers and others, had sprung nimbly from his seat, and, hooking the Pimplesque waiter deftly round the neck with his cane, caused the crockery to crash to the ground. For a breathless moment the snub-nosed one tottered on his base, then pulled himself together. "Watcherdo that for" he roared and his stentorian tones told clearly where he had been spending the last few months. "You big-footed, baggy-trousered monopoly, I'll show you.... Wait until they find your pink form my bright lad," his soldierly antagonist exclaimed. "Oh, may I be a drill-sergeant then."[13]

An advert placed in the *Bioscope* by H.A. Browne emphasized that Pimple was doing his duty:

> A Royal Engagement "Pimple" England's Greatest Film Comedian is Still Fulfilling the CONTRACT He Entered into Last Year with His Majesty the King, For Three Years or the Duration of the War, at a Salary of 1s. 2s. per day.[14]

By the time conscription for single men was introduced in January 1916 (extended to married men in May 1916) Fred claimed to have recruited between 500 to 600 men. Thereafter his activities were largely concerned with fundraising and propaganda. Through selling copies of his photograph and making collections in cinemas and music halls he provided millions of cigarettes for the serving forces. It was at a charity event, although not for a military recipient, that he sustained the injury that led to his eventual retirement from the armed forces. A boxing tournament for the benefit of a veteran pugilist and music-hall performer, Jack Wayho, was held at National Sporting Club, Covent Garden, on May 25, 1916. Interspersed with exhibition bouts by professional and amateur boxers, were several comic set-pieces, including "Pimple versus The Kaiser." Unlike the storyline of his films, Pimple for once came off second best to his imperial opponent (played, of course, by Joe). The clowning ended abruptly when he slipped and badly dislocated a knee. Six months later, on November 22, Fred was officially discharged from the army, categorized as permanently unfit. The wrongly dated and physically inaccurate reason supplied on his service record was certainly unique in British military history: "Occurred 24. 5. 16 at National Sporting Club. While giving a comic exhibition of boxing was kicked on rt. Knee instead of buttock. Not result of and not aggravated by military service."[15]

Soon after his discharge, Fred appeared in a musichall sketch that was to continue to serve him for several years. The broad humor of

A cartoon from *Pictures and the Picturegoer* (December 11, 1915) reflecting the rivalry between Charlie Chaplin and Pimple (author's collection).

Father was presented in the form of a play within a play, with Joe as a captain in a Scottish regiment searching to find a replacement actor to appear in an amateur production. When "Private Pimple" was engaged to play "the heavy father," melodrama soon turned to farce. After appearing in the sketch for a short time, Joe joined the Royal Navy on February 5, 1917. His records show that he served as an ordinary seaman until March 29, 1917, and as a deck hand in the Royal Naval Reserve Trawler Service until February 7, 1919. Like his brother, he had struck a favorable deal with the military authorities.

The Perils of Pacifism

During the latter stages of the war Fred concentrated his efforts on stiffening the nation's resolve. In 1917, in response to a perception that public support for the war was dwindling, the government supported the creation of a National War Aims Committee. Fears of civil unrest prompted by the rise of Bolshevism, mutinies in the French army and industrial disputes at home, were to be addressed by a carefully organized propaganda campaign utilizing printed material and

Rifleman Fred Evans (courtesy BFI National Archive).

special speakers. In June 1917, a Socialist convention held in Leeds to "hail the Russian revolution and organize a British Democracy"[16] helped persuade the NWAC that special attention had to be paid to densely populated urban areas—conveniently the same districts in which cinemas abounded and where Pimple comedies were particularly popular. Fred was enlisted by the NWAC as one of their regular speakers, with a car allocated to serve as a mobile platform.

Condemnations of Germany and the German nation were balanced with exhortations to pull together and to reject all subversive influences. A previously unrecorded, and probably untrue, anecdote surfaced from Fred's childhood, the *Burnley News* reporting that:

in his younger days he spent the greater part of his time in Germany as an acrobat under a German master, and his bitter experiences and the cruelties he suffered at the hands of the German people make him determined to carry his part properly out in every town that he visits in the course of his professional duties and to expose the crude and vile methods of the Hun.[17]

Of even keener concern to Fred were "The Perils of Pacifism." On the afternoon of Thursday, April 11, 1918, he addressed a mass meeting at the corner of Parker Lane, Burney. *The Burnley Express and Advertiser* reported:

"Pimple" told the mass of humanity who now surged around him that the Lancashire people did not need to be told to stick to the flag because it had been proved that they were the most loyal county in Great Britain. "I am more than pleased to be here for one reason," he continued, "and that is that last night at Mount Zion Chapel there was going to be a peace meeting." He proceeded to tell his audience that after leaving the Palace stage at eight o'clock he went to the chapel, but the meeting was not held. Was it right that anybody should ask for peace during these times. No! A voice in the crowd called out that the Mount Zion meeting was held.

"Pimple" admitted the holding of the meeting. He had denied it to see if there was anyone in the present audience who would contradict his statement. "Let me tell you as a discharged soldier," he proceeded with a penetrative look at the interrupter, "that your presence is an insult in this crowd. If you have sympathies with peace kindly leave the crowd, because I don't want you here!"

The speaker hit out at conscientious objectors, asserting that they were activated by self-ish motives. He alleged that a Burnley conscientious objector who had been released on the condition that he did not take part in propaganda work again, failed to keep his promise for the man was inside the chapel the previous night, "ready to have another pop."

"Pimple" proceeded that there were about six thousand people waiting in the neighborhood of Mount Zion Chapel. "If I had said, 'Burst those doors open, smash the chapel down,' they would have done it, but I was fair, and would not do that, because they were only silly women who were trying to hold peace meetings."

After advising the audience to do all they could to smash-up peace propaganda, and denouncing public authorities for allowing the use of their premises for peace meetings, "Pimple" said he could always be relied on to come down to Burnley to help the movement in the carrying out of our war aims.[18]

Fred's busy program to expose the perils of pacifism was undertaken as his film career sputtered towards an undistinguished close. The balance of his professional life had altered, as music-hall appearances became his major source of income. Despite making fewer movies Fred continued to present himself as a star of both stage and screen, issuing weekly adverts in the theatrical press which described him as "Great Britain's Premier Film Comedian." On the November 13, 1918, his "card" in *The Era* was, for once, not devoted to trumpeting his own successes. It proclaimed "'PIMPLE' SAYS THANK GOD IT'S OVER! AND THANK OUR BOYS FOR GETTING IT OVER."

CHAPTER 14

Pimple's Three Weeks
(Without the Option)

OF THE MANY OUTLANDISH IMAGES that Fred conjured up during his screen career, possibly the most bizarre was of himself as a "beautiful" seductress stretched out on an animal-skin rug. "Princess Pimpelina" was the doomed heroine of *Pimple's Three Weeks (Without the Option)*, a burlesque which during the first full year of World War I led to the Weston Feature Film Company appearing in the High Court of Justice and their production being described by the judge as "vulgar to an almost inconceivable degree."[1] Even harsher words were reserved for the author of the original work, who had sought to restrain exhibition of the film on the grounds that it infringed the copyright on her 1907 novel *Three Weeks*. Elinor Glyn's book was condemned as having "a tendency to elaborate incidents of sensual adultery and intrigue"[2] and was considered to so immoral that it was beyond the protection of the court. The decision on whether a burlesque or parody could infringe literary copyright established an important legal precedent, a long-standing judgment that was delivered amid courtroom proceedings worthy of a film comedy.

As with many of their productions Fred and Joe were burlesquing a film based on a book. But the production *Three Weeks* (released in the United States in December 1914 and in Britain in April 1915) was made with Elinor Glyn's approval and its adherence in places to her original novel compounded the charge of copyright infringement. For their success, the book and the film relied on readers and cinemagoers taking them seriously, finding no cause for amusement in their wildly melodramatic plots and heavy-handed attempts to suggest sexual physicality. Such notoriety was irresistible to Fred and Joe, with the added attraction that the preposterous storylines provided many comedy opportunities. More than a desire to protect the copyright of *Three Weeks*, Elinor Glyn had a strong interest in suppressing a film that exposed her work to public ridicule.

It is difficult not to identify the red-haired, green-eyed, passionate Glyn with the upper-class heroines of several of her works. Certainly, her descriptions of free-spirited women confronting hypocrisy and double standards were based on personal observation and, sometimes, direct participation. Disappointed in her marriage to a drink-dependent, debt-ridden landowner, she had conducted affairs

106

with several aristocratic lovers. Her nine-year relationship with Lord Curzon ended abruptly in 1917 when the Tory statesman decided that it might be politically expedient to marry a wealthy American widow whose reputation was not tainted by a back catalogue of erotic fiction. Glyn was a controversial figure and although the fashionable world flocked to the Adelphi Theatre in 1908 to see her play the lead role in a charity performance of *Three Weeks*, her position as mistress to the ex–Viceroy of India appears to have been unacceptable to the Edwardian establishment. She and her fictional alter egos were situated outside the generally accepted perimeters of society, a situation analogous to, but by no means like, Fred and his comic creations.

Elinor Glyn, an early portrait dating from 1903 (author's collection).

Purple Prose

The plot of *Three Weeks* opens in England, with Paul Verdayne, a lusty but sexually immature young nobleman, being sent abroad to escape the debilitating clutches of Isabella Waring, a "daughter of the middle class." But clutches of a far tighter and more exotic nature are in wait for him in Switzerland. At a grand hotel in Lucerne, he exchanges glances an attractive, influential, green-eyed older woman known only as "The Lady." They soon become lovers, consummating their relationship on a tiger-skin rug. Continuing to eschew traditional furnishings they later have sex on a couch of roses in a Venetian Palazzo. After a three-week crash-course in the aesthetics of passion and interior design, Paul is distraught when his teacher announces that she must leave him. She explains that she is trapped in an unhappy marriage to a dissolute and abusive husband, an unfortunate situation which is further complicated when she also reveals herself to be the queen of a small Balkan nation. "The Lady" and Paul never meet again. But her grand plan, to bear a royal heir with a finer pedigree than that of her obnoxious husband, comes to fruition, after which the king proves his total unworthiness by stabbing her to death. The remainder of his reign is brief, however, for he is immediately strangled by her faithful servant. After five years grieving his lost love, Paul begins to understand that life must go on. He accepts an invitation to a ceremony marking the birthday of the crown prince and for the first time sees his son—"a fair rosy-cheeked, golden-haired English child." The novel is not without its Pimplesque passages, e.g., "What a thing was a funicular railway" and "It is not a very easy thing to fold up a huge tiger-skin into a brown paper parcel tied with string."

Given her usually precarious financial situation, Elinor Glyn must have been delighted to come to an agreement with the Reliable Film Corporation of New York, guaranteeing her 25 percent of their film *Three Weeks* up to a maximum of $30,000. But she was persuaded to accept major changes for the film which lost much of the book's original impact. In an attempt to "legitimize" the central relationship, a prologue identifies Paul Verdayne as the son of the deposed king of Versilia. Now named "Sonya," the previously unidentified heroin is forced to marry the usurping king for diplomatic reasons. Meanwhile, Paul is brought up in England thinking that he is a mere nobleman. Eventually, his royal, Versilian blood rises to the occasion, providing a justification, of sorts, for the tiger-skin episode. Unlike the novel, which is related entirely from Paul's point of view, the film attempted to maximize its dramatic effect by depicting the king's dissipated behavior and the brutal murder of his wife. Several opening scenes set at the royal court completely removed the air of mystery that "The Lady" possessed in the original work. Although neither film survives, contemporary accounts demonstrate that Pimple's version clung tenaciously to the original movie.

Pimple Prose

A synopsis prepared for the court hearing shows that *Pimple's Three Weeks* matched the original films opening section scene by scene. As would be expected, Princess Pimpelina showed less dignity than Queen Sonya. In one sequence she pretended to be a portrait by standing within an ornate frame and in another defended herself from a drunken general's amorous advances by knocking him out with a carrot (a pistol was employed in the original). For the scene in which the monarch took temporary leave of her country, a street trader's donkey cart was substituted for the royal carriage.

It was with Pimpelina's and Paul's first encounter at the Swiss hotel that the burlesque began to gain momentum. The plush restaurant became Lockhart's, a popular working-man's café filled with down-at-heel rather than well-healed diners. No champagne or caviar were on offer, only mugs of coffee and thick "doorstep" sandwiches. When the couple came together for their first romantic tryst, Paul did not sink into his lover's arms as she lay on the rug but took her hands and helped her adopt a more sensible upright position. A tearful episode from the original film, when Queen Sonya penned a farewell note and tenderly placed it on the pillow next to the sleeping Paul, was reduced to absolute farce. With no suitable surface on which to pen the message, Pimpelina employed Paul's forehead as a writing slope, then posted the document into her lover's open mouth. The princess was next seen in her handsome apartments, rocking her new-born baby in a makeshift cradle constructed from a "Sunlight" soap packing case. In both films the king then entered and murders his consort, although Fred could not resist adding a hammed-up death scene. Finally, Paul was seen attending the church ceremony in honor of his son. As depicted in *Three Weeks* the solemnity of the event and the noble bearing of his young son acted as a life-affirming moment for Paul, but in *Pimple's Three Weeks* an undignified brawl concluded with the child being carelessly tossed at his father's feet.

Three Weeks in Court

Previously the victim of Fred and Joe's earliest major film burlesque, the unfortunate Charles Weston soon found his company in court defending their latest satire. One of the first batch of films released by Weston under the Piccadilly brand, *Pimple's Three Weeks (Without the Option)* was released in May 1915 and was subject to legal action the following month. Elinor Glyn, represented by Albert Clauson, K.C., alleged infringement of copyright and demanded damages, while Weston's company, represented by Henry Terrell, K.C., claimed that there could be no infringement in the case of a burlesque. After an adjournment which lasted until November, Clauson attempted to demonstrate that the Weston film had copied many episodes from both the book and the authorized film, and that legal action was his client's only option to protect her own work. It was soon clear that the judge, Mr. Justice Younger was not convinced by his argument. It was reported that:

> His Lordship said he had looked at the book, and though it could be said that whatever originality or merit there might be in it lay in its analysis of the passion of love, and the peculiarity of the feminine nature, which could not be reproduced on film.
> Another feature was that the heroine was a mysterious queen who also could not be reproduced on film. It might be said that the rest were stock incidents.
> His Lordship further observed that the fact that the hero and heroine were sitting at a table making eyes at each other was not original.[3]

Although the defense conceded that Pimple's *Three Weeks (Without the Option)* had been inspired by the film *Three Weeks*, it was contended that "copyright could not prevent anyone from caricaturing a serious work."[4] It was an assertion that caused Younger to pose a question that has been asked many times since: "You say if you try to be funny you can do anything you like?" Terrell responded "Yes. If you succeed in being funny." The defense next proposed that upholding Elinor Glyn's case would create a new and invidious situation:

> Mr Hartree, for the defendant company, said that the question was one of great importance—whether a *bona-fide* burlesque which, to some extent, adopted the plot or style of an original work was an infringement of copyright. There was no authority upon the point. There had been burlesques from the days of Aristophanes down to the present day, and it could not be denied that sometimes burlesques had much greater merit than the original works upon which they were founded. In a burlesque there was independent originality, and so it became a new work. There was no infringement of the copyright in a serious work where the other work produced a different kind of pleasure and was in no way competitive. Counsel referred to the burlesque which "intelligent people" were so fond of, and suggested that it would be casting an inconceivable burden upon the Court to ask it to stop them. His Lordship would remember the very successful Potted Plays of the late Mr. Pelissier.[5]

A Course to Dishonor

When delivered in December 1915, Mr. Justice Younger's verdict was crushing. Even though literary copyright did not extend to dramatic representations prior to an act of 1911, he was still surprised that no previous cases of alleged infringement by burlesques had been recorded. In this, the first case, he did not find that *Pimple's Three Weeks (Without the Option)* infringed Elinor Glyn's copyright in any way. In fact, even had it done so, she would not have been entitled to the court's protection. He considered that it was notoriety, created by many critics condemning the novel and library's banning the work, that had boosted its sales to well over a million copies. From the public point of view the moral stance of the book was far more important than copyright issues:

> Now, it is clear that copyright cannot exist in a work of a tendency so grossly immoral as this; a work which apart from its other objectionable features, advocates free love and justifies adultery where the marriage has become merely irksome.[6]

With a judge's traditional interest in protecting those whose resistance to corruption was less firm than his own, Younger considered that "by such books, many a poor romantic girl, striving to live a higher life, might be induced to take an easier course to her dishonor."[7]

Although Pimple burlesques were given the green light to continue, their content was severely criticized. Not surprisingly for a judge, Younger found the film "indescribably vulgar," with incidents and movements that seemed "indecently offensive."[8] Usually, the successful defendants would have been entitled to receive costs, but in this case, he felt it would offend the dignity of the court to make such a decision.

The combination of erotic novel and bawdy film appear to have put the court room in high spirits. Judge Younger whose family, as leading brewers, made a major contribution to national insobriety kicked off proceeding by asking who exactly "Pimple" was. On being instructed that he was a "humorous character well known in the kinema world"[9] the judge joined in several jocular exchanges about films and the cinema. When Terrell suggested that Younger could compare both films at "a little theatre in the Charing-Cross-road," the judge replied that they should all go together. The plaintiff's council inquired if his lordship had ever visited a picture palace, only to be reminded "Yes, Mr. Clauson, you and I went together to one in Brussels."[10] Amid loud laughter Clauson responded: "I though your lordship would have sufficient tact not to mention that incident." Despite his Belgian escapade Younger proved not to be a film enthusiast. After watching *Three Weeks* he explained: "I will tell you what happened to me yesterday. I did look at it, and after a time I found I was looking at it upside down."[11]

Elinor Glyn had received a crushing rebuke from a judge whose concern for public morals may have extended beyond "many a poor romantic girl." With large numbers of husbands at the front during World War I there was a general fear that the wives they left at home would be tempted to commit adultery, a situation not conducive to the morale of the armed forces. On a more specific level it is possible that Younger, as the brother of prominent Conservative politician George Younger, knew of and disapproved of the relationship that existed between Glyn and Curzon. Such overt and implied criticism, together with the ribaldry and sarcasm of the general public, convinced Elinor that the time was approaching to seek a less judgmental climate. She had gloried in her status as an outsider but could not accept ostracism.

In 1920 she left England for Hollywood with a £10,000 contract to write for the Famous Players–Lasky Film Corporation. Two years later she was commissioned by Metro-Goldwyn-Mayer to produce the screenplay for another version of *Three Weeks*, and to help promote the film in her own inimitable way. With a conspicuously luxurious lifestyle and willingness to make instant pronouncements on all things sexual, she quickly became a celebrity whose profile was even better known than her prose. Glyn's earliest screenplays helped boost the rapidly escalating success of both Gloria Swanson, whose exotic screen personas came increasingly to resemble the heroines of her novels, and Rudolph Valentino, who she provided with expert tuition in the art of kissing hands. For an author wedded to verbosity, Glyn's ultimate Hollywood triumph was a masterstroke of brevity. The title of the 1927 movie *It*, encapsulated the quality of "personal magnetism" or "sex appeal," an on-screen, intertitle definition being provided by Glyn herself who appeared in a walk-on role. After nine years in the United States, she found that her social melodramas were declining in popularity. Returning to England she set up her own production company to make "talkies," a venture that failed after only two films.

CHAPTER 15

Pimple in "The Whip"

ALTHOUGH ANTICIPATED, the crash when it occurred, was shocking. Immerging from the darkness of a tunnel the express train plowed into a detached carriage, smashing it into fragments. The force of the impact derailed the locomotive and, as it lay precariously on its side, it was enveloped in smoke, steam, and fiery red embers. Survivors lay amid the mangled wreckage crying for help. Yet, the disaster was only a clever illusion. As soon as the curtain dropped, the injured dusted themselves off and hurried into the wings, while a troop of stagehands quickly cleared away all evidence of the dreadful accident.

The train crash in *The Whip* was possibly the most sensational scene ever portrayed on the British stage. It represented the culmination of Victorian and Edwardian melodrama's long preoccupation with blood, thunder and, above all, spectacular effects. Over the years, developments in stage machinery had enabled increasingly realistic depictions of complex, large-scale events, but comparable sophistication had not occurred in storylines and acting techniques. Villains and villainesses remained irredeemably wicked, insatiable in their desire to destroy heroes and heroines whose goodness was almost saintly. Tired plots creaked along, with their development dependent on incredible coincidences and audience-directed asides. The incongruity between melodrama's grandiose presentation and its banal content provided Fred and Joe with richly comic opportunities, as did the willingness of audiences to abandon reason in favor of thrills.

"You Can Almost See the Whole Play from the First Act"

Predating the British release of an American film version of the play by over a year, *Pimple in "The Whip"* was a burlesque of a theatrical production, originally staged at Drury Lane in 1909. Melodrama had existed long before Drury Lane began to mount its famous epics. Originating in the late 18th and early 19th centuries with French mélodrame, equestrian dramas, musical spectacles, and Gothic romances, by the mid–1800s the form had evolved into a popular, modern morality play. Characters embodied vice on one side and virtue on the other; death and destruction abounded, but good always emerged triumphant at the end. In large working-class theaters, anti-establishment sentiments resulted in popular criminals such as Jack Shepherd and Dick Turpin being rebranded as honorary heroes with the forces of law-and-order cast as villains. But at theaters such as the Adelphi, the Olympic, the Princess's and Drury Lane the protagonists in melodrama came to be increasing represented as members of the middle or upper classes. Villains adopted top hats and, according to Jerome K. Jerome, the heroes always wore patent leather shoes. In keeping with previous "Autumn Dramas" which had been presented at Drury Lane since the 1880s, *The Whip* by Cecil Raleigh and Henry Hamilton presented a succession of set pieces which impressed either by their picturesque content or by sensational situations. The narrative which linked them was sometimes complicated, but always predictable, leading one reviewer to comment: "You can almost see the whole play from this first act, but the old material of the incessant warfare between white and black is made new by new invention."[1]

"The Whip" is an eponymous, four-legged heroine; a thoroughbred racehorse around which the action of the play revolves. A human heroine, the young and beautiful Lady Diana Sartorys, daughter of Lord Beverley, is courted for her fortune by a rapacious and repulsive relative Captain Greville Sartorys. Diana, however, falls in love with the handsome, but financially embarrassed Hubert, Earl of Brancaster, whose involvement in a car accident has caused him to temporarily forget that he is engaged to the adventuress, Mrs. D'Aquila. Joining forces with the ungallant captain, the devious divorcee claims that she was married to Brancaster, supported in the deception by Verner Haslam, a dissolute vicar. In the meantime, Lady Diana has attempted to cure Hubert of his gambling addiction by providing him with a sure-fire tip for the 2000 guineas at Newmarket—her father's horse "The Whip." Captain Sartorys and Mrs. D'Aquila hatch a plan to prevent Hubert regaining his misspent fortune by assassinating the horse in a railway collision. Curiously, they choose to discuss their scheme at Mme. Tussaud's waxworks where they are overheard by "The Whip's" trainer who, for an unrelated reason, has decided to impersonate an effigy of the notorious murderer Charles Peace. The horse is rescued from the impending crash in the nick of time and, despite last-minute machinations, manages to win the race. The Reverend Haslam redeems himself by confessing his part in the scam; Greville Sartorys and Mrs. D'Aquila are arrested; and the houses of Brancaster and Beverley are united in marriage. As Oscar Wilde wrote of fiction, "the good ended happily and the bad unhappily."

The first act of *The Whip* was played out against elaborate sets depicting the interior of the stately mansion Falconhust; its charming Italianate Gardens; and the kennels, which accommodated a pack of real hounds. In the second act the bustle of the Olympia Horse Show was recreated, followed by the gloom of the Chamber of Horrors. Scenes of the locomotive traveling at full steam and the subsequent crash occurred in the third act and in the final act, a race by 12 horses brought the play to a rousing conclusion. The plot and imagery of the play became extremely familiar to the public. Following a record-breaking Drury Lane run of 388 performances, scaled-down productions toured the provinces for several years with a London revival at the Lyceum Theatre in February 1915. For those who had not seen the play a wide selection of postcards, posters and magazine illustrations supplied a good idea of its pictorial content.

Pimple Cracks the Whip

Although the release date of *Pimple in "The Whip"* is generally given as February 1917, the forthcoming film had been announced as early as April 1915 and was certainly being shown by the summer of 1916. A surviving copy held by the BFI Archive appears to lack some footage (intertitles skip from 6 to 14), but it is relatively complete and provides a valuable example of the brothers at their belittling best. The opening credits identify the cast as "Lord Elpus (a s'nice s'man)—Pimple"; "Lord For-Givus (s'norrible man)—Joe Evans"; "Lady Bell (s'awful woman)—Miss Nina Maxwell"; and "Lady Jones (some girl)—Miss Phyllis Desmond," supported by "Jockeys, Horses. Rabbits, Mice, Chorus Girls, Parsons, etc." Animated portraits establish Joe as a profusely mustachioed, swaggering villain; Nina as a half-crazed, crouching villainess; and Phyllis as a simpering heroine, whose pretty features are delicately arranged around a snout-nose. Pimple is dressed in the bowler hat, checked clothes and knee-boots of a racing man, but he is clearly the same old Pimple.

The plot of *The Whip* is reduced to a few scenes. Curtains draw back to reveal Lord Elpus, down to his last halfpenny and "plunging" heavily at the club. After his final loss he sits abandoned by his gambling companions, hanging his head as he contemplates financial ruin. To compound his misery, he hangs it into a lighted candle. In the next scene Elpus and Lady Jones meet in a tea-room. Following Elpus' declaration: "I would ask you to marry me, only I am penniless, and I guess your father hasn't got much more," the unfortunate lovers give deep, closely synchronized sighs. Lady Jones' solution to their plight pokes fun at an inconsistent aspect of the original play: "Will you promise not to gamble if I put you on a stone ginger?" They travel to open countryside (a location shot) where they study the form of the "stone ginger," otherwise known as "The Whip." For a pantomime horse its form is impressive, sufficient to convince the villain and villainess that they need to sabotage its chances of winning the race. In an intertitle reverberating with "boom boom," For-Givus declares: "Tonight we must nobble the 'Whip.' We'll drug him with some Fast Dye so that he won't run." With nobbling in mind, he gains access to "The Whip's" stable, abandoning his Fast Dye strategy in favor of sawing off one of the horse's legs. Failing in this he removes its tail: "Now he cannot steer to victory." Following his exit Elpus enters and rectifies the steed's loss by insetting a feather duster into its backside.

As the plot thickens, so do the villain and villainess. They arrange a rendezvous in the public area of Mme. Tussaud's, where Elpus and Lady Jones are also in attendance. Several exhibits hardly support the waxwork's reputation for realistic portrayal. Von Tirpitz and Von O. Gluck ("the man who invented dinnertime," Elpus explains) are grotesque, large-headed creations, while A. Hem has a helmet, but no face and the Kaiser is presented as a pig. Charles Piece is more lifelike, largely because he is played by a live actor who pulls a succession of funny faces.[2] With Peace's place already taken, Elpus resorts to eavesdropping from close quarters, standing alongside and sometimes between the conspirators who are so engrossed in their plan to cause the rail collision that they fail to notice him.

Madame Tussaud's Waxworks. Scene from the original 1909 Drury Lane production of "The Whip" (author's collection).

With the train crash scene Pimple finally lets the audience into a poorly kept secret. All the film's a stage and all the men, women, and horses merely players. Fred and Joe had played many parts in their time, but never were their exits and entrances so poorly managed. After For-Givus has uncoupled the horsebox from its locomotive and left it to be destroyed by an oncoming express, Elpus arrives, adopting a slow-motion run. He attempts to lead "The Whip" from the wagon, but before he can accomplish the awkward maneuver a large, obviously flat train with crudely painted wheels and steam enters from stage left. Elpus reveals himself as merely Pimple as he shouts at the stage-hand: "Wait a minute, you fathead, you're too soon. I haven't got the horse out yet, go back." The express is pushed back into the wings, only to appear again before the rescue has been accomplished. Elpus/Pimple is exasperated: "You're too soon again. Wait until the Horse is out, and when I say SAVED, you come on and make the collision." He raises his arm skyward to demonstrate the dramatic pose with which he will accompany the cue. When he eventually manages to drag the horse—and its diminutive jockey—from

Parallel scene from Pimple in *The Whip* (1916). Left to right: Fred Evans, Joe Evans, Geraldine Maxwell (courtesy BFI National Archive).

the wagon he strikes the pose and declares "Saved." Nothing happens. Once more, he lifts his arm in triumph and yells "Saved." Still nothing. Looking off-stage he shouts in annoyance: "I've said 'Saved' twice you fool, come out." The temperamental express finally comes out, knocking Elpus and "The Whip" flying.

Suffering no ill-effects from their encounter with the locomotive Elpus and "The Whip" arrive at Newmarket. The racecourse is initially depicted as a painted backcloth before which stand a small crowd of extras. In one final act of wickedness, Lord For-Givus contrives to have the small jockey arrested for menacing behavior. His villainy is to no avail, for Lord Elpus borrows the jockey's outfit (a surprisingly good fit) and leaps into the saddle.

The novelty of real horses racing on a theater stage is inverted in *Pimple in "The Whip"* which shows obviously artificial horses racing in actual locations. Most of the race takes place on an area of common land with ditches, paths, and a few distant houses. Two rudimentary "fences" are introduced into the normally flat 2,000 guineas, causing chaos as the jockeys are forced to push and drag their mounts across the obstacles. Occasionally, a soldier is seen in the background, a reminder of the real world and the ongoing war. Actuality and whimsy are mixed to an equal extent in a shot of the horses rounding the corner of a suburban green and approaching the camera. Crowds of ordinary men, women and children line the roadway, while, at first glance, the horses seen from head-on seem almost real. There is no doubt of the artifice involved when "The Whip" is seen approaching the winning post. Back in front of the painted backcloth, the horse stops and throws Elpus who is unable to coax or force it over the line. Perhaps there is a fragment missing, but, as it stands, the film ends with Elpus a few inches short of winning both a fortune and the hand of the woman he loves.

Melodramatic Mishaps

With "The Whip," Fred and Joe were, proverbially speaking, flogging a dead horse. Although melodrama persisted (and still persists), it had long been a target for comedians and humorists. From the 1880s Harry Pleon had frequently lampooned the form in a series of songs, sketches and playlets typified by his "Sensational Melodrama" from 1894 which was advertised as:

> "THE LOW-BORN PEASANT," Or, "The Pirate-Lover, the Village Maiden, and the Soldier Bold"—Murder!—Suicide!—Love!—Revenge!—Pistols!—Daggers!—and Onions!—the Explosion on Board the Orange-Box—Great Excitement—Death of Everybody.[3]

Like Fred and Joe, Pleon also guyed current successes, as in his 1901 version of Sir Arthur Wing Pinero's "problem play" *The Notorious Mrs Ebbsmith*, retitled *The Notorious Mrs Eggflip*. By 1890 melodrama's stock characters were so set in their stereotyped rut that Jerome K. Jerome was able to produce a whimsical, but acerbically accurate guide to *Stageland: Curious Habits and Customs of its Inhabitants*. The hero's "chief aim in life is to be accused of crimes he has never committed"; the villain "wears a clean collar, and smokes a cigarette; that is how we know he is a villain"; and the adventuress "is fond of married life ... and she goes in for it pretty extensively."

When he came to direct his Hollywood version of the play in 1916, Maurice Tourneur aimed for a high degree of realism. Although the titles declared it to be "the Great Drury Lane Melodrama 'The Whip'" the original production's evocation of rural Yorkshire became the wide-open spaces of California. The extensive longshots that were required to depict automobiles careering down country roads and a real locomotive hurtling along its track were visually striking but lacked the immediacy of the stage presentation. In the theater the very closeness of the train crash made it more spectacular than Tourneur's "real-life" collision. But the heightened impact of live performance came with the ever-present danger of technical malfunctions. On the opening night of *The Whip* at Drury Lane, the race scene ended in chaos when the judge's box was accidentally raised into the air and, worse still, the wrong horse was first past the winning post.

The concentration on theatrical glitches in *Pimple in "The Whip"* may have reflected technical issues in the Drury Lane production but it became even more appropriate for a series of itinerant versions of the drama. Following the acquisition of the play's touring rights by the impresario Charles Dance, mishaps became even more likely as the production moved between theaters on a weekly basis. At the time that *Pimple in "The Whip"* first appeared, a scaled-down and speeded-up version of the play had been devised for music hall consumption. To enable the play to be staged twice nightly, Dance compressed the original four acts into two, telling the story in just fifteen scenes. Audiences had little time to digest the plot, or to recover from the sensational effects that unfolded in rapid succession. Acting performances became even broader as actors attempted to emphasize their roles. Scenery and machinery were under considerable stress as they were quickly adapted to fit a variety of differently sized stages.

Fred and Joe had seen it all before. During their long apprenticeship in pantomimes and music-hall they must have encountered many situations when accidents and malfunctions had shattered theatrical illusion. Occasionally such events involved extreme danger to performers, as in the case of their mother whose lace collar once caught fire after brushing against gas-lighting at the front of the stage. At other times small, but embarrassing errors might be spotted by the audience, particularly in theaters in which performers were closely overlooked. Dave Aylott remembered that the auditorium of the Palace Theatre, Dover (where Joe appeared in melodramas) was so small that a performer on stage could almost shake hands with someone in the balcony. But, unless confronted with irrefutable proof of the artificiality of what they were watching, it seems that audiences were generally content to temporarily suspend their disbelief.

Even before Fred started to send-up film and stage productions, he had used the world of entertainment as the starting point for many of his comedies. Pimple was often depicted as a member of an audience who became so enthralled by the skill or power of a performance that he attempted to replicate it, usually with catastrophic results. Like William Costagliola, the would-be Zigomar of the "Black Hand Gang," his character had a fertile and impressionable imagination. While young William was sentenced to a spell in the local reformatory for pursuing his fantasies, Pimple's preoccupation with acrobats, dancers, singers, and actors resulted in him becoming a national laughingstock. Eventually, Fred decided to concentrate on the style and content of entertainment rather than its effect, producing versions of popular productions that were based on skepticism and not the power to suggest. In both his "imitation" comedies and longer burlesques, Pimple presented the audience with two propositions; the first was that performance was not quite as easy as it looked, and the second that fiction was not half as real as it sometimes seemed.

CHAPTER 16

Our Old Pal Pimple

FRED AND JOE DID NOT make films for posterity. Theirs were ephemeral productions, aimed at audiences who appreciated them for their current appeal and not their abiding aesthetic qualities. The unfavorable comparisons that have been made between Pimple pictures and American and European counterparts fail to consider that the brothers' primary objective was to provide topical humor derived from a widely shared indigenous culture. Fred and Joe were chiefly motivated by a traditionally satirical, not cinematic, intent as was evidenced in their stage, film, and, later, puppet-show endeavors. In addition to burlesquing the subject matter of more pretentious productions, Pimple movies poked fun at the escapist nature of filmmaking and the artifice by which it was achieved. In a sense, they represented a form of anti-film, cheerfully running a corrective commentary alongside the objects of their travesty. Pimple's relationship with his audience was multi-layered and more complex than that existing between other film characters and their public. Often referred to in the press as "our old friend" or "our old pal," he was omnipresent in cinemas for five years, providing not only a series of comic capers, but an ongoing process by which filmgoers could examine their own relationship to the movies.

The nature of his audience meant that Fred did not have to rely so heavily on the carefully arranged stunts and visual tricks that were typical of many American productions. Unlike the comedies of his rival Chaplin, which involved much editing and re-shooting, his films were straightforward observations of comic situations, directly photographed as if the camera were transcribing a theatrical performance. Joe explained to Denis Gifford that after a brief rehearsal the cast would usually ad-lib its ways through a scene which, unless a major accident occurred, was taken only once. He recalled: "I actually took the first few films on a 'De Brie' camera ... and then E.T. Williams came up and took them himself whilst I produced (I don't think my photography was too good)."[1]

An attempt to introduce Fred's comic character to the American public was unsuccessful. In January 1916, the Nestor film company began to release Pimple comedies with titles altered to reflect national differences. Fred became "Charles Evans—the famous English comedian," while Pimple was re-named "Flivver," U.S. slang for a runabout car, but also for a hoaxer or failure. Although they were widely shown the films seem to have aroused little enthusiasm. They did how-ever come to the attention of American and Canadian censors who occasionally found their humor too robust. *Flivver's Dilemma*, which showed Flivver/Pimple attempting to hide several young women from his clergyman father, was banned in Quebec because of its religious content (Pimple's ruse of persuading his female guests to impersonate items of furniture echoed one of Grandfather Fred's most famous pantomime routines). In Chicago, the cuts demanded by the munici-pal censorship board before allowing the exhibition of *Flivver's Good Turn* were: "Real Burglars jimmying window and entering house; comedy burglar spanking woman; policeman pulling trousers off men and scene following showing trou-serless men sitting on wall"—objections which appear to have struck at the very heart of Fred's comedy.[2]

The failure of Pimple films in the United States suggests the extent to which Joe and Fred's comedy was directed at British audiences. The American cinema-going public was extremely diverse. As Charles Musser writes:

> Inside the new movie houses, particularly in the downtown areas, an Italian carpenter in need of a bath might sit in an orchestra seat next to a native-born white-collar salesman or a Jewish immigrant housewife—in short, next to anyone who shared with him a some-times secret passion for what might flicker across the screen.[3]

Such a cosmopolitan alignment was certainly possible in Britain, but generally audiences were of a more homogenous nature, well able to appreciate cultural and historical references. Whereas films made in the United States were likely to pres-ent a strongly visual form of comedy that could be comprehended irrespective of social or ethnic background, Pimple productions often depended on a mutually understood context for their effectiveness. With their extensive theatrical expe-rience, enhanced, perhaps, by a degree of inherited wisdom, Fred and Joe were acutely aware of the psychology of their audiences.

Fred entered films towards the end of the picture palace's first phase of devel-opment, at a time when those who attended were exhibiting much of the uninhib-ited behavior that was commonplace in proletarian music halls and fairground exhibitions. However, increasingly sophisticated pricing-structures and closer supervision in music halls meant that they excluded many individuals who trans-ferred their patronage to cinemas. Picture palaces were cheap, local, and offered a continuous program of short films that allowed the audience to attend when and for how long they desired. As Dr. Luke McKernan observes:

> Cinemas provided conviviality, warmth, music and entertainment at a price that put it in the reach of all. They were readily available. And put no social constraints on those wish-ing to attend. The phenomenon of the continuous show, combined with the heterogeneous program of one-reelers promising an ever-changing roster of comedies, dramas, travel-ogues, industrials and newsreels. Offered not only an escape through the film's subject matter but through the very act of attendance.[4]

The sense of escapism created by the films was matched by the liberating nature of the cinemas themselves. Even the humblest establishments aimed for an exotic appearance to set them apart from their workaday surroundings. Festoons of electric lights and large colored posters decorated the exteriors, while inside extensive use of mirrors, gold paint and plush curtains provided a marked contrast to the cramped and dreary homes of many of the audience. Entrances and auditoriums became community areas in which it was commonplace to pass audible judgment on the character, clothes or company of friends and acquaintances. The darkness required for viewing films enabled clandestine acts, ranging from hurling pieces of fruit at the pianist to "snogging" in the more private sections of the hall. The entertainment elicited a vociferous response—with catcalls, boos, whistles, cheers, and "raspberries" indicating approval or approbation. Children, especially, had discovered a wild and woolly wonderland in which they could fuel their gun-toting, train-wrecking fantasies largely beyond the reach of adult intervention.

Towards Gentrification

To manage progress towards a more profitable future, cinema needed to attract new, more easily managed audiences. A major step towards gentrification occurred in January 1910 with the enforcement of the 1909 Cinematograph Act. The safety requirement to obtain a license led to the closure of many penny-gaff/converted shop establishments and the increased construction of purpose-built establishments. With local authorities realizing that they could employ the act to impose additional controls on cinema-owners, the industry looked towards self-regulation to help protect itself from over-zealous moral supervision. An independent British Board of Film Censors became operational in January 1913, possessing the authority to authorize or refuse exhibition. Initially, two classifications were issued. "U" certificates indicated that productions were suitable for viewing by children, while "A" certificates required children to be accompanied by an adult. Such improvements, together with the added refinements of afternoon teas and orchestral accompaniments, encouraged the growth of middle-class attendances. It was only a matter of time before films began to reflect the changing nature of the audience.

Pimple was created at a time when a degree of order was beginning to be imposed on cinema chaos. The subjugation of unruly audiences was under way, with children having to resort to subterfuge to see many of the shows. In a wider context, the effects of certain types of films on the juvenile mind was increasingly preoccupying educationalists, religious authorities, and local magistrates. While one-reel westerns, comedies and crime thrillers remained popular, feature films began to dominate exhibition practice. Continuous film shows, with the inherent problem of audiences overstaying their welcome, were replaced by programs in which feature-length and short films were combined to form a package of set duration. Although many feature films included spectacular and exciting sequence, a greater reliance on narrative resulted in challenges to members of the audience accustomed to basic storylines. There were problems, too, for those who had difficulty reading the increased numbers of intertitles necessary for sustaining complex plots. Similarly, the "art film" (usually of European origin,) caused a degree of bewilderment and boredom by the extensive deployment of dramatic camera angles, colored tints, and other overtly cinematic techniques. Many welcomed the sophisticated pleasures of extended storytelling, but there were others whose experiences of cinema going were irretrievably linked to the maximum action and minimum explication of shorter films.

At first comedies were largely unaffected by the rise of feature films, showing little sign of employing more complex plots. Although they had gradually increased in length, they had done so by an additive process which simply linked one similar incident to another. With a succession of comic mishaps or a frantic chase taking place through several scenes, the effect was cumulative rather than narrative. Fred's comedies had conformed to such stereotypes from his earliest Cricks and Martin appearances, through to his creation of Pimple. But the public's seemingly insatiable appetite for such repetitive fare began to weaken. An attempt to unify Fred's madcap chases with a more realistic chain of incidents played at a slower pace is provided by a long "orphaned" film, now re-united with its title. The subject of the British Film Institute's crudely catalogued *Fat Man on a Bicycle* is Pimple acting as a cycle instructor.

Pimple Turns Honest

Shot on the waterfront opposite Eel Pie Island and in the neighboring streets, the 2:25-minute fragment of *Pimple Turns Honest* (August 1914) opens with the intertitle "W.H.O.R.K a la Pimple." Pimple and his large male companion are shown bidding goodbye to a woman at a front door. Although Pimple is dressed in his usual striped blazer, tiny cap and light-colored sports shoes, his pupil has opted to wear a suit and tie for his first cycling lesson. In the next scene the pair approach the camera from the far end of a curving street—Lebanon Park, Twickenham.[5] They lean heavily against each other—the cyclist struggling to achieve balance and Pimple exerting all his strength to keep him from toppling over. Eventually they collapse and, extricating himself from the tangle, Pimple throws his cap to the ground in frustration. They are next seen on another street, repeating the same desperate attempt to maintain equilibrium until a costermonger pushes his handcart across their path. The resulting collision spills baskets and their contents into the road, with the irate trader pelting the pair with his ruined fruit and vegetables. Bystanders watch with interest; a woman is seen in the distance with her hands on her hips and small boys run back and forth. By now

Scene from the previously unidentified 1914 film *Pimple Turns Honest* (courtesy BFI National Archive).

those other onlookers, the cinema audience, would be eagerly anticipating the next disaster. In a quite lane that runs behind Orleans House and Gardens, Pimple and his friend crash into a nursemaid, upending her perambulator and spilling her infant charge onto the floor (shades of the ill-used babies in Victorian pantomime). After pacifying the child, she displays her anger by kicking both men in the backside. A final, very brief shot shows the pair struggling past Bowyer's riverside coal-yard towards other unseen catastrophes. It is clear that Pimple's attempts to lead an honest life are just as disruptive as if he were following a criminal career.

A Friend of the Audience

Fred needed a new type of comedy which retained his audience's support, and which did not, like increasing numbers of dramatic films, confuse or intimidate them. The answer lay close at hand in the form of burlesque, a process which allowed him to stay on familiar terms with his many fans. As Rachael Low observed "as a friend of the audience he made nonsense of the ambitious Art which impressed and dazzled them."[6] It must be said that Pimple was an assiduously good friend—keeping appointments, staying in touch, sharing jokes and secrets and, above all, providing continuous reassurance. His audience of friends knew that Pimple would be available in picture palaces at any time, with new adventures released every month. He was also readily accessible via chatty communications in the entertainment press and through regular live appearances to support his films. In February 1915, the *Bioscope* reported a packed itinerary of music-hall appearances in which Fred was to perform as both as a serious actor and a comedian.[7] The audience themselves received a personal invitation to share the screen in a film shown at the Hippodrome, Coventry, soon after his live performances there in the first week of October 1917. At the start of the engagement, he announced that he would "be making a film in Coventry in which local faces, local streets and scenes will be depicted."[8] The surviving copy of *Pimple's End of a Perfect Day* (BFI Archive) contains a scene in which the camera lingers on a happy crowd of adults and children following Pimple as he takes his leave of them in an automobile.

Cinemas seemed almost to be imbued with Pimple's presence. When the editor of *Pictures and the Picturegoer* interviewed Fred at the Central Hall, Tooting, South London, in 1915, he reported:

> "Pimple," said Mr. Chapman, the genial manager, "is crawling around somewhere among the audience selling autographed copies of your paper for your cigarettes for soldiers fund. I'll tell him you've arrived." Boy-Scouts were sent out "Pimple" hunting in the semi-darkness of the crowded hall, and five minutes later he was embracing me.[9]

On screen, Pimple's burlesques of current hits and his references to contemporary concerns insured that he always made a fresh and relevant contribution to the friendship. For his *Ins and Outs* (October 1918) Pimple became a potential member of the audience when he was depicted trying to gain entrance to 11 different Manchester cinemas without paying for admission.[10]

Suspension Suspended

Pimple involved audiences directly with his comedies either by acknowledging them from the screen or by revealing to them the inner workings of plots and cinematic techniques. Such an approach often resulted in his productions becoming an early form of meta-film, in which the viewers were vigorously encouraged not to suspend their disbelief. In *Pimple's Eggs-traordinary Story* (February 1913) he colluded with the audience to present a farcically unreliable narrative. As an errand boy he was seen explaining to his employer how a basketful of eggs came to be broken. The account was illustrated in graphic detail, with a sequence showing three "bloodthirsty ruffians" attempting to steal the fragile delivery and Pimple dispatching them with a trusty knife. For a time, the gullible grocer was in a position comparable to a cinemagoer swept away by a convincing narrative. But the audience of *Pimple's Eggs-traordinary Story* were already party to the "truth"

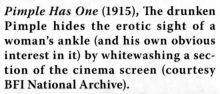

Pimple Has One (1915), The drunken Pimple hides the erotic sight of a woman's ankle (and his own obvious interest in it) by whitewashing a section of the cinema screen (courtesy BFI National Archive).

of the situation, having already seen Pimple meeting another errand boy with whom he played the gambling game "Pitch and Toss" until an argument caused the eggs to be smashed.[11]

Pimple's unreliability could always be relied upon. Attempting another delivery job in the extant *Pimple Has One* (October 1915) he starts to consume the alcoholic contents of his basket. Soon he is uproariously drunk, a state that is indicated by scenes showing him clinging to house-railings, a policeman and a lamp post. His difficulties in staying upright are made worse by the pavement rocking from side to side, a simple cinematic trick achieved by tilting the camera. Pimple only feels that the ground is shifting beneath him, but the viewer, who is hopefully not intoxicated, sees the imagined movement. At one time Pimple performs a series of forward rolls "down" what the observer knows to be a subjective incline. Later in the film, Pimple is sitting on the ground when a woman rests her foot on his basket to adjust her shoe. The erotic exposure of her ankle to the cinema audience—and his own equivocal response to it—is too much for Pimple to tolerate. With a knowing look to camera, he reaches for a conveniently placed bucket of whitewash and paints out the provocative section of the screen. A similarly obliterative process is present in *Pimple's New Job* (February 1914). As an

Pimple's Part (1916). The shadows of Pimple and his wife rehearsing a violent scene for the "Brewery Lane Theatre" demonstrate that things are not always what they appear to be, especially on screen (courtesy BFI National Archive).

unlicensed bill sticker, Pimple plasters posters for "Spinks Soap" on all types of surfaces with his usual careless abandon. His papery pursuits are finally halted by three policemen who paste him onto a wall with one of his own posters. The bill sticker is absorbed into the bill and the moving picture in which he appears is momentarily rendered static.

On several occasions, Pimple demonstrated that things were not always as they appeared. A silhouette scene in *Pimple's Part* (March 1916) showed that the eyes might easily be deceived in the case of a perceived situation or even a film. As an actor, Pimple is depicted rehearsing a violent scene with his wife. Although the audience can see that his wife is laughing and that his dagger is a crude wooden prop, a policeman viewing the event from the other side of the window-blind is tricked into thinking that a real murder is taking place. In *Pimple's Wonderful Gramophone* (September 1913) a piece of obviously fake machinery supplies a metaphor for technology-based theatrical/cinematic deception. Pimple has constructed a large box with a protruding funnel and the painted notice: "Wonderful Gramophone—Put a Penny in the Slot—Ask for Any Tune You Like and You Will Hear It." Hiding inside the ramshackle construction, Pimple, equipped with a collection of musical devices, struggles to fulfill the public's increasingly challenging

Fred Evans plays a huckster in the 1913 film *Pimple's Wonderful Gramophone* (courtesy BFI National Archive).

requests. Eventually the scam is ended when someone with no investment in its "wonderfulness," a drunk, crashes into the show. The inspiration for *Pimple's Wonderful Gramophone* was perhaps provided by a full-page cartoon appearing in *Ally Sloper's Half Holiday* twenty years earlier. Sloper, a disreputable character not dissimilar to Pimple, adopts the persona of a scientific mountebank and employs one of his many children to hide under a pretend phonograph to provide imitations of famous politicians and singers.[12]

With his numerous live appearances at cinemas and theaters establishing that he was a real comedian who played the fictional Pimple on screen, Fred demonstrated that film personas were easy to fabricate. In *Pimple, Himself and Others* (April 1916) he was approached at his studio by an associate who has boasted, falsely, to his lady friend that he was acquainted with "all the cinema stars."[13] Fred supported his friend's claim by making himself up and appearing as Max Linder, Ford Sterling and Charlie Chaplin, his impersonations proving so convincing that, when he appeared as Pimple "Himself," he entirely captured the affections of the young woman.

Fred's continuing expose of the film game reached new levels in *Oliver Twisted* (October 1917), his send up of an American version of Charles Dickens' *Oliver Twist* (Paramount, 1916). Unlike the original film which starred

34-year-old Marie Doro in the title role, Pimple's production cast a male actor as Oliver, although not quite as junior as conventionally depicted. Surviving footage shows Pimple as a swaggering Bill Sikes, with his ferocious Bull Terrier "Bull's-eye" (represented by a stuffed toy) tucked under his arm or sometimes dragged on a piece of string. Bill's partner Nancy and the villainous Fagin are recognizable from earlier portrayals, but a totally unexpected character appears in the form of the film's director (referred to as "the producer" in the film's inter-titles). The director is first seen before the camera when he tells Pimple that he is "not brutal enough" and urges him to "knock the stuffing" out of Oliver with a large cudgel. He then interjects during the famous scene depicting the death of Nancy when the lead actress resigns her part because she is being treated too vio-lently. Pimple is assured by the director that there is a substitute, a young lady "doesn't mind a little bit of knocking about." Unfortunately, the degree of "knock-ing about" is too extreme for the second Nancy and she also leaves the set. Finally, the director supplies a Nancy-sized rag doll which Pimple proceeds to pummel with his club. In a red mist Pimple kills Fagin, much to the annoyance of the director who requires him to die in a later scene. The director's concerns are soon immaterial as he is the next to be dispatched, taking his place on the pile of bod-ies on the floor. Surveying the carnage, Pimple is phlegmatic. Having killed every-one, apart from the camera operator, he declares: "I suppose I had better hang myself and get it over."

In *Oliver Twisted* the horrors of Nancy's murder in the original novel and subsequent recreations of the scene are transformed into humor as Pimple shows cinemagoers that the savage dogs and murdered heroines portrayed are only dummies or puppets. More than anything the mock violence of the film is remi-niscent of the traditional Punch and Judy show in which the truncheon wielding Punch (accompanied by his dog "Toby") annihilates the rest of the cast to the vast amusement of the audience.

It seems that the cinema industry gradually became less tolerant of Pimple's subversive comedies. In reviewing *Pimple Acts* (January 1916) the *Bioscope* struck a cautionary tone:

> Pimple is engaged by a motion picture company, but his efforts to please only succeed in landing everybody into a terrible muddle. Amusing in its way, but we are inclined to ques-tion the wisdom of allowing the public to "go behind" the scenes of film production.[14]

Most of Pimple's fans knew that when he appeared as a billsticker, an errand boy or as a more exotic character he was just "taking people off"—a process of impersonation which, though varied, did not obscure his basic personality. There was a limit, however, to how often the overpowering presence of Pimple could inhabit such flimsy simulacrums. Although music-hall comedians and clowns such as Grandfather Fred Evans had followed comparable courses, their routines had not been exposed to the public on a near weekly basis over a period of several years. Even the burlesques in which he appeared as named characters in specific productions began to lose their appeal as a limited number of satirical devices were constantly recycled. Five or so years after his emergence Pimple was becoming predictable and repetitive, losing the power to hold his audience's attention. The best of friends can sometimes drift apart.

The End of a Beautiful Friendship

In 1914, 53 Pimple films were released, with 49 in 1915, 31 in 1916, shrinking to 10 in 1917[15] and five in 1918. Why Fred and his cinema audience finally went their separate ways is not clear—changing tastes, personal matters or lack of investment may all have contributed to the rift. Fred felt that both he and the British film industry had been badly let down by lack of official support. In 1923 he complained:

> The people here are struggling to get a foothold in the world's market for pictures, yet not the slightest official help or encouragement is forthcoming. In America if a film producer wanted a battleship he could get one. And look at the railways there. Film producers can do almost what they like on the trains. The United States Government does all it can to help the industry. This country will not grant us facilities. American firms can get more concessions in London than British Films. While American and foreign films form the greater part of our programmes at the present time we cannot get our pictures into America unless we are in the trust.[16]

The trade press had become increasingly critical of his style of comedy. At the start of 1917, The *Bioscope* questioned the wisdom of re-issuing of the 1914 film *Lieutenant Pimple Under Sealed Orders*:

> This burlesque is by no means one of Pimple's best. It is extravagant and elementary, and was one of the films that showed how very dependent Fred Evans was on cleverly ridiculous parodies for his success. It is certainly not worth re-issuing.[17]

A year later the same publication considered that the content of one of Fred's last films, *Rations*, was excluding a large part of the audience:

> The one pity is that comedy sometimes oversteps the bounds of good taste and is apt

THE ONE AND ONLY

"PIMPLE"

FIRST RELEASE OF THE PICCADILLY SERIES

IMPLE'S MILLION DOLLAR MYSTERY

"The One and Only Pimple" salutes his public (courtesy of Glenn Mitchell).

to be somewhat broad. It seems a pity to limit a film to a certain type of audience by introducing situations that might be regarded as offensive.[18]

It would probably not have occurred to Fred that many of his once faithful followers were moving on. When he introduced Pimple in 1912, the public were pleased to meet him. To some, particularly children, his wild antics reflected their own unruly behavior or disruptive daydreams. Others found him a reassuring influence, identifying with his familiar music-hall humor and recognizable urban settings. With the introduction of new forms of film exhibition and expression, he was present to help audiences retain ownership of the picture palace experience. But, by the end of World War I, the once-unsettling changes made to cinema and cinemas had become accepted to such an extent that few wished to challenge or subvert them. The war too, had altered people's perception of Pimple films. There was declining enthusiasm for films which made light of hardships encountered on the home front. And when watching escapist feature films, audiences had probably decided that they could do without the company of a pugnacious, piss-taking pal.

CHAPTER 17

Pandora B9/877

B9/877 IS THE CATALOGUE NUMBER of a Pandora's cardboard box kept securely in the vaults of the UK National Archives. It is tightly bound with linen ties and when these are loosened the opening of the closely fitting lid sounds strangely like an inhalation of breath. There are no evils stirring within, however, for the contents have long since lost their ability to cause hurt or harm. Now the records of Fred's 1920 bankruptcy—the undignified maneuvers as he frantically attempted to avoid his many creditors—take on the qualities of film comedy rather than personal catastrophe. More than anything the assortment of yellowing papers provide an insight into the life of a variety performer struggling to make a living in a cash-strapped, socially changing wartime and post-war environment.

Although Fred was fortunate to have avoided the horror of the trenches, he appears to have felt disregarded and ill-used in the years immediately following the war. In 1920 he complained:

> The people for whom we worked were making thousands of pounds out of us! And that has been my experience throughout my picture career—cheapness. And where there is cheapness where is opportunity—and encouragement?
>
> You know I have never had a proper chance as an Englishman. I spent two years in the service, and yet, after making an enormous personal success in films, and then throwing up my place in the film market—for two years in the Army means something to a film actor—I wasn't given a chance, though, as regards to my work on the halls, I have just signed through the good offices of Lew Lake, a contract for £40,000.[1]

At his bankruptcy hearing Fred painted a gloomy picture of how his "war" injury had led to a lengthy period of unemployment, with later propaganda activities often resulting in physical exhaustion. His finances, he claimed, had also suffered though having to fund his War Aims Committee appearances at the rate of £15–£18 a meeting.

In later years Joe suggested that the brothers were phlegmatic about the change in their fortunes. He wrote to Denis:

> You see when war (1st World War) broke out that practically ended our film activities, as I joined the navy & my brother Fred (Pimple) joined army, and when war was over, we were forgotten. And so we embarked on a successful tour of the music halls, being top of the bill on all leading syndicates Moss-Stoll-Gulliver-independent theatres etc, and we were so busy writing & producing shows & sketches that I soon forgot film days, being young—we soon forgot one thing to take up another.[2]

Despite the theatrical successes indicated by Joe, Fred's actions suggested that he was still eager to revive his film career. Long after his final screen appearances as Pimple, his advertising continued to refer to his status as a "film star" with frequent allusions to the possibilities of renewed moviemaking. But financial expediency required that, while planning a triumphant cinema comeback, he continued with his career on stage. From simple comic sketches, Pimple's stage shows (usually written by Joe) were expanded into multi-scene productions featuring several performers. Although comedies, the shows often had a military or war theme, as in a six-scene drama which was announced in the spring of 1919, but apparently never produced:

BRITAIN'S
MYSTERY SHIPS
BEAT ALL HUNS
"PIMPLE'S"
"MYSTERY SHIP"
WILL BEAT ALL RECORDS
It is NOT a War playlet, BUT an intensely dramatic comedy written
by Joe Evans (the author of "Pimple's" present success) featuring
"PIMPLE" Britain's Greatest Film Comedian[3]

Pimple Bankrupt

Fred's wayward attitude toward financial matters had been evident for several years. In May 1919, a judgment was made against him for £78 owed for rented apartments and goods, and, on November 19 of the same year, newspapers carried the headline "Pimple Bankrupt" stating his liabilities to be £336 (£645 by April 1920) and his assets nil. On February 18, 1920, Mr. Registrar Hope accepted Fred's "scheme of arrangement" to reimburse his creditors at the full rate of 20s. to the pound, putting aside £10 a week from his earnings to make repayments.

Some individuals and businesses had been waiting for years to receive money that they were owed. The James Cycle Company, of Birmingham, had been paid £1 10s 6d on account of a "Record" bicycle purchased on June 23, 1911, but were still attempting to obtain the balance of £5 4s 6d. W. Poupart, Dairy Farmers, of Heath Road, Twickenham, claimed £5 14s. 6d for the supply of milk and goods for nine months up to June 12, 1914. And William Knipman, of the St. Margaret's Hotel Stables, Twickenham, was hoping to retrieve £1. 15s 6d in connection with a horse, saddle and "loose boxes for pictures" hired on October 29 and December 14, 1915. J.D. Brumfitt was owed almost £40 for the rental of a furnished house at 26 Wilton Grove, Wimbledon, and Rose Cross £78 for board and lodgings at 6 Gloucester Road, Regents Park. In the absence of hard cash Rose had taken the law into her own hands and impounded Fred's (not so wonderful) gramophone. The Inland Revenue was demanding a large sum, as were the *Era* and

Fred Evans, Joe Evans, and Lily Poole return to the variety stage in the comedy sketch *Father.* **Program for the Finsbury Park Empire, February 7, 1921 (author's collection).**

Encore periodicals which had carried Fred's lavish advertising. Under an agreement dated May 9, 1919, Fred had also been loaned £278 11s 6d by his agent Lew Lake.

In his "Debtor's Statement" Fred attributed his insolvency to:

the illness of his wife and himself soon after he came out of the army in November 1916; to heavy business travelling and general expenses since then; to his expenses estimated at between £140 and £150 in connection with certain war work (propaganda) and to losses over card playing and horse racing, such losses being estimated at £210 for the period of three years preceding the Receiving Order.[4]

Fred explained that after being discharged from the army he had been ill for 14 weeks which exhausted his saving. Before the war he had never paid more than 25s–30s for lodgings, but recently he was charged five guineas for two bedrooms and a sitting room in Manchester. His war work had cost him approximately seven pounds a week.

By 1920 projected income from stage appearances represented a viable means of rectifying his financial situation. His arrangement with Lew Lake was expiring in February of that year and he had negotiated several lucrative new contracts. He was to receive £130 a week for a 14-week engagement at Moss Empires Ltd. in 1920, and there was a further contract with London Theatres of Variety Ltd. for two 12-week tours at £100 a week.

Social Stigma and Slamming Doors

Alongside rising costs, Fred, along with other variety performers, also started to encounter social prejudice. In November 1919 he wrote:

When I returned to the stage after doing my bit with the 1st Surrey Rifles, I naturally took it for granted that I was coming back to that life which, with all its drawbacks, is dear to me. Like hundreds of others, I had been up and down the country for years, playing a week here, a week there, always seeking the "digs" where I was known. and everywhere feeling I was among friends.

I never thought that the day would come when I would knock at the doors of former landladies to have the door slammed in my face by women who curtly intimated that I was no longer welcome.

In Glasgow recently I was driving round in a cab for four hours searching for rooms, and at last I found shelter at a hotel where the bill for myself and Mrs. Evans came to £15 for the week, exclusive of "extras." There were other theatrical people who had to shelter in railway waiting-rooms and even sleep in their dressing-rooms.

Friends of mine who recently went to Manchester paid £5 5s for two tiny bedrooms and a shabby little sitting-room in a back street.

Everywhere it is the same story. Theatrical people spend hours hunting for lodgings, and have to endure most insulting remarks about "pros."

"We only take in respectable lodgers now," is a formula among present-day provincial lodging-house people.

How the unfortunate revue girls fare on their 50s. a week's salaries is too terrible to contemplate.[5]

Having toured with *Father* for a prolonged period, Joe wrote the same characters into a new sketch, which was first produced early in 1921. The ill-disciplined Private Pimple had now fallen foul of Sergeant Major Ferit (played by Joe), his resulting court-martial leading to *Fourteen Days C.B.* Another stock Pimple character, the naval lieutenant, resurfaced a year later in *The Hidden Terror. The Stage* explained that it was "a familiar story of stolen plans, a naval hero, a pretty adventuress, and the triumph of right, with an unusual finish concerning a hidden terror that turns out to be an ape with a desire to jazz with the man he is supposed to destroy."[6]

Not only the story, but, apparently, the jokes in *The Hidden Terror* were familiar. Following the Fred's appearance at the Royal Hippodrome, Belfast, for the week commencing March 5, 1922, the theater's manager reported back to head office:

The Company this week is extra good and went extra good at both houses last night "A very long programme but we will get over this" BILTON & MAX very good. GRANDE STELLA'S EXTRA GOOD and went specially good (One of the best Musical Acts we have had). BETH TATE Very good. MAPLE & MAY very good. LESLIE WARD & partner very good. PIMPLE & CO Just fair. This sketch takes far too long and he will not take any-thing out. The sketch is poor and the comedy is not good and consists of a lot of old chestnuts only did fair at each house. JOE O'GORMAN very good and went as well as ever. THE HUNTINGS Quite good. On the whole a good programme if the sketch would play in Twenty minutes and give the other turns a better chance.[7]

For *Her Ladyship*, produced during the summer of 1922, Fred adopted drag, playing a butler persuaded to impersonate a Charlie's Aunt–type character to help facilitate the engagement of a young couple. Such 30-minute comedies were relatively new to the music-hall stage, but similar productions had been a mainstay of Victorian theater in the form of curtain-raisers supporting full-length plays. Both Pimple's stage comedies and their earlier counterparts were linked by farcical plots, frequent puns, and the use of aptronyms—in *Her Ladyship* Joe played "Lord Noswen" (Lord knows when).

Revue

Detecting a change in popular taste, Fred and Joe decided to abandon comic playlets for a more up-to-date form of entertainment. Their first revue, *Punch*, was presented on October 30, 1922, at the Elephant and Castle Theatre, close to Fred's Kennington birthplace. Rather than forming a single "turn" on a longer variety bill, the revue now provided a complete package of entertainment, combining comedy and drama, song, and dance. Described as a "Pot Pouri in Eight Scenes," the show had a "slender plot"[8] which appears to have been stretched to breaking point by a series of disparate episodes.

Scene one opened with a line of chorus girls in Scottish uniforms performing a dance based on military drill. Somehow, this merged into a rewritten version of Private Pimple's court martial. In scene two, the soprano Betty Trix (Fred's stepmother Beattie Evans) sang the ballad "I Want a Man." Scene three consisted of the Brothers Walsh performing a dialect comedy song "Two Lads fra Lancashire," while scene was taken up by a sensational sketch. Fred played a husband returning home to find his wife embracing his best friend (played by Joe). After she had fled the room both men decide to test her love by pretending to shoot themselves. As the shots rang out the wife returns, but instead of cradling one of the prostrate bodies she ran to take solace in the arms of yet another lover. A hard act to follow, but in scene 5, Beatty did her best with the ballad "Orange Blossom Time in California." Pimple returned for scene six, creating havoc and confusion by walking an imaginary dog. An eccentric dance in scene seven featured Joe and Jack Walsh as a couple of drunken Broadway swells. In the last scene, Pimple appeared as a comedy dame causing chaos in a high society setting. As a finale the ladies of the company warbled "Way Down Upon the Suwanee River" and the gentlemen reciprocated with a rag-time version of Dvorak's "Humoresque." *Punch* proved a popular vehicle for Fred and Joe, continuing to tour provincial theaters until the summer of 1924. In an updated version the "Punch Jazz Band" was introduced, with Fred performing Eddie Cantor's universally popular novelty song "YES! We have no bananas."

In acknowledgment of the mushrooming popularity of American-style dance-bands, music became an increasingly important ingredient of Pimple revues. In June 1924, the 13-scene *Lucky 13* was advertised as having 28 artists, including the "Lucky 13 Girls."[9] Among performers appearing in the show during its year-long tour were Fred's singing stepmother, billed as Beattie Trix, and his dancing older daughter "Little Betty Evans." Once again Fred performed a comic song, "Why Do the Ladies Follow Me?" In line with the show's strongly musical emphasis, Fred tried his hand at something new. The closing section of the revue was devoted to the "Saveloy Banana Band" (a comic reference to the famous Savoy Havana Band), an ensemble that consisted of first and second saxophones, saurosophone, banjo, cornet, trumpet, piano, bass, and drums in the hands of the celebrated jazz-musician, Pimple.

By December 1925, when *Stand and Ease* opened, the Saveloyards had been provided with a more dignified title, "Pimple's All British Band of Novel Syncopators." "Little Betty" was joined in dance routines by her younger sister Josey. At one point in the show Fred played a pacifist gladiator, supplying "a sly burlesque on Shaw's Androcles, including the lion."[10] Fred's performance in another sketch particularly impressed a Northern reviewer:

In one scene, a really gripping drama and quite a novelty for revue, he gives a wonderful impression of a gorilla, and holds the audience breathless with suspense while he breaks from his cage and saves two young girls from African natives. It is one of the best things ever seen in revue in Burnley.[11]

Sheet music for "Another Little Glass," a song featured by "Pimple and his All-British Band" in stage shows during the late 1920s (author's collection).

Pimple's most successful revue was named after a piece of music, though not as elevated as Dvorak's "Humoresque" or even Cantor's "Yes, We Have No Bananas." *Mademoiselle from Armentieres* was calculated to raise a snigger from ex-servicemen who remembered singing the bawdy ballad about an elderly French lady who (in the polite version) "hadn't been kissed for forty years." First presented at the Grand Theatre, Luton, on September 19, 1927, the revue's first scene presented Fred, playing a film and revue comedian, in his dressing room at the Frivolity Music Hall. To help win a bet for an old friend of army days he agreed to impersonate the mythical mademoiselle, and thereafter the plot became virtually impenetrable with most of the cast adopting a variety of disguises. Music was provided by "The All British Cabaret Band" conducted by Pimple, with Josey and Betty providing energetic displays of the "Black Bottom" and "Yale Blues." Except for *Vim*, which appeared briefly in 1929, *Mademoiselle from Armentieres* continued to "inky pinky, parlez vous" until 1930.

The close and complex alignments of friends, family and working practices which Fred had been used to since childhood, continued into his theatrical life during the 1920s. Familiar faces came and went, often resulting in unlikely combinations. Lily, usually billed as "Lilian Poole," produced each show and sometimes played in them. Betty and Josey Evans were regular performers, and occasionally appeared alongside their father's stepmother Beattie and her son, and Fred's half-brother, Frank. From early film-making days came Jimmy Reed and Pimple's younger self, Tommie Collett. Two close family members who did *not* appear in Fred's shows during the 1920s were his father and brother. Fred Evans Senior had returned to England on Saturday, April 8, 1922, announcing his arrival home by telegraphing his son from Waterloo Station. Immediately after his music-hall appearance at Preston, Fred caught the midnight express back to London where he found his long-absent father "being given a hearty welcome by his grandchildren."[12] Perhaps they had not been told of Fred and Joe's long and fruitless walk to Southampton. With his "hard case" father stating his intention to remain in England, Joe decided that it was once more time to try his luck in the United States.

The decade finished for Fred as it had started—with landlady problems. Relationships between touring music-hall "pros" and those who provided their "digs" were often strained, as the former group seeking to maintain a bohemian lifestyle untrammeled by rules and regulations and the latter attempted to preserve their reputation, property and supplementary "perks." Despite, or because of, their formidable attributes, landladies provided comedians with rich material. In the "The Pro's Lament," dating to the mid–1920s, an anonymous performer penned an unflattering portrait:

> The landlady's plump with two chins and a hump
> And about her late husband she bleats'
> She tells you with tears she's been letting for years
> And you know that it's true by the sheets.[13]

Earlier, George Robey had acted as a more sympathetic mouthpiece for the long-suffering theatrical landlady, commonly addressed as "Ma":

> You can see by my demeanor I'm an actress.
> Or at least I was a year or two ago.
> Ah me! I never thought I'd come to this game.

Letting lodgings to the gay and frenzied "Pro."
In fact, I have to live out in the suburbs,
When I'm sure by now I should have been a star
And to have to serve up ham and eggs and haddocks.
And let those saucy actors call me "Ma."

For when the boys and girls begin to kid me
I know it's only jealousy because
Its better far to be a good old has-been
Than a never-will-be or a never-was.

Fred came off second-best in his fiercely contended battle with a formidable Exeter landlady, Mrs. Catherine Ley. The local court was told how he had rented rooms at 23a Longbrook Street, while appearing at the Exeter Hippodrome at the end of December 1928. Although the original arrangement was for four persons, Fred's party consisted of five, to which a nurse and child were later added. Mrs. Ley declined his offer of £2 rent and insisted on £3. Matters came to a head after his final show when the landlady refused to let him into her house until the bill was settled. Having failed to gain entrance by enlisting the aid of a policeman, the comedian brought the manager of the Hippodrome to intercede. Mrs. Ley was resolute and eventually an irate Fred was forced to hand over the amount demanded. On gaining admittance, he threatened Mrs. Ley that he would "do her in" and that he would "break every stick" in the house. She retreated to the police station and returning to her home at 3:30 a.m., found that her lodger had been on a destructive rampage. He had caused damage to walls, electrical fittings, furniture and to a player piano. Fred was fined 20s, ordered to pay costs of £3 3s and to compensate Mrs. Ley to the sum of £3.[14]

Chapter 18

Joey, Jimmy, and Gerry

Having acted for years as Fred's writer, co-star and protector from angry actresses, Joe walked, or, rather, sailed away from his older brother in 1923. Whether the decision to travel to Canada and the United States was motivated by career prospects or personal reasons, the move was long-term and lasted for seven years. Even prior to leaving, Joe had not been entirely committed to supporting Fred's film and stage efforts. While continuing to make a major contribution to Pimple productions, he participated in two further screen partnerships, one with James Godden Reed, a young comedian who was already a veteran filmmaker, and the other with Geraldine Maxwell, an actress who also starred in her own comedy films. Joe's relationship with Geraldine was more than professional. In 1914 she became his wife.

Gerry

As with many other early film actors, the dearth of film footage means that Geraldine has been almost entirely wiped from film history. She is significant, however, as one of a limited number of women achieving success in a male dominated profession. Within this small group of female contemporaries, she is also worth examination for her untypical social background. Cinema actresses (and in some cases writers and directors) such as Laura Bayley, Jackeydawra Melford, Nell Emerald, Violet Hopson, Gladys Sylvani and (from Ec-Ko and Homeland) Blanche Kellino had all previously appeared either in legitimate theater or on the music-hall stage. Geraldine's previous employment experience appears to have been limited to artistic needlework, a genteel occupation pursued at her parent's home in a leafy London suburb.

Ada Mary Bowles, or Geraldine Maxwell as she became known, was born in 1888 in the Borough, Southwark, where her father was employed as a police constable. After serving in the force for 23 years and 28 days, Frederick Gentry Bowles retired in 1899 and became landlord of "The Carpenter's Arm," a pub in the Buckinghamshire village of Saunderton Lee. By 1906 the family had returned to London, where they settled at 15 Ashbourne Road, Chiswick. At this time Frederick Bowles' benign and bearded features were widely depicted in a newspaper advertisement for the patent medicine "Bile Beans." In a fulsome testimonial he explained that he had been invalided from the police with rheumatic gout, bent double with pain until he sent for a course of the miraculous curatives.

In her early twenties Ada began to find work as a bit player in films made by British and Colonial, London Films and Hepworth. It is possible that her engagement with the latter company was brought about by a young neighbor, who was to become one of Hepworth's principal leading ladies. Chrissie White (1895–1989) was born in Chiswick and by 1911 was lodging close to the Hepworth studio in Walton on Thames. Her family, however, continued to live in Holly Road, within a short walk of Ashbourne Road. Perhaps Geraldine was a friend of Chrissie's older sister Rosina, an actress, or worked with her widowed mother who was a dressmaker (Geraldine's mother was also a dressmaker). By whatever means Geraldine entered the film industry, her qualifications for screen appearances were immediately apparent. She had long, delicate features; full lips; heavy lidded eyes; and a mass of wavy, fair hair. Although classically Pre-Raphaelite in appearance she was far from languid in behavior, participating in comic, and sometimes dramatic, action with energy and enthusiasm.

Geraldine started to work with Fred and Joe in 1913. Within a short time, it was decided to cast her as the central figure in a feature length dramatic film. It was a new departure for the brothers, and one possibly dictated by Geraldine's striking presence. In the sensational detective drama, *The Pearls of Death*, she played a titled lady with a dark secret. Before marrying into the aristocracy, she had belonged to a secret criminal society. Unwilling to accept her resignation the organization decided that she should be eliminated, arranging for an agent to be planted in her household. After gaining access to her pearls, the gang employed fiendishly clever technology to convert them into an explosive device which would detonate when the clasp of the necklace was fastened. Fortunately, Lockwood Beck, a detective played by Joe, uncovered the plot and was able to fling the deadly jewelry through the mansion's French windows. As usual Joe wrote the scenario, later telling Denis Gifford that "this plot would not stand up today but way back in those early days it was accepted as good drama."[1]

The Pearls of Death appears to have been shown extensively following its release late in 1913. Its success persuaded Joe to produce another feature length drama, again revolving around Geraldine. Set during the Boer War of 1899–1902, *Stolen Honours* told a tale of sibling rivalry. Two brothers, officers in the same regiment, fell in love with Isobel Drummond, the colonel's daughter (played by Geraldine). In keeping with her military background, she informed them that she would wed the one who gained the most honors during the war. Lieutenants John Weston (Joe) and James Weston (Fred) were soon in action. During a battle, the regiment ran low on ammunition and the colonel (who must have been somewhat confused by having two Lieutenant J. Westons under his command) sent James with a dispatch to headquarters. Being of a cowardly disposition he froze under fire, causing his considerably braver brother, John, to take the message himself. Although successful in his mission, John was wounded and developed amnesia. His craven brother stole the dispatch and claimed the honor of delivering it. Despite harboring a secret passion for the wounded John, Isobel felt duty bound to keep her commitment to the, apparently, braver brother. The plot was further complicated when a blackmailer discovered the deception, but eventually the truth was revealed, and John/Joe secured the hand of Isobel/Geraldine.

The *Kinematograph and Lantern Weekly* devoted almost a page to the film and its potential effect on an audience:

> Who can withstand the plaintiff appeal of a dispossessed hero? Who can repress a sensation of loathing and repulsion when cowardice and crime seem to be winning the day? What just man or woman can witness the spectacle of a bad man just about to steal a woman's love by a base-trick without feeling a desire to rise and protest.[2]

More prosaically, the *Bioscope* observed "audiences who like the colours laid on thickly will find plenty to please them in the film."[3]

The on-screen romance between Geraldine and Joe in *Stolen Honours* (June 1914) reflected real life. On May 9, 1914, the couple had married at Brentford Registry Office, West London. *The Bioscope* reported:

> Pimple in a new role. Last Saturday, at Chiswick, Joe Evans, brother of Fred Evans ("Pimple"), was married to Miss L. Maxwell. Both Joe and Miss Maxwell are members of the Phoenix-Pimple company of players, well-known out Twickenham way. We heat that Mr. F. Evans gave a present which was both ornamental and useful.[4]

Following their marriage, no further feature films were produced, but Geraldine, or Gerry as she was familiarly known, became a regular player in one-reel Phoenix and Piccadilly productions. During 1915 there were two attempts to provide her with her own series. In *The Lady Detective* and *The Kidnapped King* (both released August 1915) she created Sally, a persistent but disaster-prone sleuth. Later in the year Joe adopted a popular stereotype to provide Geraldine with a new character, Liza, a cockney flower girl whose ambitions to better herself inevitably ended in chaos. Culture and class provided the comic themes for *Liza on the Stage* (November 1915) and *Liza's Legacy* (March 1916). In the former film Liza bribed a theatrical manager to allow her to play the lead in Shakespeare's *Romeo and Juliet*. Regrettably, Liza had not anticipated the disruptive conduct of her costermonger friends whose presence in the audience brought the performance to a riotous conclusion.

The second Liza production ventured into territory already explored by George Bernard Shaw in *Pygmalion*. As the humble flower seller, Geraldine was summoned to a solicitor's office where she was informed that she had inherited a fortune. Her desire to enter society was soon achieved when she married Lord Pembroke, an impecunious nobleman, but their honeymoon party proved a fiasco with the arrival of her uninhibited working-class guests. The film concluded with the discovery that there was no legacy, reducing Lord Pembroke to the humble rank of gentleman flower seller. Geraldine's portrayal of Liza seems to have offended the sensibilities of the *Bioscope* reviewer who complained: "the mannerisms of the coster girl are not particularly pleasing."[5]

A similarly broad approach was taken by Geraldine in *When Women Rule* (December 1915). She was seen attempting a selection of occupations usually reserved for men, but her disastrous efforts to act as a female coalman and policeman caused some adverse comment in wartime Britain. In a letter to the *Middlesex Courier*, F. De Fontslanque complained:

> There is a poster in Ealing called "When Women Rule." Its purport is to ridicule women; when that sex is working so splendidly and bearing its sacrifice so nobly, it ill behoves us to allow it to be sneered at. Let us rather remember it was under woman's rule (Queen Elizabeth's) that England obtained her supremacy, and pray that under man's we may still retain it.[6]

In search of extra income through added variety, Joe labored and gave birth to "Joey." The new character not only shared his name and was played by himself but was also provided with a "Mrs. Joey" portrayed by Geraldine. Their domestic exploits included Joey being terrified by his wife's beauty mask in *Joey's Night Escapade* (March 1916) and the couple losing all their pay-for-use furniture when they ran out of shillings for the meter in *Joey's Automatic Furniture* (May 1916). *Joey's Pluck* (June 1916) was described as a "very amusing screen adaptation of the well-known music-hall sketch 'Her Burglar,' briskly acted by Mr. and Mrs. Joe Evans."[7] Geraldine's position as a leading comedian in British films during the World War I period was extremely unusual. The rarity of a home-grown female cinema star was such that the appearance of Bella Blanche (Blanche Kellino) in *Economy* (April 1917) promoted the *Kinematograph and Lantern Weekly* to observe that "it is claimed that she is the first lady to play the principal part in a British film comedy."[8]

The few surviving glimpses of Geraldine on screen occur in Pimple films. She is seen as one of a group of relatives in *Pimple's Uncle* (December 1915) and as the comedian's wife reluctantly taking part in rehearsals in *Pimple's Part* (March 1916). In the first production she carries a small child and in the second she works on a piece of sewing before helping to act out a murder scene. Throughout both films she an active and enthusiastic participant. Happily, a sequence from the extant *Pimple's Pink Forms* provides an excellent example of her comedic abilities. In the film Pimple is becoming exasperated by his lack of success in persuading military-age men to complete the official registration forms. Calling at one home he prepares to strangle the person answering the door, only to find that his intended victim is an attractive young woman. Immediately his mood turns to bashfulness, which is expressed by some comic byplay with his cap. The woman, played by Geraldine, is playful and winsome. Although the official forms are specifically intended for men, Pimple offers to assist her to fill one in. Their intertitled conversation runs:

PIMPLE: Are You single?—if so how many children have you?
MISS: I am single—but I am looking for a handsome man.
PIMPLE: I've clicked!

As they take their seats at a table, Pimple prepares for the collaborative effort by flicking his clogged pen. Suddenly splattered with ink, "Miss" retaliates by smearing Pimple's blazer. His next move is outrageous. He wipes his inky fingers on Geraldine's blouse just above her breast. But "Miss" is forgiving of such ungentlemanly conduct and puts her arm around him as they continue their form filling. Their flirtation continues as, seated side by side, they playfully bump against each other. Geraldine's bumping soon proves to be the more vigorous than Fred's and he is pushed from his chair onto the floor. But Pimple has so enjoyed his encounter with the exuberant "Miss" that he proposes a return visit: "Well good-bye dear! I must go now—I'll bring you some more forms nest week!"

The most complete record of Geraldine as an actress is found in *Pimple in "The Whip"* in which she is billed as "Nina Maxwell." With hair dyed black and dark shadows painted around her eyes, she strikes every histrionic pose associated with the villainesses of popular melodrama. It is a bravura burlesque performance, although one which is not typical of much of her high-spirited comedy work. Geraldine's extant film appearances and reviews of titles such as *Liza's Legacy* and *When Women Rule* suggest a well-developed sense of comic physicality.

Geraldine Maxwell and Fred Evans in an ink splattering scene from the 1916 film *Pimple's Pink Forms* (courtesy of Bob Geoghegan, Archive Film Agency).

In many ways her background, appearance, and introduction to filmmaking parallel those of the American slapstick comedienne Louise Fazenda, but unlike Max Sennett's irrepressible star, Geraldine's talents are now largely a matter for conjecture.

With the decline in popularity of Pimple comedies, Joe and Geraldine found that their own screen careers also came to a stuttering halt. The unemployed film actors transferred their talents to the music-hall stage, appearing in the sketch *Father* with Geraldine playing Captain Raffle's fiancé. But presenting a live show twice nightly for months on end called for more resilience and discipline than the ad hoc art of moviemaking. A degree of friction seems to have arisen within the group. causing Fred to place a curious advert in *The Era* in August 1920:

> PIMPLE, The Undisputed King of British Film Comedians, wishes Managers and Proprietors to know that his Brother, JOE EVANS, assisted by Miss Nina Maxwell in A TELEPHONE ENTANGLEMENT (Own Scene carried) A Clean and Very Funny Fifteen Minute Act, is open for immediate dates. Owing to rumours afloat that we parted bad friends PLEASE NOTE that I released my brother from his engagement with me to play this show, as it made such a BIG HIT on my Combination Tour, that I realised it would be selfish of me to keep him back from MAKING GOOD. I STRONGLY RECOMMEND THIS ACT.[9]

Although Joe had re-joined his brother's troupe by 1921, Geraldine was not in evidence. Similarly, she did not sale with him to the United States, remaining at home with their young son, Joseph Frederick Gentry Evans.

Jimmy

For several months during 1915 *Pictures and the Picturegoer* invited readers to choose their "Greatest British Film Player," listing hundreds of actors under the companies for which they worked. There were four names given for Phoenix—Fred, Joe, Gerry Maxwell, and James Reed. Like Fred and Joe, Jimmy came from a theatrical background. His father, Bob Reed (Robert Godden Butt, 1869–1927) claimed to have been born in Drury Lane (the street, not the theater) and he was one of several siblings who all became well-known in the circus ring and on the variety stage. In addition to heading one of Europe's most successful pantomime troupes (at one time including the future movie star Stan Laurel), Bob Reed became a prodigious player in silent films, claiming that by 1925 he had appeared in almost 1000 productions. Jimmy's uncle, Johnny Butt (George John Butt, 1878–1931), also graduated from the family act to become a similarly prolific early films actor. The extent of Johnny Butt's contribution to British film-history has been largely obscured by the uncredited nature of his appearances during the 1900s. From 1914–1930, however, he was widely recognized as a leading film comedian and character actor, continuing in the industry long enough to appear in the early talkies *The Informer* and *Blackmail*. Many of his comedies were made for Cecil

Hepworth, including ten one-reel "Exploits of Tubby" (1916) in which he played a mishap prone, middle-class husband to Violet Hobson's "Mrs. Tubby."

Young Jimmy's introduction to films occurred at the age of nine, in 1906, when he joined his father, who was working for Hepworth. Later, the family's acrobatic talents were in evidence at the Cricks and Martin studio at Mitcham, making it likely that it was it was there that Fred and Joe first encountered their future colleague. By his late teens Jimmy had made his way to the Folly studio where he was engaged to help with scripts and to appear in films. For the first time Fred's younger brother, now aged 24, became the senior member of a screen partnership, the "Terrible Two." Previously, amongst many supporting roles, Joe had played Pimple's comic sidekick "Captain Scuttle" (the name usually given to sea captains in pantomime) in several films in the summer of 1913. "Scuttle" was soon cut adrift, being replaced in 1914 by "Raffles," a criminally inclined character very loosely based on E.O. Hornung's gentleman burglar. Although referred to as the "exceedingly funny Raffles series,"[10] the central figure remained Pimple, with Joe playing a subservient role as seen in *Judge Pimple* (February 1915):

> In order to help his friend, Raffles escape the law, Pimple disposes of the Judge, then appears as dispenser of justice. A ludicrous burlesque, in which sentences are grossly misapplied, female offenders are liberated, and which ends with a bustling finale. Quite a good item of its particular kind.[11]

For the "Terrible Two" series there was little difference in the comedy characters allocated to Jimmy and Joe. Their wildly acrobatic antics as "Lemon" and "Dash" had more in common with the Brothers Egbert's "Happy Dustmen" routines than the comedies and burlesques in which Pimple took central stage. Starting with *The Terrible Two* (November 1914), the series included *The Terrible Two on the Mash* (November 1914); *The Fiery Deeds of the Terrible Two* (November 1914); *The Terrible Two on the Wangle* (December 1914); *The Terrible Two, Kidnappers* (January 1915); and *Ye Olde Waxworks: By Ye Terrible Two* (March 1915). The synopsis for *The Terrible Two on the Warpath* (November 1914) reveals strong similarities to slapstick music-hall sketches:

> Knockabout business of a strenuous nature is the main feature of this release, which deals with the false behavior of two lady companions and a vengeful attack by their beau upon a treacherous looking foreign gentleman, in which a garden roller and other handy implements are wielded in alarming fashion.[12]

When Fred left Ec-Ko in 1913 his place as principal comedian was taken by 22-year-old Sam T. Poluski, who introduced the character "Nobby." A similar process occurred when he departed from Folly in 1915, with Jimmy stepping in to replace "Pimple" with a comedy detective named "Lynxeye." Jimmy's new character was pitted against the ferocious villainess "Arabella" (played by an actress named "Little Chrysia") who was occasionally aided and abetted by Joe as Raffles. Arabella was apparently too much of a handful for just one adversary, so "Sergeant Lightning" of the River Police (also played by Jimmy) was drafted in. Soon, however, war put a temporary halt to Jimmy's involvement with the cinema industry. An ominous reminder of the hostilities and their effects occurred on July 8, 1915, within a short boat ride of the Phoenix Eel Pie Island studio. Mrs. Chancellor of the imposing River Deep house, Twickenham, hosted an entertainment for wounded British, Australian and Canadian soldiers convalescing at nearby Richmond Hospital. As well as strawberries and cream enjoyed on the riverside lawns, there were exhibitions of Phoenix films and live performances by members of the company. Jimmy was much in evidence acting as both projectionist and comedian. Four months later he joined the Royal Flying Corps.

Jimmy served as a flying officer on the eastern front for two years. By 1920 he was reunited with Fred and Joe, appearing in their music-hall sketches until 1922. Subsequently, he became a leading figure in cinema management in the north of England, running the Picture Palace Theatre and then the Tivoli in Barrow in Furness. His imaginative use of live entertainment to enhance feature films included an appearance by his father as a Chinese mandarin in an oriental themed prologue to the 1918 Selznick Pictures *The Forbidden City*.[13] For the showing of Chaplin's *The Circus* at the Capitol cinema, Glasgow, in November 1928, Jimmy arranged an introductory Harlequinade which featured his wife and himself as Columbine and Clown. An actor portraying Charlie was "burnt by the poker in real old-fashioned style in the real old-fashioned place" and then subjected to a shave with a gigantic razor.[14] It was the sort of scene for which his father, who had died the previous year, was famous.

Joe in the USA

On the other side of the Atlantic, Joe had also been evoking nostalgia. Largely directed at Canada's British immigrants, the dramas, and comedies that his repertory company staged were often echoes of the pre–World War I variety theater. At the end of October 1924 Joe and his fellow performers had arrived at the Playhouse in Victoria, British Columbia, to offer their version of John "Humanity" Lawson's melodramatic sketch *The Monkey's Paw*. The following week Joe was still in reflective mood, offering a comedy farce whose title evoked an unhappy episode in his own career. Fortunately, *Archibald, Certainly Not* was more successful than its song counterpart, a number performed once—and only once—by Joe in New York.

The Playhouse provided another reminder of the old country with a Christmas production staring "Joseph Evans, of English Pantomime Fame" in "The Best of All the English Pantomimes ... Cinderella."[15] Like most of Joe's Canadian productions the pantomime was supplemented by feature length movies; two rather than one for this seasonal extravaganza, George M. Cohan's *The Meanest Man in the World* and Charles Chaplin in *The Idle Class*. To pack all the contents into a bulging program of entertainment, the pantomime was played without intervals in an hour and a half. A cast of 20 actors rattled through the familiar riches to rags, rags to riches story of Baron Stonybroke's beautiful but soot-smeared daughter. As usual, Cinderella's tormentors, the Ugly Sisters, were the main comic element, with Joe representing the repulsive Ermantrude. The role of his repugnant sibling, Priscilla, was not played by a male comedian (as tradition dictated), but by a 22-year-old soubrette named Maisie Carr. Joe and Maisie had formed a long-term partnership and, soon after the pantomime, they set off on a two-year theatrical tour of the United States. Sometimes the pair performed as individual acts in variety theaters, but more often than not they played the leads in farces, revues, and music comedies such as *Harem Scarem*; *A King for a Day*; *The Luck of the Army*; *Poor Old Gran' Pa*; *Sponging on the Spencers*; and—shades of Pimple— *Lieutenant Potts, R.N.*

From September 1929 Joe's company was based at the Strand Theatre, Winnipeg, Canada. At the end of December, he mounted another production of *Cinderella*, with a cast of 30. He was at pains to inform the local press representative that he had appeared in every pantomime back in the "old country" and that the current show adhered closely to traditional lines.[16] Remembrances of pantomimes past may have persuaded Joe that it was time to return home. He had asserted his independence by appearing with other artists and in other countries, but now perhaps he should return to check on the progress of his older brother.

CHAPTER 19

An End to Filming

IN 1929 FRED CLAIMED that he had received a "tempting offer" to appear in the new "talkies."[1] There would be no triumphant comeback, however, and, apart from some uncredited work in the early 1930s, he did not appear on screen again. His film career had been in a rapid decline from the latter stages of World War I, with the British public forgetting that his popularity once rivaled that of the great Charles Chaplin. But despite the waning of his film-star status, Fred remained true to the spirit of burlesque. Towards the end of his life, he found a different means of satirizing contemporary life and events, a comic mirror that, although new to him, was as ancient as the entertainment business itself.

Although embarking on a third tour of the re-written comedy sketch *Father* in 1919, Fred was anxious to re-assert his position as a film comedian. On January 1 of that year, he had announced: "I am taking over new studios and am starting films again, those interested write to E.W. Horder (sole film manager for 'Pimple'), Cinema Exchange, The Parsonage, Manchester."[2] Six weeks later plans seemed more advanced:

> Pimple having secured a Studio in Manchester is now busy on his next Film Production—
> *Pimple's Peace!* Wanted: Artistes suitable for Film Work (living in and around Manches-
> ter) to write "Pimple Film Productions," 12 Ducie Street, Oxford Street, Manchester, Busi-
> ness Manager E.W. Horder.[3]

Pimple's Peace failed to appear. It was a pattern of unrealized come backs that was to persist throughout the latter part of Fred's career.

In March 1920 it was reported that Fred had signed a three-year contract with the British Film and General Trading Company for Pimple comedies "to be produced on a very elaborate scale."[4] Joe was to revive his Raffle's character and work had already begun on their first film which was titled *An Honest Life*. Filming may well have commenced at a studio (located at a skating rink in Macclesfield, Cheshire), but it seems unlikely that it ever concluded. Despite lack of output, Fred continued to present himself as a film star. On June 8, 1920, he wrote to the Premier Cinema School, Southsea, Hampshire, from the Rink Studios. With its publication in the *Portsmouth Evening News* the letter promoted both recipient and sender, acting as an endorsement for one of many establishments offering film acting as a way of escaping from everyday drudgery and affirming

Fred's continuing high status in the industry. Addressing his comments to Will (probably the film-actor Will Asher) Fred promised:

> I should not hesitate to take any of these pupils and place them in any of my Film Productions knowing that you have trained them.... As soon as I start filming I am quite ready to offer parts to any one you might recommend.[5]

To demonstrate that he was still active in the cinema industry Fred contrived several events that savored more of street theater than organized filmmaking. While appearing in *Father* at the Palace, Derby, in June and July 1920 he advertised that "the Derby public will be able to see a 'Pimple Film' being made," giving a precise time and exact location for the event.[6] The publicity generated by the stunt was considerable. Under the headline "FILMING A COMEDY. SHADOW OF TRAGEDY IN DERBY PICTURE," the *Derby Daily Telegraph* reported:

> Derby picturegoers have plenty of opportunities for viewing the latest films for the town is excellently served with picture houses, but chances of seeing films in the making are rare. To-day, however, such a chance was offered, and Derwent Bridge was crowded with spectators when "Pimple," the well-known screen comedian, at present visiting the Palace, filmed a scene from one of his "blood-curdling melodramas." For upwards of half an hour before the comedian arrived crowds of people were congregating on the bridge watching the preparatory arranging of the camera and properties. The comedian arrived at length amid the applause of the onlookers. Attired in a schoolboy's cap and a striped blazer much the worse for wear, he proceeded to give instructions to the camera man, and, all being ready, embarked upon his perilous journey. Accompanied by a small gentleman with a large moustache and a silk hat, he rowed to the middle of the stream where furious argument commenced. Pimple, evidently annoyed, commenced to attack his companion with bags of flour, and after both actors had received numerous duckings, the scene ended with them both in the water.
>   The comedy now assumed a serious aspect. Both oars being lost, the boat was being rapidly borne down the stream by the strong current, and resisted all the efforts of the two comedians, who were endeavouring to swim upstream and push it before them. Pimple's companion ultimately succeeded in getting aboard, and Pimple swam away and secured the oars. The boat was then rowed back to Graham and Bennett's timber yard, where the company were waiting, Pimple hanging on to a chain in the bow of boat and being towed to safety. The crowd was unstinting in its appreciation of a plucky act. Truly a film comedian's lot is not a happy one.[7]

A month later Fred promoted a similar event at Nottingham. Publicity for his engagement at the Empire Theatre again offered the chance to see a movie being made, claiming that scenes for a new cinematic departure, *Pimple's Topical Gazette,* would be filmed in the city including a shot of the comedian diving into the River Trent.[8] Fred also tried a less dramatic way of securing public interest by placing an advert in the local press seeking four ugly women to appear in a filmed beauty show scene.[9] Occasionally, his theatrical appearances, film-making and charity work coincided. In February 1921, his engagement at the Nottingham Empire was combined with a visit to Vickers engineering works to help raise funds for the National Sailors Society. It was stated that the event, in which he was accompanied by "The Sailors Chaplain" G.H. Mitchel, was also to be filmed.[10]

The News Before It Happens

Having satirized all form of fiction film, Fred and Joe decided to extend their ridicule into the sphere of factual newsreels. Single themes such as "Prison Reform" had always provided filmmakers with starting points for whimsical comedy, but now it was decided to emulate the format of the various "Gazette," "Graphics" and "Topical Budgets" which had become a standard feature of cinema programs. In October 1920 it was announced that "Pimple's Topical Budget" would soon be available as a weekly, half reel (500 ft.) subject, and that it would introduce the remarkable innovation of covering news events before they occurred.[11] The following month "Pimple's Burlesque Topical Gazette, No. 1" was advertised, featuring "Fred Evans (Pimple)" and "Ernie Mayne and his Corporation" (Mayne was a well-known music-hall comedian with a large stomach, i.e., "corporation").

It seems that the spoof newsreels failed to appear as regularly as promised for there was little reference to them in cinema reviews. An indication of their proposed content is provided by a double page advert which appeared in the *Kinematograph and Lantern Weekly* for February 17, 1921. A series of vignette cartoons by Gerald Somers pretend to show the contents of a typical "Gazette," amongst which "The Premiere and the Italian Ambassador" depicts a Pimplesque David Lloyd George making a purchase from an ice-cream vendor—with the "American Representative" represented by a Ford automobile. "Scenes of the Recent Gale—A Terrible Wreck on the North Coast" shows a drunken tramp laying in the surf at the seaside. The "Aeroplane Two Million Miles High" is too far away to be captured in the frame, and a piece of helpful household advice "How to Prevent Fish Smelling in the Summer" is merely an opportunity to repeat the old joke "Cut their Noses off in Winter." On a more controversial level, "Wonder of the Universe, A Discharged Soldier Gets a Job!" focuses on an ex-combatant expiring from shock after being offered work.

Another three-year contract, with "a well-known company," was announced in February 1922, with Fred revealing that he was working on what appears to have been a second edition of the comedy newsreel:

> Pimple, Britain's Greatest Film Comedian, now busy on his "Grand National film burlesque" which will be released in Pimple's Topical Gazette, the Greatest Series of Film burlesques ever shown, which will prove a record for British Film comedies. Where are all these so-called British Film Comedians? "Pimple" 1910 to 1921 and still Britain's Greatest Film Comedian.[12]

Pimple's The Three Musketeers

For their final burlesque Fred and Joe identified a suitable subject in a film version of the Alexander Dumas novel *The Three Musketeers* produced by United

The famous clown Grock visiting the set of *Pimple's The Three Musketeers* in 1922. Left to right: Joe Walsh, Mr. Vanham (Grock's partner), Jack Walsh, E.T. Williams, Fred Evans, Grock, Mrs. Grock (author's collection).

Artists. Provided with a glittering UK launch at the Royal Opera House, Covent Garden, on December 19, 1921, the film was a lavish costume drama featuring a bravura central performance by Hollywood's leading male star Douglas Fairbanks. Despite its high production values, the film was ripe for caricature, overlong and with a myriad of intertitles explaining its convoluted plot.

As the fiery Gascon D'Artagnan, Fairbanks stretched the audience's credulity in different directions, playing a teenage character although looking every one of his 38 years, but then belying his mature appearance by performing a series of remarkably athletic stunts. A contemporary reviewer found the overwhelming odds in numerous swordfights difficult to accept: "There must be a limit to the number of enemies one man can fight. Once he appears miraculous the thing ceases to interest. The risks are no longer real risks."[13]

It is unfortunate that so little is known about *Pimple's The Three Musketeers*. Fred's stage commitments meant that, unlike most Pimple films, production took place over several months in widely spread locations. In March 1922 scenes were being shot in the neighborhood of the Newcastle beauty spot Jesmond Dene,[14] while five months later filming was proceeding in Swansea.[15] Co-starring as musketeers were Joe and Jack Walsh who were part of Fred's touring troupe and the camera was operated, as usual, by E.T. Williams. Two publicity photographs demonstrate that Fred continued to employ incongruity and anachronism as part of his comedy; in one he is seen performing a spirited Scottish Sword Dance before a group of bemused French courtiers and in the other he poses beside a modern bi plane wearing his 17th-century costume.

When the film was released by Shadow Play Ltd. in September 1922, Fred had every reason to be optimist. Extending over two reels it was one of his most ambitious productions and it was initially exhibited at the newly opened Tivoli Picture House in central London, a 2000-seat luxury cinema

Advertising brochure for the 1922 film *Pimple's Three Musketeers* (author's collection).

which replaced the music hall of the same name. But a promised series of "super comedies"[16] failed to materialize and although continuing to advertise himself as a cinema star Fred was left to concentrate on stage work. Pimple's film career had finally run its riotous course.

Filming as a Public Entertainment

Although no further Pimple productions appeared, Fred continued to organize public displays based upon the process of filmmaking. As with the staged events in Derby and Nottingham in 1920 and other towns on his music-hall itinerary, the people of Hull turned out *en masse* on September 12, 1923, to see Pimple perform before the camera. Whether the camera was loaded was another matter, for no film resulting from the event appears to have been shown. Given widespread notice of the event, thousands arrived at the Prince's Docks, crowding the Myton and Monument Bridges and the quayside. Joe Walsh acted as director and E.T. Williams performed the function of camera operator as Pimple climbed aboard a sailing boat occupied by two "crooks" and a "vamp." The usual comic combat ensued with Pimple pitching his two mail antagonists into the water. Finally, he "booted" the vamp (played by long distance swimmer Molly Spevington) overboard, quickly joining her when a diminutive policeman appeared on the scene.

Why Fred should "make" such similar films and then, apparently, not exhibit them is open to question. Certainly, he was aware that his activities had been viewed with skepticism. On his next visit to Hull, he wrote to the editor of the *Hull Daily Mail*:

Sir,—It has been a source of much pain and regret to me on my return with the revue "Punch" at the Tivoli this week, to find that a good deal of doubt and suspicion seems to exist in the mind of the Hull public, in respect to my film making exploits in your city last September.

I have been told that the general gossip is to the effect that it was a mere stunt. That the camera was "dud" and that not a scrap of film was exposed. Heaven forbid that I should cause my fellow artists to run such grave risks for the sake of a "mere boost."

I should be grateful if you would grant me the privilege to state most emphatically that it was a genuine film-making exploit and to substantiate what I saw, I am prepared to give £50 to any of your local charities if anyone can prove otherwise, if they will put down a similar sum to meet my challenge.[17]

The 1930s

Joe returned to England on May 11, 1930, accompanied by Maisie Carr (Gladys Ethel Carr). Although Fred might have benefited from his creativeness, and from new material developed in the U.S. and Canada, Joe did not immediately join his brother. Instead, he and Maisie operated as a double comedy act into 1932, at one stage adapting the old war-horse *Father* to their own requirements. Meanwhile, Fred had temporarily abandoned touring revues to manage his own variety theater in the coal-mining town of Cannock. Like its new owner, the Hippodrome had undergone a checkered existence. Opening as a music hall in 1912, it had offered live entertainment and films until 1925, in which year it was converted into a Palais de Dance. Fred took possession in the spring of 1931, advertising:

New Hippodrome, Cannock, Staffordshire. Newly Decorated and Renovated. Now under the personal management of "Pimple," the Universal Favorite and his Famous Comedy Stock Company playing to capacity's. A Victory for Variety.... All Old Friends, those who have worked for me, write in.[18]

Fred had ambitious plans for the Hippodrome. On April 22, 1931, he wrote to Charles Chaplin:

Dear Mr. Chaplin,

I daresay you will remember me in the old days when we were boys together and later as "Pimple" of the films.

I would very much like to book "City Lights" at the above. I am now leasing this theatre, capacity 650, can play to £35 night (twice nightly) with matinees about £225 on the week.

I should be grateful if you would give me an option of Booking your film.

Every Success
Yours Sincerely
Fred Evans "Pimple"[19]

Within a short time, Fred also took over management of the Electric Palace at nearby Hednesford. In an attempt to secure variety acts for his two theaters he advertised that, with the exception of one cinema showing talkies, they were the only entertainment venues serving a local population of 100,000.[20] Irrespective of such potential audiences, the enterprise lasted only to the end of the year, after which both theaters became cinemas under new ownership.

Money Talks *and Talking Pictures*

Fred and Joe were briefly reunited for a remarkable revue which had been created by the inventor, musician, and producer Harry Wilkinson. Opening at the Royal, Barnsley, on February 22, 1932, *Money Talks*, combined several new technologies to create a startling theatrical experience. A pre-recorded soundtrack synchronized with live performances and speakers were situated around the auditorium to relay special effects and the voice of a compere. Films were shown, including recently taken views of the locality, and the latest wonder, television, was demonstrated. The public were featured in the show as well as being immersed in it, with on-stage gramophone recordings being made of members of the audience and film-tests offered to a lucky few. As a personality strongly associated with films, albeit of the silent variety, Pimple was a suitable choice for the show's principal comedian. Despite its undoubted novelty *Money Talks* was not a success and by the summer of 1932 Wilkinson had replaced it with one of his earlier productions. The brothers had left the revue by the end of April; Joe to resume his partnership with Maisie Carr and Fred to contemplate yet another return to filmmaking.

It seemed that a long called for government initiative might rekindle Fred's career. For many years he had complained about unfair competition from American productions, hosting a meeting in 1926 at which he protested that:

> After a film had earned its profit in America it was dumped in this country and could be rented to the exhibitor for 30s. to £3 a week. The British producer could not let a film for less than ten to twenty times that sum. It was impossible for a British film to enter America, and yet there was no restriction on the entry of American films to this country. The system of block booking must stop. It meant that when a big American film was produced the British exhibitors were allowed to rent it only on condition that they took other films with it. The result was that British theatres were booked up foy years ahead with American films, and there was no room for British films.[21]

In 1927 the British government bowed to such arguments by introducing the Cinematograph Films Act which specified that cinemas should exhibit a quota of at least 7.5 percent British films. The economic stimulus given to home-produced films resulted in the formation of several new companies, one of which provided Fred with hopes of a cinema comeback. In the summer of 1932, it was reported that a disused temperance hall in Bispham, Blackpool, had been transformed into the United British Film Studio. By July 2, full sound-recording equipment, powerful arc-lights and four cameras had been installed and shooting of the company's first feature *Love's Dream* was about to commence. Telling the story of a romance between a rich man's daughter and a seaside Pierrot, the production was to star the up-and-coming movie-actress Dodo Watts (1910–1990), supported by the veteran film-comedian Fred Evans. Although the studio became functional, nothing further was heard of *Loves Dream*.[22] It is possible that Fred's involvement had been organized by Harry Wilkinson, who, in 1933 was appointed manager for the North Regional Film Corporation at Bispham.

Downward Path

As the decade progressed the name "Pimple" slipped inexorably down and finally from variety bills. The fulsome, self-congratulatory adverts that were so much part of Fred's comic profile, ceased to appear as he was forced to accept more menial and less lucrative engagements. His appearances took place increasingly at clubs, roadhouse taverns and in cinemas-variety. Sometimes he reverted to his earliest role in the entertainment business. For three weeks at Christmas 1932–33 he played clown in Pat Collin's Christmas Fair and Circus at Bingley Hall, Birmingham, sharing the arena with elephants, performing horses, dogs, and a donkey.[23] The presence of "Sonnie Jinks and Pimple" as clowns at John Sanger's Circus at the Metropole, Hulme, in 1935, might indicate a new and temporary partnership, although the nickname may have been generic in Sanger productions.[24]

Early in 1933 Fred and Joe came together once again to present a topical comedy sketch *The Peace Conference*. Their new act featured regularly at music halls throughout the first half of the year, in addition to which they appeared in a one-off revival of the *Punch* revue at the Pavilion, Southport.[25] Although the brothers ceased to perform as a double act after June 1933, they found employment playing minor roles in a few early talkies. Joe told Denis Gifford that he had worked at Elstree, Welyn, Shepherd's Bush and Shepperton studios, and that he and Fred (as a clown and ringmaster) had appeared together in at least one production.[26]

There was one final episode in Fred's quest to regain his previous cinema celebrity. On March 11, 1933, the *Daily Herald* reported "'Pimple' To Come Back":

> A house and seven acres of ground in Dublin have been bought as the first Irish film studio by Mr. E. Henderson for the Irish Free State Film Company, and fully equipped floors are to be built. Work on the first subject *Paddy Wins the Sweep* will begin in Spring. It will bring back Fred Evans ("Pimple") one of the first comedians of the early days of silent British pictures.[27]

Needless to say, neither Paddy nor Pimple won the sweep.

Into Obscurity

In November 1933 Fred appeared at the Regent Cinema, Truro, Cornwall, placing the last traceable advert in which he employed his screen nickname:

"MONDAY Next, One Night only at 8, the One and only 'Pimple' (as funny as ever) AND CO., including 'Argus,' the World-famed 'Thought Reader.'"[28] From 1934 Joe combined his acting and creative talents by becoming an actor and scenic artist with several touring repertory companies, particularly the Charles Denville Players with whom he was associated before and after World War II. His wandering profession sometimes made him difficult to trace, at one time defeating the efforts of an Ottawa lawyer who had a piece of good news to convey to him. During the early 1930s Adam Goodhall had been entrusted with a legacy $118.80 (possibly from the estate of Joe's great-aunt Amy Howes) to deliver to Joe, but after tracking the elusive performer from Ottawa, Montreal, Hamilton, and Calgary, he finally lost him in Islington, London.[29]

While Fred and Joe's whereabouts during the 1930s and early 1940s are often unknown, those of their father and stepmother can be pinned down with exactitude. Like his own father Fred Evans had become an alfresco street entertainer and in his old age could be found playing an accordion to the queues waiting to buy tickets for the Empire and Odeon cinemas in London's Leicester Square. When the *Sunday Chronicle* ran a piece about Fred and Beattie in 1933 the couple had already been busking in central London for several years. Following the publicity, they made a handful of variety appearances, but soon returned to their open-air careers. Bannister Howard, in his 1938 autobiography, recalled a poignant meeting:

> One evening in 1937, while walking through the West End, I heard the accordion being played very beautifully and someone singing.
> Turning round in curiosity I saw a bent, white-haired old chap to whom someone was giving a copper.
> He was wearing a card round his neck bearing the inscription: "Old Timer."
> I went up to him and asked him who he was. "I'm Fred Evans," he said, "brother of Will Evans, the comedian."
> I was very much touched by this, for the poor old fellow looked so much in want.
> "My name is Bannister Howard," I said. "I bought *Tons of Money* from your brother Will and it made £100,000 for us."
> "I've earned twopence in the last two hours," said the old man, bursting into tears.
> I took him to a pub and, after telling the story to a little crowd of sympathetic listeners, I organised a collection on his behalf. We raised just over eight shillings, which he received very gratefully. He played "Romance" for us and we all joined in the chorus.
> And—would you believe it?—he vanished before I thought of asking where he lived, or had made other inquiries about him and I never found out what has since become of him.[30]

Howard was as unobservant as he was tactless, for following their encounter Fred Evans continued as a very visible busker in the West End for several years. In 1939 he and Beattie were living at 95 Sandringham Buildings, Charing Cross Road, a block of artisans' dwellings which, though grim in appearance, had the advantage of being situated adjacent to the queues of London's theater land. Shortly before Christmas 1944 Fred was interviewed by a reporter from the *Daily Herald*. Described as the oldest busker in London, the 81-year-old exercised a veteran's prerogative by comparing the present unfavorably with the past:

"There's little honour left in the square these days," he said tugging at his beard. "Too many bullies threaten to bash your face in unless you clear off a pitch." "Many's the time I've played in big pantos. We were gentlemen in those days. Why, when my dad was playing at Drury Lane in the '70s and '80s King Edward would go to his dressing room. Those were decent days. Now you've got too many beggars and bullies."[31]

Marionette Follies

For their last collaboration Fred and Joe could not have worked more closely together. Shoulder to shoulder, they hunched over a miniature stage, manipulating the strings of an array of 18-inch-high puppets. Their *Marionette Follies* show was launched in January 1944, although the construction of the models and their synchronization to a specially prepared soundtrack must have taken several months of prior planning. Given the brothers' lifelong commitment to topicality, it was not surprising that their puppets more frequently portrayed film-stars, radio-personalities, and politicians than the conventional fairy tale characters commonly associated with such entertainments. Once more Fred and Joe were in complete control of the process, sharing concept, creation, exhibition, and exploitation. And, as usual, their focus was on burlesque.

Various productions of *The Marionette Follies* toured—largely in Cornwall, Devon, and Somerset. When the show opened during the latter stages of World War II, the West Country was heavily fortified by coastal defenses and airfields, with a massive military build-up preparing for the D-Day invasion of Europe in June 1944. A sparse local population was inflated by the presence of armed forces and by large numbers of young evacuees from Britain's major cities. Added to the economic advantages provided by larger potential audiences, Fred and Joe could rightly claim that they were helping to boost national morale. A 35 percent part of their box-office receipts was donated to charity, allowing them to state they had raised £700 between March–September 1944.[32]

Thirty years after Fred and Joe had lampooned Kaiser Wilhelm, they sunk their satirical teeth into another German war-leader. At a show booked by the Penzance Young Liberals in June 1944 the *Marionette Follies* included "a great topical burlesque" titled "The Bogey of Europe," a nickname coined for Napoleon Bonaparte, but now re-allocated to Adolf Hitler. Joining the miniature form of "Adolf" were similar caricature puppets representing his allies "Musso" (the Italian leader Benito Mussolini) and "Tojo" (the Japanese Prime Minister Hideki Tojo). In contrast, a patriotic tableau illustrated "Sons of the Lords of the Air," a popular song that had been adopted as the anthem of the Air Training Corps.[33]

On a return visit to Penzance the following month there was less emphasis on the war. Appearing once again at the Congregational Hall, the show provided a new selection of figures including Jack Payne with members of his famous dance band and a cabaret presenting the singer Ann Shelton, film star Fred

Astaire and variety favorite George Formby, complete with ukulele. Less familiar faces were seen in a parody of a well-known BBC radio discussion program "The Brain's Trust." If younger members of the audience were not familiar with the philosophical prognostications of Professor Joad, Commander Campbell and Ellen Wilkinson, the Seven Dwarves were on hand to rescue Snow White from an evil giant. The display was mounted within "an exact replica of one of London's finest theaters."[34]

The Marionette Follies toured extensively throughout 1944, playing for short runs at community halls and other venues in Cornish towns such as Sennen, St. Buryan, St. Just, Pendeen, Helston, Goldsithney and St. Ives. Special shows were given to the armed forces, evacuees, and hospital patients. In following years, the brothers took their puppets beyond Cornwall, although they were not able to fulfill their objective of appearing in every county of the British Isles. A projected tour of Canada also appears to have been abandoned.[35] Occasionally, they presented the show without the assistance of the other. In December 1946, Joe's name alone appeared in connection with an engagement at the Empire, Woolwich, South East London,[36] while in February 1949 it was Fred and his wife who appeared in Ballymena, Northern Island. A review of the latter entertainment at the Variety Theatre, Mill Street, confirms that Fred was still acting as a mediator between entertainment and those entertained:

> At the beginning Mr. Fred Evans, writer and producer of the show, gave some of the history of the Marionettes. They were introduced to this country from Italy, in the 13th century when there was a law forbidding live actors to appear on the stage. Puppets were, however, known 4,000 years ago, for when the tombs of ancient Egypt were opened some were found.[37]

New chapters in the Evans' family history also appears to have been specially invented for the entertainment. In February 1944, an advert referred to the Evans Brothers as being: "from an old Welsh-Cornish family, and who are now domiciled in Cornwall."[38] Ten months later a review of the performance at the Small Hall, Market Place, Wells, Somerset, reported that "the show is presented by the Evans Brothers, and for 200 years members of the Evans Family have handed down, from generation to generation the scientific art of puppetry."[39]

Sigh No More, Landladies

There was no place for "Pimple" in the *Marionette Follies*. Like George Robey's "Ma" he had become a good old has-been, his failure to re-engage with movies after World War I resulting in a steady decline in popularity. The very name, if remembered at all, only served to remind the public of a lost age of silliness and naivety. At a stretch "Pimply" might have become an honorary dwarf, but when it came to the remainder of the cast of *The Marionette Follies*, he lacked

Pimple, the winning post, a painted backdrop, and a pantomime horse. The finish of *Pimple in "The Whip"* (courtesy BFI National Archive).

the one quality that Fred and Joe valued most highly—topicality. The joint creator and operator of the show was now billed simply as "Fred Evans," no longer "Britain's Most Famous Film Comedian." His family relationship to famous clowns and music-hall stars was not featured in his publicity and instead he was claimed to be the descendent of a long line of marionette showmen.

With childish Pimple no longer available to take his bows, Fred adopted the character of the elderly puppeteer, a guardian of a time-honored and arcane lore. Although overstating his association with puppetry, Fred would certainly have experienced marionette exhibitions in their nineteenth and early 20th-century heyday. He might even have met one of the most famous Victorian puppet showmen, Harry Wilding (1857–1941), who lived close to the Cannock Hippodrome during the early 1930s. The Evans brothers' involvement with *The Marionette Follies* was not, however, an exercise in nostalgia, rather a pragmatic approach that mirrored their earlier decision to embark on careers in filmmaking. During the 1930s and 1940s puppetry had undergone a major revival with innovators such as Harry Whanslaw and Waldo Lanchester (film-actress Elsa Lanchester's brother) devising fresh ways of presenting the ancient entertainment. Like movies, puppetry provided Fred and Joe with a popular "new" medium, offering a considerable degree of autonomy and ample scope for exploiting their artistic and performing talents.

The reduced scale of their new enterprise meant that the Evans brothers concentrated on personal caricature. Employing the close-up instead of the long shot, they directed the audience's attention inward toward a small stage rather than outward to a large screen. As usual, their main target was entertainment, with individual performances being subjected to close and witty scrutiny. Fred and Joe had become skillful miniaturists, drawing on the distilled experience of a lifetime in show-business to guide the actions of their puppet creations.

By the start of the 1950s, Fred's world had become extremely small. He had moved into a caravan on a plot of land adjoining Webster's Garage, at Montpelier Terrace, in the Cornish town of Torpoint. The concerns and complications involved with live performers had long since vanished and his company now occupied a trunk, much as family and colleagues were stowed away in the recesses of his memory. Like the cast of the *Marionette Follies*, the figures from his past could be resurrected, re-assessed, and sometimes renovated. They were a motley collection that included Fred the comical old clown; Minnie the dashing bareback rider; Trick and Trixie whose tricks were not always very amusing; Will, the always merry "Musical Eccentric"; the Brothers Egbert endlessly linked in a round of double trouble; and a discordant chorus of disgruntled landladies. Whether Joey the long-suffering stooge had been consigned to storage or was still an active participant in his life is not clear. Alone, or with an assistant, Fred soldiered on. He died on August 21, 1951, having collapsed as he lifted the heavy trunk of puppets on his way to a performance.[40]

CHAPTER 20

Family Affairs

"In Loving Memory of FRED EVANS (Pimple) who took his Final Curtain Aug. 31, 1951 and his wife LILY EVANS who joined him Sept. 2, 1951. Always remembered by their family."

THE COMMEMORATIVE NOTICE inserted by two of his daughters in *The Stage* four years after Fred's death was a standard expression of respect that gave no indication of an often disruptive and disrupted relationship. Lily's life with Fred was anything but straightforward. Despite many years spent together the couple appear never to have married. While Lily continued to produce his shows and to bring up their three daughters, Fred wed a young dancer with whom he had four children. On becoming divorced, he married again, adding another three offspring to the Evans' family tree. Fred's professional legacy might have been one of laughter, but his personal conduct was apparently the cause of distress and dismay. Although Lily may have joined Fred in music-hall heaven, their final years on earth were spent living a long way apart.

The variety profession was not conducive to domestic life. Relationships were fluid and frequently unstable; gambling and heavy drinking were commonplace; and the stresses associated with performance sometimes resulted in violent and erratic behavior. Fred's extended family was large and its marital misadventures many. The rapid re-marriage of Fred's father after his wife's sudden death—indicative of a previous relationship—had been foreshadowed by his uncle Will. Only six months after his wife, Ada Luxmore, died from cancer in May 1897, Will married Evelyn Poole. He had also conducted an affair with an actress Ethel May Thomas during the last months of Ada's illness. After Will's decision to leave Ethel and their child to marry Evelyn, his jilted lover sued unsuccessfully for breach of promise. Will and Evelyn (affectionately nicknamed "Dinkie") remained together until 1920 when the comedian walked out on his family to set up home with the performer, Nora Emerald.

Fred's uncle, "Happy Dustman" Albert Jee, had also been involved in a breach of promise case. During a lightning courtship he had sent the music-hall singer Gladys Mavius a succession of presents and passionate letters declaring himself to be her "ever loving sweetheart." Albert's ardor quickly cooled, leaving him to pay £75 damages settled in a 1908 court hearing. Gladys, whose heart seems to have remained unbroken, provoked admiration for a diamond ring that she proudly exhibited to the courtroom: "It's a beauty—a single diamond and I love single stones" she informed the judge.[1] Having been cleared of breach of promise in his own case, Will Evans decided that the subject represented excellent material for his music-hall act. In his song "A Breach of Promise Case" (1908) he represented a female plaintiff who had met the defendant after being thrown out of a public house:

> Oh, a breach of promise case is very peculiar.
> They ask you things you wouldn't like to tell your Ma,
> They put you in the box and then begin to preach,
> I prefer a case of champagne to a case of breach!

The Dream Man

During research for this biography, two marriages involving a variety performer named "Frederick Evans" were uncovered. Given that Fred had a relationship with Lily throughout the period it seemed likely that a second Fred Evans might explain the apparent anomalies. The name Fred Evans is not uncommon, nor is it remarkable for two variety artists with the same name to be performing during the same period. Another Fred Evans was duly discovered, billed as "The Dream Man" in music halls during the 1900s and enlisting in the armed forces in the early part of World War I. It eventually transpired that, despite his long-term association with Lily, the bridegroom in both marriages was Fred "Pimple" Evans. But it also became apparent that the "Dream Man" had unsuspected links to "Pimple."

The other Fred Evans was older than Fred "Pimple" Evans by 12 years, having been born in Poole, Dorset, in 1877. It seems likely that both Freds met in 1900 when *The Era* for March 24 reported:

> Mr. Fred Evans, a member of the Florador Troupe of musicians and pantomimists was married on Thursday at St. Joseph's Church, High-street, Deptford, to Miss Kate Leary. Though bearing exactly the same name as the chief of the above combination, the bridegroom is no relation whatever.[2]

By 1901 Fred Evans had left the Floradors to become one of Fred Karno's company of knockabout comedians. Significantly, in the light of a future development, he often appeared alongside the Scottish performer Billie Ritchie. For some time, Fred Evans toured in a series of sketches presented by T. Reed Pinaud who had bought the European rights from Karno. Among his roles were "The Terrible Turk" in *Mumming Birds*, and the drunken dude, famously associated with Charles Chaplin, in a later version of the same sketch. It was possibly his portrayal of a "Fagin-like old clothes man" in *Early Birds* that provided the inspiration for his later one-man act.

In March 1909, *The Era* reviewed his performance at the Grand, Clapham Junction:

> Fred Evans in a novel absurdity, *Dreaming*, in which he represents the characters he sees in his dreams—Fagin and Bill Sikes—was heavily received, the murdering of Nancy (represented by a dummy) by the latter being accompanied by roars of laughter.[3]

With its unusual content and remarkable display of acting, the sketch proved successful at major music hall throughout the UK from 1909 to 1914. At some stage, its popularity came to the notice of Fred Evans' old colleague, Billie Ritchie, who had become a solo comedian after traveling to the United States with a Karno company in 1905. Acquiring the American performance rights, Ritchie presented the "protean" sketch as *A Dream of Dickens* on the vaudeville circuit in 1912. Ritchie went on to become one of Charles Chaplin's main rivals in early film comedies, although he appears not to have filmed the sketch. In October 1917 Piccadilly released *Oliver Twisted*, a two-reel comedy in which Pimple sent up the 1916 American film of the novel. With its scene of Pimple as Bill Sikes murdering a dummy, the film was also perhaps a homage to Fred's older namesake.

After volunteering for the King's Colonial Infantry in September 1914, Fred "Dream Man" Evans becomes difficult to trace. Whether he resumed his theatrical career after military service is not known, but by the outbreak of World War II he had become a commercial traveler in the tea trade. He was still married to Kate after 39 years.

Marriages

The confusion created by an unrelated Fred Evans alongside a pair of related Fred Evans in the variety profession does not conceal the difficult facts of Fred "Pimple" Evans' two marriages. On August 15, 1923, he married 16-year-old Daisy Victoria Stiles at Hendon Registry Office. She was already three months pregnant, and it is likely that she was a minor performer in his show *Punch*. Fred's identity was confirmed by his age, 34; his father's details; and by the witness, Jack Walsh, who was appearing in his current production. Daisy and Fred had four children between the years 1924 and 1930, their birthplaces Wirral, Cheshire; Brighton, East Sussex; Eastry, Kent; and Hendon, Middlesex, suggesting a life spent on tour. It is possible that Daisy was a member of the group that caused the dispute with Exeter landlady Catherine Ley in 1928 and that the child mentioned in newspaper reports was one of Fred's new family.

Fred referred to his children in an interview given to the *Coventry Evening Telegraph* in December 1927. He explained that the entire Jee family were to benefit from the will of his "aunt" Amy Howes who had died at the age of 85 in Brewster, Putnam County, New York. Former bareback-rider Amy had been left a fortune from her husband Seth Benedict Howes, one of the biggest circus proprietors in the United States. Fred and Joe's relationship to Amy Howes was, to say the least, complicated. Her husband Seth Howes was the brother of Nathan Howes who was the father of Egbert Howes, the brother-in-law of Fred and Joe's maternal grandfather Joseph Jee. The inheritance apparently consisted of at least a million pounds of gilt-edged stock to be shared by 42 nephews and nieces. Fred may have been drawing on stories told by his mother when he related that, as a boy, Seth Howes gave "circus" shows to other children in Brewster. "In the end" Fred continued "he had three big ranches, to supply his circuses with bronchos." Asked by the reporter what he intended to do with the money, Fred seemed uncertain about how many children he had when he answered:

> Settle it [the inheritance] on the four kiddies. For the present I shall go on getting a fortune, under certain conditions, in "Mademoiselle from Armentieres." You can't retire from our job. After the footlights, any other life is much too slow. It's the only profession that claims you, body and soul, until you have to stop altogether. I can't go into business—or quietness—on a fortune. But I shall be just as good a comedian if I know my children are secure for their lives.[4]

Amy's Howes' estate was eventually distributed to many of her relatives and several charitable institutions. Whether Fred or Joe received a share has not been established, but Fred's later behavior in the 1930s showed that the security of his children was not his main concern. In 1936 Daisy sued for divorce, claiming that he had frequently committed adultery with a neighbor in St. Mark's Crescent, Regents Park. At the time of the case his whereabouts were unknown, Daisy supplying the information that he had recently been acting in a production at the Theatre, Benwell, near Newcastle on Tyne.

In 1941 Daisy married Stanley J. Overbury, an ex-actor who was actively involved with wartime charities. By this time, ex-husband Fred had also remarried and had already started another family. When he married again, in Swansea in 1938, Fred gave his age as 40, rather than 49, while his new wife, Virginia Gladys Brooker, claimed hers to be 23. Although stated to be a professional dancer, her experience must have been limited for she was only 16 years old. The three children from the marriage (born in August 1939, July 1940, and June 1941) knew little of their father and in later years were merely told that he was not a good person.

Pimple's People

Fred was survived by his father, who died, aged 88, in the spring of 1952 and by Beattie who passed away in 1964. In 1939 his partner Lily Evans (recording herself as "divorced") was living in Streatham, South West London, with two of their daughters, Josey Lilian and Betty May (whose husband the musician Dante Alphonso Palmerino Mancini had died the previous year). Betty was at times employed as a screen and film make-up artist and a dance teacher at the Arthur Murray Studio. She later married a major in the Canadian army, ending her days in California, aged 90. At the age of 20, Fred and Lily's third child. Peggy met a rope spinning, knife throwing, joke-telling variety performer with whom she appeared for many years as "Don and Honey Ray." During the late 1930s they began to construct dioramas and tableaux which featured hundreds of intricately carved, tiny figures. Their historical and fantasy scenes occasionally reflected Fred's marionette show. Alongside series depicting the Royal Artillery through the ages and a history of torture, they exhibited fairy tale and pantomime subjects such as *Robinson Crusoe, Red Riding Hood, Cinderella,* and *Snow White*. Following their move to Canada in the 1950s they continued model making, achieving a major success when their work formed the basis for "Miniature World" in Victoria. Peggy or Honey as she had become known died in Calgary, aged 90.

Joe's first wife, Geraldine Maxwell, appears to have abandoned performing by the early 1920s. Nothing is known of her later life with the exception that at the outbreak of World War II she was living with her mother and married sister, having reverted to needlework to make a living. Although apparently still married to Geraldine, Joe appears to have lived with Maisie until her death in 1959. During the late 1950s and early 1960s he appeared in an amateur concert party in the Hove area of Sussex but in 1961 a thrombosis necessitated the removal of one of his legs. Despite his poor health, in 1963 Joe courted and married Barbara Gertrude Tibbetts, an ex-professional ice skater who was 25 years his junior. He lost his other leg in 1964 and died on October 31, 1967. There were few surviving mementos of Fred or of their most famous comic creation. A month later Barbara wrote to Denis Gifford: "On looking through Joe's photos etc. I found that he had a few clips of Pimple film—a frame of which I am enclosing—would you like to have them?"[5]

If Barbara had passed the clips on to Denis, they would have soon been submerged as he added layer upon layer to his collection. Despite the meticulous research demonstrated in his publications he never compiled a catalogue of the many thousands of items crammed into his home. It was, as his friend Bob Monkhouse described, "a vast gathering of treasures," but one to which Denis alone held the key. When he died—suddenly and alone—in 2000 the wholesale clearance of his house threatened to scrap many items that may have appeared to have little or no value. Fortunately, friends realized the significance of the recorded interviews and the audio tapes were saved from an uncertain fate. They eventually found their way to the British Film Institute library where Denis's conversations with elderly cinema pioneers may now be heard.

CHAPTER 21

Postscript

HISTORY CAN BE DEFINED as what historians choose to write about. In the quest for clear and coherent narratives, those discussing the development of early film have sometimes put problematic areas to one side, either ignoring them completely or downplaying their relevance. The comedian Fred Evans has fallen foul of such a process, with a dogmatic emphasis on the evolution of cinematic art causing his films to be dismissed as inferior to the work of several less successful music-hall contemporaries and to most American comedians of the period. Yet Fred's popularity and his prolific output deserve explanation.

Fred's claim to fame rests on the enthusiasm that the public demonstrated for his 200 silent comedies made shortly before and during World War I. During the period Fred rivaled Charlie Chaplin as the nation's favorite comedian, but his approach to filmmaking was extremely different. His childhood friend Charlie was catering for diverse American audiences, adopting a strongly kinetic humor that also resulted in his films becoming accessible to the entire world, irrespective of languages spoken. Fred, on the other hand, was largely influenced by the burlesque, satirical and topical traditions of British music hall and pantomime, thereby ruling out a large degree of international appreciation. Relying so heavily on movement, Chaplin's comedy transcends not only the spoken word, but time, whereas Fred's had so many connections with the popular culture of the 19th and early 20th centuries that it rapidly became obscure and difficult to comprehend. Chaplin's output found its way into archives and museums while Fred's productions were consigned to the trash can. In 1970, Denis Gifford could write of Fred and Joe that "both were forgotten and will probably remain so as hundreds of their films seem to have vanished."[1]

Charlie Chaplin endeared himself to those seeking aesthetic legitimacy for the film industry with his innovative and beautifully crafted movies, while Fred chose to subvert the new medium by sending up its more grandiose output and poking fun at cinematic techniques. As the "Little Tramp" Chaplin charmed movie goers with his visual artistry and the universality of his themes. In the character of "Pimple" Fred Evans provoked laughter by demonstrating that cinema was just the latest, and perhaps not the greatest, development in the long history of popular entertainment.

Appendix:
The Films of Fred Evans

FRED EVANS IS KNOWN TO HAVE APPEARED in over 200 films, most of them as the character "Pimple." Survival rates are low, with only 20 entire or fragmentary films preserved in the BFI Film Archive and an extremely small number held in private collections. In the following filmography release dates are given in brackets, although the films were often shown some time earlier. Contemporary reviews are given to supplement those already included within the text. Many other reviews will be found in cinema-related publications of the time.

1910

1. *The Last of the Dandy* (Cricks and Martin, April 8, 1910)

2. *A Costly Gift* (Cricks and Martin, August 19)

3. *The Marriage of Muggins, V.C. and a Further Exploit* (Cricks and Martin, September)
   Archive: BFI National Archive.

4. *Prison Reform* (Cricks and Martin, October 25)

5. *As Prescribed by the Doctor* (Cricks and Martin, November 26)

1911

6. *Charlie Smiler Joins the Boy Scouts* (Cricks and Martin, May 18, 1911)
   Archive: BFI Archive.
   Smiler is alternatively described as "Charlie" and "Charley" in contemporary reviews and advertising.

7. *Charlie Smiler Takes Brain Food* (Cricks and Martin, June 8)

8. *How Puny Peter Became Strong* (Cricks and Martin, June 29)
   Archive: BFI National Archive.

9. *Charlie Smiler Completes in a Cycle Race* (Cricks and Martin, July 6)
   "Charley, after an initial essay with his bike in his bedroom, takes to the road

and makes the best of his way to the starting point of a road race. One of the wheels of his mount comes off, and the only substitute at the local cycle shop is one of the old 'ordinaries' with the big wheel. Charley takes this, and gets off in advance of the others, leading until a brick brings his mount and himself to grief. Charley gets another spill in trying to avoid a dog, and then decides to take a short cut. He rides into a clothes line, and gets warm treatment from an irate lady; and later charges full at a party sitting round a table outside a village inn, turns a somersault into a horse trough, dives clean through a cottage window, and takes a flying leap right into a mud cart." Supplement to *The Bioscope* (June 29, 1911): xiii.

10. *Charlie Smiler Takes Up Ju-Jitsu* (Cricks and Martin, August 10)

"Smiler is one of a number of people who gather outside a booth, inside which a troupe of Japanese wrestlers are performing. He files in with the rest, and is so impressed by the skill of the performers that he seizes a member of the audience and tries to throw him, only himself to be roughly handled by one of the Japs, who throws him over his head, and finally pitches him out of the tent. Smiler, once he has recovered from the shaking, begins to practice on others the falls he has been so painfully acquainted with. In a stout farmer, Smiler meets more than his match. All the holds Smiler has learnt fail to move him off his pins; even when a walking stick is brought into play he stands fast, and then he joins in himself, and Smiler has such a rough time that he limps away with his liking for ju-jitsu almost cured., though a bout with a tailor's dummy revives him a little, and he is still further exhilarated by the ease with which he topples over a row of bobbies one after the other. The next person he runs across, however, though she is only a slight girl, throws him over her shoulder with the greatest of ease, ending by presenting him with her card, which shows her to be 'Madame Thrower,' a well-known teacher of the art." Supplement to *The Kinematograph and Lantern Weekly* (August 10, 1911): iii.

Archive: Three scenes from the film are contained in the James M. Anderson compilation of silent film comedy *All in Good Fun* (1955). Further sequence contained in Anderson's *Crazy Days* (1962).

11. *Charlie Smiler is Robbed* (Cricks and Martin, August 27)

"A really clever chase subject full of ingenious and mirth provoking incidents. Our old friend Smiler is one of the leading characters, the other a pickpocket who takes advantage of Smiler's abstracted air as he gazes into a shop window, to become possessed of his watch and chain." Supplement to *The Kinematograph and Lantern Weekly* (August 24, 1911): xx.

Archive: Huntley Archives.

12. *A Bag of Monkey Nuts* (Cricks and Martin, September 7, 1911)

"A roughly dressed young man of the labouring class purchases a bag of monkey nuts and the effects of eating these are remarkable in the extreme. He has barely swallowed the first before he begins to act exactly like a monkey himself, takes to the railings as a means of progression instead of the road, swarms a lamppost, and then takes a return visit to the stall where the nuts were bought, and brings everything to the ground in confusion. Later, he upsets a guardian of the law and order who tries to restrain him and takes a flying leap through a shop window. He makes his way to the top of a factory chimney, dives down the chimney, and immerges in the furnace room below, with his mania apparently burned out of him, for he accepts the proffer of refreshment made by the astonished workmen, with every appearance of sanity." Supplement to *The Bioscope* (October 12, 1911): viii.

A surviving still from the film identifies the comedian as "Fred Evans," suggesting that similar uncredited appearances were made for Cricks and Martin in the 1910–1911 period.

13. *Charlie Smiler Is Stage Struck* (Cricks and Martin, November 2)

14. *Stop the Fight* (Precision Films, c. December)

1912

15. *Wanted: A Wife and Child* (Precision Films, c. January 1912)

16. *Fred's Police Force* (Precision, c. February)
    Archive: BFI National Archive. Incomplete.

17. *Cowboy Mad* (Precision, c. February)

18. *The Little General* (Precision, c. April)

19. *Fifty Years After* (Precision [MP], c. May)

20. *A Novel Burglary* (Precision [MP], c. May)

21. *Pimple Does the Turkey Trot* (Ec-Ko/Cosmo, November 10)

22. *The Taming of Big Ben* (Ec-Ko/Cosmo, November 17)

23. *Pimple and the Snake* (Ec-Ko/Cosmo, November 24)
    Archive: BFI National Archive.

24. *The Whistling Bet (Ec-Ko/Cosmo, December 2)*

25. *Grand Harlequinade* (Ec-Ko/Cosmo, December 15)

1913

26. *Pimple Gets a Quid* (Ec-Ko/Cosmo, January 5, 1913)

27. *Pimple Wins a Bet* (Ec-Ko/Cosmo, January 12)

28. *Pimple's Fire Brigade* (Folly Films/Cosmo, January 19)
    "The house is on fire, and Pimple's fire brigade is summoned. Picture the doors of a stable-yard opening, from which there proceeds two donkeys harnessed to a

broken-down wagon, on which stands smoking a hot-potato baker. Pimple, in fire-man's outfit as captain, drives with his gallant crew seated behind him. The spec-tacle arouses the mirth of the populace. The fire brigade is in no hurry, and stops at a water trough to give the mokes a drink. Then a couple of carrots on the end of a long pole are used with a view to getting up speed. But a newsboy comes along announcing 'all the winners!' and it is necessary for the fire brigade to discuss the news before they can go any further. Having said all they have to say on the subject of sport, the great engine once more gets on the move. It pulls up later on near some cottages to inquire of a small boy if he has seen a fire anywhere. The small boy leads them to the burning cottage they are too late, the fire is already put out. Pimple is not to be done, and taking no notice of the occupants, he runs up the fire-escape, enters the building, and begins to fling out the furniture. But he catches sight of a football match in the next field, and he and his gallant band crowd on the roof to watch it. When a goal is scored they are satisfied, and descend to knock off, as it is one o'clock, and time for some baked potatoes. There luncheon is interrupted by one of the firemen discovering that the fire engine is on fire, and we leave the party amongst the ruins. This is broad farce, and it is quite impossible to convey any use-ful idea of the humor of situations by mere description. We are quite sure that this film will be extremely popular." *The Cinema* (January 1, 1913): 66.

29. *Pimple Becomes an Acrobat* (Folly Films/Cosmo, January 26)

30. *Pimple's Eggs-Traordinary Story* (Folly Films/Cosmo, February 2)

31. *Pimple as a Cinema Actor* (Folly Films/Cosmo, February 9)
    "Pimple sees an advertisement for a moving picture actor and applies for the same. The secretary tells him he must be able to cycle, juggle, wrestle and perform on the trapeze. Our hero sets off to learn these things and as well may be imag-ined his is not a triumphant course." Supplement to *The Kinematograph and Lan-tern Weekly* (January 16, 1913): xxix.

32. *Pimple as a Rent Collector* (Folly Films/Cosmo, February 23)
    "By the side of the cold, dark water Pimple, tired of life, is intent upon mak-ing away with himself. He pauses to take the temperature of the juicy depths, then makes a frantic rush, but is dragged back by friendly hands. His rescuer leads him off to where one more chance more awaits him. A rent collector is wanted, and he is given the job, with instructions to be sure to collect the rent. At his first call he meets with apologies, and regrets, but no rent. Disappointed and a bit angry, he vows to make the next beggar pay. He strips off his coat and hat, and bangs vigorously upon the door. But cold water runs down his spine, and his heroic intentions vanish when the door opens, revealing six feet of massive humanity. He reassumes his coat and proffers a timid request for the rent, getting by way of reply a sound cuff and a kick that sends him flying. He knocks very gen-tly at the next door which is opened by a pale thin young man. Immediately Pim-ple becomes pugnacious. He strips off his coat, rolls up his shirt sleeves, bullies

the poor young man, ends up by shaking him like a rat and flinging him into the passage. At the next house he is greeted by a dainty apparition that drives all sordid notions of rent out of his head. He indulges in a little flirtation, kisses the lady's hand, and so departs. His next call brings him upon the affectionate attentions of a slut with her hair in curl papers. This is more than Pimple can stick, and he beats a hasty retreat. At the next house he finds a large board, 'Beware of the dog,' which announcement satisfies him, and he departs without investigating further. Returning to the office he has only apologies and no money to tender. He gets kicked out, and we next see him leaning sorrowfully against a large door. He steps pensively through the door, and then we observe painted upon it in large letters this word, 'Workhouse'; it is a conclusion that will fetch the house down." *The Cinema* (January 22, 1913): 58.

33. *Pimple as a Ballet Dancer* (Folly Films/Cosmo, February 16)
 "Watching a ballet dancer perform, and with a graceful kick reach a tambourine she holds above her head, Pimple is seized with the desire to do likewise. He begins to practice and kicks a tray out of a waiter's hand. He gets flung out of the show. He goes dancing through the streets, and lifts the tray off a muffin-man's head. When the muffin-man has done with him he goes on his way, and this time kicks a satchel out of a young lady's hand. He creates a disturbance at a pot-shop, upsets a street-seller of 'Wait-and-see' Pills, and waltzes into a circle, where some street minstrels are passing round the hat. His flying foot catches the hat, and scrambles the cash amongst the crowd. There is a rush for it on the part of the spectators, and a rush for Pimple on the part of the minstrels. They turn him upside-down, shake his pockets out, gather up the spoil, and leave him weeping in the roadway." Supplement to *The Bioscope* (February 6, 1913): xiii.

34. *Pimple Goes A-Busking* (Folly Films/Cosmo, April 6)

35. *Pimple Joins the Police Force* (Folly Films/Cosmo, April 20)

36. *Pimple, Detective* (Folly Films/Cosmo, April 27)
 "Pimple is summoned to discover a stolen baby. In his attempts he does some fairly funny things. When he sees a man holding a baby he thinks he is on a clue, but on reaching the man's house he is ordered away. The missing baby is finally found in a dog's kennel, and the detective is given the order of the boot." *The Bioscope* (April 17, 1913): 99.

37. *Pimple's Motor Bike* (Folly Films/Cosmo, May 4)
 Archive: BFI National Archive. Incomplete.

38. *Pimple Writes a Cinema Plot* (Folly Films/Cosmo, May 18)
 "Pimple sees an advertisement offering £5 for a picture plot. An incident in the park gives him a base upon which to found his story, which is soon written. He reads his plot to many passers-by and all die with laughter. At last the kinema factory is reached but when the plot is recited to the manager, he merely looks

puzzle. Exasperated, Pimple fells him with a bludgeon." Supplement to *The Kine-matograph and Lantern Weekly* (May 1, 1913): xxv–xxvii.

39. *Pimple and the Gorilla* (Folly Films/Phoenix, May 26)

40. *Miss Pimple, Suffragette* (Folly Films/Phoenix, June 2)

41. *Pimple Meets Captain Scuttle* (Folly Films/Phoenix, June 16)
"Pimple decides to shuffle off this mortal coil, Captain Scuttle, happening to look round, sees the would-be suicide, and at once rushes to the rescue. Under threats of shooting him, he persuades the unhappy Pimple to refrain from hang-ing himself. How the precious couple join hands and obtain a good meal and a pair of boots for nothing affords a theme for some uproarious fun." *The Bioscope* (June 19, 1913): 87.

42. *The Indian Massacre* (Folly Films/Phoenix, June 23)

43. *Two to One on Pimple* (Folly Films/Phoenix, c. June)

44. *The Story of "Hy-Am Touched or the Triumph of Lady Bird"* (Folly/Phoenix, June 9)
"Pimple (our greatest tragedian?) specially wrote this great drama in order that he might assume the title role, for which he is to receive he enormous sum of £500 (perhaps)....

C.V. Paterson plans to ruin our hero and, at a grand assembly, 'Hy-am Touched' loses his all at the glorious game of halfpenny nap. Broken to the world 'Touched' is just going to go, when C.V., Paterson suggests they should play for his lady love, Lady Bird. Seizing a chair, 'Touched' is about to brain his antago-nist when Lady Bird intervenes and cooing sweetly bids him play. Fortune is at last touched by 'Touched,' the first two tricks are won by the anxious hero. Alas, from the depths of his patent boots the villain brings the ace and ... 'Touched' has observed the action and striking his opponent with a champagne bottle, he fells him to the floor. (He didn't really hit him, so don't be alarmed).

I must fly, fly to foreign climes, and 'Touched,' bidding goodbye to his Lady Bird, gets.

The subsequent scenes take us to gay *Paree*? where, after various adventures, 'Touched' reads in the agony column, 'Come back at once. The man you killed is not dead—Lady Bird.'

That fetches him and he hurries back home in a hurry...."
Synopsis probably supplied by Joe Evans, *The Kinematograph and Lantern Weekly* (June 5, 1913): 697.

45. *Pimple's Complaint* (Folly Films/Phoenix, July 14)
Archive: BFI National Archive. Incomplete.

46. *Pimple's Motor Trap* (Folly Films/Phoenix, July 21)
"Again in trouble for rent, which Pimple and Capt. Scuttle cannot pay, the landlady puts them into the street. Pimple soon hits on a plan to replenish the

exchequer. Annexing a policeman's uniform and helmet, he unfolds the idea of disguising himself as a minion of the law, stopping motor cars under the pretext that they have exceeded the speed limit and taking bribes. Scuttle will not have anything to do with the plan, but Pimple proceeds. The first attempt is a fiasco, the car, instead of stopping, goes round the corner, leaving Pimple in the middle of the road. Hearing a motor horn Pimple thinks he has a capture this time, but it only turns out to be a small box on wheels pushed by a small boy. The next deal comes off. Pimple artistically receives his bribe with his hand outstretched behind him. The motor moves off, Pimple looks at the bribe, but, alas, it was but a halfpenny. The next episode promises better, for Pimple handles banknotes, but fickle fortune deserts him. A real policeman comes along and amid desperate expostulations, Pimple is arrested and taken to the County Police Station. Here Scuttle puts in an appearance as Police Inspector and effects Pimple's escape and the two annex the car, which they proceed to sell at the first garage they come to." Supplement to *The Kinematograph and Lantern Weekly* (July 3, 1913): xxiii.

47. *Pimple's Sporting Chance* (Folly Films, Phoenix, August 4)
"In the first scene, Mrs. Jones is found to be assailed by two queer looking specimens of the genus Bailiff. The valiant Pimple and his friend Scuttle happen in, and 'gently' dismiss the two bold men. The next problem is that of 'raising the wind' for the saving of Mrs. Jones' household goods. A means quickly presents itself when the two heroes see the 'Palace of Boxingland.' Within ten minutes a match has been sealed between Pimple and another Bantam.

On the following evening, before a packed assembly of the 'fraternity,' the great match is announced, and Pimple, attended by Scuttle, enters the ring. Three rounds of a mystifying nature follow, in which boxing, Ju-Jitsu and Graeco-Roman are impartially applied, amid great excitement. In vain does the referee appeal. His sallies, even secure him several nasty 'chin-enders,' while Scuttle's excitement leads to even worse results.

In the end, after a furious bout, Pimple knocks out his adversary in great style, and gets the purse of gold. Not a second is to be lost, for already the bailiffs may be 'on the job,' and' as a matter of fact, Pimple and Scuttle just get to Jones' in times to avert the great catastrophe. A final display of Pimple's 'form' in 'chucking' the villain concludes a very laughable comic." *The Bioscope* (July 3, 1913): 69.

48. *Pimple Takes a Picture* (Folly Films/Phoenix, August 11)
"*Even the taking of a picture can be made humorous.*—Pimple is a kine cameraman and sets out to photograph a series of scenes. The results cannot be described, neither can Pimple's condition when everything has finished." Supplement to *The Kinematograph and Lantern Weekly* (July 24, 1913): xxiii.

49. *Pimple Gets the Sack* (Folly Films/Phoenix, August 18)
"Pimple again enters the thorny path of evil-doing. Our picture opens with a real burglar breaking into a house. Hardly have we seen the entrance effected

than on the scene comes Pimple. Armed with a hammer and saw, he is just helping himself into the window when a limb of the law appears. Pimple just asks the officer to bump him up,' but gets flung violently out of the picture. Hardly has the constable turned his back, when Pimple makes a rush for it and lands inside the open window. Here he finds himself covered with the revolver of the burglar and is forced to submit to being bound with a rope. Thinking the intruder is safely trussed up, the burglar gets on with the business in hand. Wriggling himself free, Pimple gets into a sack and terrifies the burglar on his return. Out of the window they go, the poor burglar flying as if for his life, until they are brought up short by three policemen. The sack is taken to the police station. The magistrate, to make the punishment fit the crime, orders the sack to be thrown into the river. This is accomplished, and we see an extremely woebegone figure being hauled out of the water." Supplement to *The Kinematograph and Lantern Weekly* (July 24, 1913): xxiii.

50. *Adventures of Pimple—The Battle of Waterloo* (Folly Films/Phoenix, August 25)

51. *Pimple's Wonderful Gramophone* (Folly Films/Phoenix, September 1)
Archive: BFI National Archive.

52. *Pimple's Rest Cure* (Folly Films/Phoenix, September 8)

53. *Pimple Joins the Army* (Folly Films/Phoenix, September 15)

54. *A Bathroom Problem* (Folly Films/Phoenix, September 22)

55. *A Tragedy in Pimple's Life* (Folly Films/Phoenix, September 29)

56. *Dicke Turpin's Ride to Yorke* (Folly Films/Phoenix, October 6)
"The latest adventure of the amazing Pimple carries him into a region of romance which is always certain to make an appeal to popular fancy, but no knight of the road has ever proved so mirth provoking as this representative of the famous highwayman.

Dick Turpentine and his wonderful steed, Elizabethe, go through all the adventures that tradition has ascribed to their famous original, and serve them up with an addition of humour and wit which are entirely their own. The gallant steed displays far more than equine intelligence, and the robbery of the mail cart, and the subsequent ride to York, will delight young and old alike, while the intensely pathetic death scene will certainly bring tears of laughter to every eye.

The whole film is an excellent joke from start to finish. There is never a dull moment, and the fun is infinite in its variety. Even the last sad scene, which pictures the obsequies of the faithful mare, is relieved of its gloom by the evident satisfaction shown by the cat, who officiates as sexton and undertaker." *The Bioscope* (September 4, 1913): 799.

57. *Pimple Does the Hat Trick* (Folly Films/Phoenix, October 13)

58. *Pimple's Wife* (Folly Films/Phoenix, October 20)

59. *Pimple's Inferno* (Folly Films/Phoenix, October 27)

60. *Pimple Goes Fishing* (Folly Films/Phoenix, November 10)

61. *When Pimple Was Young* (Folly Films/Phoenix, November 20)

62. *Pimple the Sport* (Folly Films/Phoenix, November 24)

63. *Pimple Gets the Jumps* (Folly Films/Phoenix, c. November)

64. *Pimple's Ivanhoe* (Folly Films/Phoenix, December 8)

65. *Once Upon a Time* (Folly Films/Phoenix, December 15)

66. *Slippery Pimple* (Folly Films/Phoenix, December 22)

67. *Lieutenant Pimple on Secret Service* (Folly Films/Phoenix, December 29)

1914

68. *Pimple's Kissing Cup/How Pimple Saved Kissing Cup* (Folly Films/Phoenix, January 5, 1914)

"Who has not heard of Kissing Cup, the great racehorse, whose famous feats on the course have been the theme of countless 'recitaters' the world over. Our worthy friend Pimple has cottoned on to the idea, and has given us his version. Lord Rothkid receives a visitor early one morning, in the person of the great Baron von Baron, his rival for the hand of Lady Muriel. He has come to press for the immediate payment of a debt of honour, but Lord Rothkid has not a sou wherewith to liquidate his debt, and asks as a favour to wait until the great race is run, as he has placed his all on Kissing Cup. 'She is bound to win, and then I can pay you in full.' Baron von Baron decides in his mind that Kissing Cup shall not run, and leaves the house to put his idea into practice. Next morning, on going the rounds of the stables, Lord Rothkid discovers that Kissing cup has gone. Utterly astounded and bewildered, he rushes with the stable lad to tell the police. They were on the way, when they meet our friend Pimple. The stable lad happened to know Pimple, and introduces him to Lord Rothkid with the remark that he might be able to help him, to which our worthy friend, after hearing the story, agrees. Telling them to leave it to him, Pimple goes with them to the stable, and there picks up a clue. This he follows, and it leads him to the gates of the Baron's residence. Effecting an entrance to the grounds, Pimple finds the trace leads him to a high window, and, hoisting himself up, he sees with joy his quest is not in vain, for within, seated on a chair, gagged and bound, is the missing Kissing Cup. Getting into the window, Pimple soon releases the horse, and they make their escape...." Supplement to *The Cinema* (January 1, 1914): 125.

Archive: BFI National Archive. Incomplete.

69. *Pimple's Great Bull Fight* (Folly Films/Phoenix, January 12)

"Our one and only Pimple decided to go to Spain for his holidays, and while there he reads in the 'Spanish Onion' that Bombita has resigned his job as a bull-fighter. This conjured up visions to him, and he offers himself as a substitute, and is accepted. We see him dancing the tango—we mean the fandango—with his Spanish landlady, for joy. The day of the great fight arrives. Pimple, as a Toreador, makes a handsome figure. While he makes his bow to the public the bull goes to sleep. You have heard the proverb that it is better 'to let sleeping dogs lie.' Well, Pimple would have done better if he hadn't woke the bull up, for it tossed him in the air several times, and finally chased him into a shed, where we can only imagine what took place, for the walls got knocked out, and Pimple is left, seated among the ruins, where, after collecting his scattered wits, he finally announces that 'Bombita can keep his job—I'm going home.'" Supplement to *The Cinema* (January 1, 1914): 126.

70. *Pimple's Midnight Ramble* (Folly Films/Phoenix, January 19)

"There's been trouble at the Cottage, and Pimple is as nervous as a cat. The other night, whilst reading the newspaper in bed (a bad habit, by the way), he reads that there has been a goodly number of burglaries in his neighbourhood, and the miscreants had not hesitated at murder. With this pleasing subject on his mind, Pimple falls asleep. Any wonder, then, about two hours later, we see him arise, fast asleep, seize the poker, and go in search of the burglars. Various people get the shock of their lives. On he goes until, passing an open door, he enters, still fast asleep. Into the drawing-room he goes, where he terrifies two gentlemen of the housebreaking fraternity, busy on the silver. Their cries of terror bring the police and the householder on the scene, and the now awakened, bewildered Pimple is congratulated for capturing the culprits single-handed." *The Cinema* (January 1, 1914): 126.

71. *What Happened to Pimple, No.1—The Suicide* (Folly Films/Phoenix, January 29)

72. *Pimple's New Job* (Folly Films/Phoenix, February 2)
Archive: BFI Archive and Archive Film Agency.

73. *Pimple's Humanity* (Folly Films/Phoenix, February 9)

"As 'Johnny Walker,' the Scottish Jew in 'Humanity,' Pimple literally carries the burden of the piece on his shoulders, for, his fellow-actors, objecting to the way in which their heads are used for the smashing of crockery, he dispenses with their services entirely, and, with the assistance of two amenable dummy figures and the assistant stage manager, puts up a fight such as has never been seen in the most transpontine melodrama." *The Bioscope* (January 22, 1914): 337.

74. *Lieutnant Pimple and the Stolen Submarine* (Folly Films/Phoenix, February 16)
Archive: BFI National Archive.

75. *What Happened to Pimple (No.2)—The Gentleman Burglar* (Folly Films/ Phoenix, February 16)

76. *When Pimple Was Young—Young Pimple's Schooldays* (Folly Films/Phoenix, c. February)
Listed in Gifford, *The British Film Catalogue 1895–1970* but not traced in *The Bioscope* or *The Kinematograph and Lantern Weekly*.

77. *When Pimple Was Young—His First Sweetheart* (Folly Films/Phoenix, March 2)

78. *Pimple Elopes* (Folly Films/Phoenix, March 9)

79. *Lieutenant Pimple's Dash for the Pole* (Folly Films/Phoenix, March 30)
Archive: BFI National Archive.

80. *Pimple in the Hands of London Crooks* (Folly Films/Phoenix, April 6)
"Our worthy friend Raffles was thinking of a plan whereby the valuables of Lord and Lady Courtney could be transferred to his own pocket. At that moment who should come by but Pimple. Under the threat of telling the passing policeman of the last affair, he consents to help. The plan evolved is that the pair should go to the reception in evening dress and seize any opportunities. The situations that crop up are side-splitting in their absurdity, especially the effort of Pimple to annex the pearl necklace of Lady Courtney, and the raid of the 'owdacious' couple on the bedroom of Lord and Lady Courtney, whilst the latter are sleeping the sleep of the just.

It ends in flight, however, and when they get out of the house into the grounds, they find to their dismay the whole place is surrounded by police. At once there is an exciting chase and but for the overturning of a four-wheeler, they would have got away. As it is, we see the corpses being conveyed into the drawing-room, tenderly laid on the carpet and covered with winding sheets. This is naturally a dry job for the police, and they are invited to the 'below stairs' to have s 'livener.' They had but turned their backs when the corpses came to life. And when the police return they find, instead of the dead bodies, there are sundry cushions and rags under the sheets in their place, and Lord Courtney also makes the discovery that his silver from off the sideboard has vanished also.

Leaving them bewildered, we revert to our two rascals to find them sharing out the spoil, Pimple taking a hand in this in a manner quite worthy of his style of beauty." *The Kinematograph and Lantern Weekly* (March 26, 1914): 90.

81. *Pimple and Galatea* (Folly Films/Phoenix, April 13)

82. *Pimple in the Grip of the Law* (Folly Films/Phoenix, April 20)

83. *The House of Distemperley* (Folly Films/Phoenix, April 27)

84. *Young Pimple and His Sister* (Folly Films/Phoenix, May 4)

85. *Pimple Goes to Paris* (Folly Films/Phoenix, May 11)

86. *The Battle of Gettysownback* (Folly Films/Phoenix, May 18)

87. *Lieutenant Pimple's Sealed Orders* (Folly Films/Phoenix, May 25)
  "Lt. Pimple is taking his ease at the Riviera. A telegram is received: He is wanted by his grateful country to take sealed orders to the great War Lord. The wretched spy, Von Skinski hears of his mission and tries to waylay him. Lieut. Pimple will leave the War Office in naval costume, wearing a rose. The resourceful Pimple lets many men leave the office all wearing roses. Disguised as an old sea salt he puts the villains on the wrong track. Starting upon his mission, he is soon shadowed, but ever alert, he gives his followers the slip. Arrived on H.M.S. Impossible, the real work starts. Von Skinski is there. He will have the papers at all costs, 'Ah!' he says to the woman he is trying to dishonour, 'if you do not get me the papers from Pimple I will tell your husband and then—ah! Then.' At a ball Pimple and the husband are dressed as pierrots. The woman drugs the wrong pierrot. Too late she finds it is her husband. One last resource awaits Von Skinski. Gun practice is about to start. 'Give me the sealed orders,' he yells, 'or else I'll tie you to the practice target.' Pimple is seen out at sea, the shots flying around him. At last he is rescued. The resourceful Pimple finds a way to deliver his sealed orders to the great War Lord, and is afterwards received in loving adoration by his grateful country." Supplement to *The Kinematograph and Lantern Weekly* (January 4, 1917): ix.

88. *How Pimple Won the Derby* (Folly Films/Phoenix, May 28)

89. *Stolen Honours* (Phoenix Film Agency, May)

90. *Pimple's Burglar Scare* ((Folly Films/Phoenix, June 1)

91. *Lieutenant Pimple Goes to Mexico* (Folly Films/Phoenix, June 8)
  "Pimple meets with General Hurt-yer, is ordered to be shot at cock-crow, but kills 'the bird' which has to crow out the death signal. Pimple is put out of action for a time, but ultimately meets the American general, and there's a shaking of hands under the old flag!" *Hull Daily Mail* (May 8, 1913): 6.

92. *The Whitewashers* (Folly Films/Phoenix, June 8)

93. *Pimple 'Midst Raging Beasts* (Folly Films/Phoenix, June 22)

94. *Pimple in Society* (Folly Films/Phoenix, June 29)

95. *Pimple's Advice* (Folly Films/Phoenix, July 6)

96. *Pimple's Trousers* (Folly Films/Phoenix, July 13)

97. *Big Chief Little Pimple* (Folly Films/Phoenix, July 20)

98. *Pimple Turns Honest* (Folly Films/Phoenix, July 27)
  "Of a more humorous nature is 'Pimple Turns Honest,' and in his good resolve and hard work in learning a ponderous gentleman to cycle, Pimple has the

sympathy of the audience and the laughter as well. It was left to the man who has his milk-barrow overturned and the nurse who has her charge nearly killed to supply the dramatic situation, as well as the crippled old gentleman who got so unceremoniously turned out of his hand-coach." *Perthshire Advertiser* (October 7, 1914): 5.

Archive: BFI Archive: Incomplete.

99. *Pimple, Anarchist* (Folly Films/Phoenix, August 3)

"The anarchist club with its bogey-like president, and ridiculous ritual, is an excruciatingly droll scene and Pimple, needless to say, does full justice to it. He is entrusted (just his luck) with a bomb and told to blow up the King of Whitechapel. His entry into the palace, in the disguise of a reporter for 'Komic Kuts' (pencil two inches in diameter) is rich fun—and so also is his exit, with the bomb (though unbeknown to him) still in his own pocket. Arrived home he is tickled to death at the thought of how the Monarch of Mile End will 'get a rise' at 12 o'clock—the time at which the bomb is wound up to go off. He laughs uproariously, when—tic-toc-tic-toc, the familiar sound of the deadly explosive is heard quite close—and it only wants a minute to the hour.... We leave poor Pimple hanging high up in the air on the telegraph wires." *The Kinematograph and Lantern Weekly* (August 6, 1914): 81.

100. *Broncho Pimple* (Folly Films/Phoenix, August 10)

101. *Pimple, Counter Jumper* (Folly Films/Phoenix, August 17)

102. *Pimple's Vengeance* (Folly Films/Phoenix, August 24)

103. *Pimple Pinched* (Folly Films/Phoenix, August 31)

104. *Pimple's Last Resource* (Folly Films/Phoenix, September 7)

105. *Pimple Beats Jack Johnson* (Folly Films/Phoenix, September 14)

106. *Pimple's Escape from Portland* (Folly Films/Phoenix, September 21)

"Pimple overpowers a warder, gets into his clothes, steals his keys and lets all the prisoners out. One of these turns up with Pimple at a fancy dress ball and they are 'holding up' all their guests for their jewelry when the officers arrive and another stern chase takes place, in which Pimple gives us a brilliant bit of running and some comic quick changes." *The Kinematograph and Lantern Weekly* (August 6, 1914): 81.

107. *Lieutenant Pimple, Gunrunner* (Folly Films/Phoenix, September 28)

108. *Pimple, M.P.* (Folly Films/Phoenix, October 5)

109. *Pimple's Proposal* (Folly Films/Phoenix, October 12)

110. *Pimple Enlists* (Folly Films/Phoenix, October 19)

111. *Pimple's Charge of the Light Brigade* (Folly Films/Phoenix, October 19)
Archive: BFI National Archive.

112. *Lieutenant Pimple and the Stolen Invention* (Folly Films/Phoenix, October 26)

113. *Pimple's Great Fire* (Folly Films/Phoenix, November 2)

"As chief of a very curious brigade, whose engine is a particularly nondescript affair, Pimple takes advantage of a faked-up conflagration to remove the numerous presents on show at a reception. An almost too ridiculous, yet laughable episode, the 'engine boiler' serving to conceal the booty." Supplement to *The Bioscope* (October 15, 1914): ix.

114. *Pimple, Special Constable* (Folly Films/Phoenix, November 9)

115. *Pimple's Prison* (Folly Films/Phoenix, November 16)

116. *Lieutenant Pimple, King of the Cannibal Islands* (Folly Films/Phoenix, November 23)

117. *Pimple's Leap to Fortune* (Folly Films/Phoenix, December 14)

"For the fire scene in 'Pimple's Leap to Fortune,' a gentleman gave me permission to put smoke-rockets and fire-boxes under one of his front windows. I saved the daughter from a fiery furnace, my firemen dashed up, put the fire out, and cheered me for my bravery and we all started back to the studio. Suddenly, a shriek for help reached us. The gentleman of the house was shouting that his curtains were on fire. Back we dashed, and my 'firemen' put the real fire out—without water." Fred Evans interview in *Pictures and the Picturegoer* (week ending April 3, 1915): 10.

118. *The Clowns of Europe* (Folly Films/Phoenix, December 21)

119. *Inspector Pimple* (Folly Films/Phoenix, December 28)

120. *How Lieutenant Pimple Captured the Kaiser* aka *Pimple Captures the Kaiser* (Folly Films/Phoenix, November 30)

1915

121. *Pimple and the Stolen Plans* (Folly Films/Phoenix, January 11, 1915)

122. *Pimple on Football* (Folly Films/Phoenix, January 18)

123. *Young Pimple's Frolics* (Folly Films/Phoenix, January 21)

124. *The Adventures of Pimple—The Spiritualist* (Folly Films/Phoenix, January 21)

125. *The Adventures of Pimple—Trilby*/aka *Trilby. By Pimple and Company* (Folly Films/Phoenix, February 1)

"Like a certain well-remembered comedian, our genial friend pimple has acquired a reputation for the burlesquing of famous specimens of the dramatist. So successful, in fact has he become in this direction that we feel sure, that were it not for the limitations of 'the silent screen,' the popular comedian would at once soar to the realms of fictionalized grand opera. In the feature under review the arch conspirator, whose fun is of the broadest, yet never offensive, is cast for the *role* of Trilby, and is certainly 'all there,' even to the Montmartre wig and the classic (?) pedal extremities.

In the famous studio of the three British artists we are initially regaled with very taking scene in wherein a number of obviously Futurist works are in progress of development. Trilby, light as the zephyr, arrives as the trio, with Svengali and Gecco as musicians, raise the welkin, and adds her sawmill screech to the discordant din. The hypnotist, although near to flight, agrees that latent talent is there, and a very laughable mesmeric *séance* follows.

Another very comical burlesque upon the posing incident is witnessed; then we hurtle through the main incidents of the play, all neatly and cleverly held to folly. The climax arrives when the faithful chums arrive at the theatre where Trilby, under the direction of Svengali, is the star attraction. We see the tragic end of her mentor and poor Trilby's attempts to appease an angry audience with a dance *a la* Pavlova. The film ends with a shower of tributes (from Covent Garden) and the hurried exit of the fair artiste to the green room, where the ever-faithful Billee explains that Svengali has gone to 'the Land of his fathers.'

The film is cleverly played, and owes not a little of its interest to the very humorous subtitles, all, as in Pimple productions, destined to point a more or less obvious moral. A burlesque which should evoke nothing but good-humored comment, and which deserves much more appreciation ordinarily shown to comic items." *The Bioscope* (December 24, 1914): 1366.

126. *Mrs. Raffles Nee Pimple* (Folly Films/Phoenix, February 8)
"Fairly efficient comedy item, Raffles prevails upon Pimple to pose as his better half in order to secure a cheque from a very ingenuous relative. The episode of borrowed children not quite original, but serving quite well to complete the broad humour of the tale." Supplement to *The Bioscope* (January 7, 1915): vii.

127. *Pimple in the Kilties* (Folly Films/Phoenix, February 15)

128. *Judge Pimple* (Folly Films/Phoenix, February 22)

129. *Sexton Pimple* (Folly Films/Phoenix, March 1)
"In which Sexton Pimple, with his gallant assistants, Tinker and Pedro, save the life of H.R.H. the King of Cork, who is beset by foreign spies." Supplement to *The Kinematograph and Lantern Weekly* (March 5, 1915): xxxi.

130. *Pimple's Storyette* (Folly Films/Phoenix, March 8)

131. *Pimple's Dream of Victory* (Folly Films, Phoenix, March 15)
"After a heavy meal (presumably of lobster) the naval hero falls asleep and dreams of quaint 'goings on' at the bottom of the ocean. Admiral Von Tirpy, the *bête noir* of Pimple, has a particularly warm time with patent torpedoes, ere our

comical friend awakens to the sound of 'Reveille.'" Supplement to *The Bioscope* (February 11, 1915): vii.

132. *Pimple, the Bad Girl of the Family* (Folly Films/Phoenix, March 22)

"A release which should certainly link among the very best of the Pimple potted plays. Everyone concerned, from the sporting damsel (Pimple *a la* Watteau), the wicked sporting squire and his myrmidons, to Jack, the blacksmith hero, play well indeed. While the various 'sets' (not by Hemsley) are wonderful scenic constructions. A very amusing, yet quite inoffensive burlesque of the popular melodrama—titles and 'comments' also good throughout." Supplement to *The Bioscope* (February 18, 1915): vii.

133. *Flash Pimple, the Master Crook* (Folly Films/Phoenix, March 29)

134. *Pimple, Child Stealer* (Folly Films/Phoenix, April 5)

135. *Pimple Copped* (745) (Folly Films, Phoenix, April 12)

136. *Pimple's New Job* (Piccadilly/Browne, April)

137. *Pimple's Three Weeks (Without the Option)* (Piccadilly/Browne, May)

138. *Pimple's Royal Divorce* (Piccadilly/Browne, May)

139. *Pimple's Million Dollar Mystery* (Piccadilly/Browne, June 17)

140. *Pimple's the Man Who Stayed at Home* (Piccadilly/Browne, June 24)

141. *Pimple's Past* (Piccadilly/Browne, July 1)

"Employed by the Government—in the capacity of a convict!—Pimple makes his escape, and first robbing a convenient scarecrow of its clothes, wanders into the grounds of an adjacent hostel, where he joins a merry party, to whom he relates the sad story—highly coloured, by the way—of his past life. At the conclusion of his tale, which has earned him a glass of beer, he is suddenly confronted by a warder, who promptly hauls him back to prison. Fairly effective comedy in which much of the humour is derived from its quaint 'verses' that act as sub-titles." Supplement to *The Bioscope* ((June 3, 1915): i.

142. *Pimple's the Case of Johnny Walker* (Piccadilly/Browne, July 8)

143. *Pimple's Peril* (Piccadilly/Browne, July 15)

144. *Pimple's Art of Mystery* (925) (Piccadilly, Browne, July 29)

"Pimple visits a theatre and sees a very clever conjuring turn. He decides to go to the conjuror and ask him to teach him his tricks. He is received very kindly by the professional, who advises him to buy his 5s. book. Pimple sets himself to work, and on the night of his grandparents' party he arrives carrying a bag containing the paraphernalia. But, notwithstanding his careful attention to all details given, he is met with failure with every experiment. In his attempts to copy the conjuror, he only succeeds in injuring nearly every member of the party. He is, however, undaunted, and caps all his past efforts by nearly blowing up the whole house with gunpowder. We see him later sitting disconsolately on the pavement trying to collect his thoughts, and from the expression on his face, one would imagine that the conjuror who sold him the book of tricks will have an unpleasant half-hour next time he chances to come across Pimple's path." Supplement to *The Kinematograph and Lantern Weekly* (June 24, 1915): xxvii.

145. *Pimple's Rival* (Piccadilly/Browne, August 12)

146. *For Her Brother's Sake* (Prieur, August 16)
Fred Evans in a straight dramatic role.

147. *The Smugglers* (Prieur, August 23)
Fred Evans in a straight dramatic role.

148. *Pimple's Dilemma* (Piccadilly/Browne, August 19)
"The Reverend Pimple, our hero's father, accompanied by the curate, decides to visit his son. Alas! The visit is too unexpected for Pimple, who is at his wit's end to know where to hide the girls he is with. Three are bundled into his bedroom and hidden in the bed; two are transformed into armchairs; and the remaining one, by placing a tray on her bac, is made into a table. The preparations are only just completed in time, for papa is so eager to see his son that he bursts into the room as Pimple is giving final instructions to them to keep still. Both father and curate evince a strong desire to sit, and Pimple has hard work to prevent them. Papa feels the bed to see if his boy is sleeping on a feather bed, only to discover a form there. Poor Pimple is at first at a loss to explain, but gets over it by saying they are wounded Germans! Pimple, fearing discovery, determines to do away with himself and returning to confess the deed, finds his father in one chair with three girls, and the curate in the other with the remainder. The Reverend Pimple, to silence his son, gives him a cheque for £1,000 and departs, much to the joy of all, who foresee a rollicking time in store." *The Kinematograph and Lantern Weekly* (July 8, 1915): xxx.

149. *Pimple's Holiday* (Piccadilly/Browne, August 26)
"Fairly amusing comedy, taken at the Karsino, Tagg's Island, and introducing some well-known vaudeville actors." *The Bioscope* (July 8, 1915): 103.
"The visitors to the 'Karsino,' Fred Karno's popular river resort, on Sunday last were much amused at the antics of Syd Walker and Pimple, who were taking part in a cinema comedy on the island. Pimple is, of course, well known in the cinema world, but it was Syd Walker's debut into those regions. The members of the 'Parlez-Vous Francaise' revue company [a Fred Karno production] also took part in the film which will shortly be showing at all the leading cinema theatres. The party were afterwards entertained to lunch by Mr. Kano who gave them all a good time." *The Era* (May 26, 1915): 12.
Possibly the only Pimple comedy for which an exact filming date is known, i.e., Sunday, May 20, 1915.

150. *Tally Ho! Pimple* (Piccadilly/Browne, September 2)

151. *Driven by Hunger* (Prieur, September 6)
Fred Evans in a straight dramatic role.

152. *Pimple's Scrap of Paper* (Piccadilly/Browne, September 9)

153. *The Kaiser Captures Pimple* (Piccadilly/Browne, September 16)

154. *Pimple's Boy Scout* (Piccadilly/Browne, September 23)

155. *Mademoiselle Pimple* (Piccadilly/Browne, September 30)

156. *Pimple's Burlesque of "The Still Alarm"* (Piccadilly/Browne, October 4)

157. *Pimple Has One* (Piccadilly/Browne, October 7)
Archive: BFI Archive: Incomplete.

158. *Pimple's Good Turn* (Piccadilly/Browne, October 14)

159. *Ragtime Cowboy Pimple* (Piccadilly/Browne, October 21)
"'I've just seen Broncho Billy on the films, and I think he's lovely.' 'Lovely,' answered Pimple—'Lovely—my dear girl you should have seen me when I was a cowboy—listen, and I'll tell you my experiences.' So Pimple poured forth his wonderful adventures into the listening ears of the believing Amelia. How he was made sheriff, how Big Jim robbed the coach (incidentally a perambulator) and out he was run to earth by our hero, who, with big guns, bombarded his trenches—how Jim was lucky enough to escape from Pimple's clutches—and all the thrilling episodes were poured into the wondering ears of the beautiful Amelia. Unfortunately the story was unfolded in a farmyard, and at the most exciting part a drove of cows came along and Pimple hurriedly sought shelter on the nearest lamp-post, where discretion was the better part of valour." Supplement to *The Kinematograph and Lantern Weekly* (September 16, 1915): xxxii.

160. *Pimple's WillIt—WasIt—Isit* (Piccadilly/Browne, October 28)
Filmed at Hastings, East Sussex

161. *Pimple's Some Burglar* (Piccadilly, Browne, November 4)

162. *Pimple's Motor Tour* (Piccadilly/Browne, November 11)

163. *Pimple's Three O'clock Race* (Piccadilly/Browne, November 18)

164. *Pimple Up the Pole* (Piccadilly/Browne, November 25)

165. *Pimple's Three* (Piccadilly/Browne, December 2)

166. *Pimple's Road to Ruin* (Piccadilly/Browne, December 2)

167. *Pimple Explains* (Piccadilly/Browne, December 16)
"Excellent Pimple comedy, in which that gentleman, by pretending to be a special constable, is enabled to spend many a riotous 'evening out,' until his wife fathoms his secret." Supplement to *The Bioscope* (October 28, 1915): i.

168. *Aladdin* (Piccadilly/Browne, December 27)

169. *Was Pimple (W) Right?* (Piccadilly/Browne, December 23)

170. *Pimple's Uncle* (Piccadilly/Browne, December 30)
Archive: BFI Archive.

171. *Some Fun* (Sunny South/Comedy Combine, c. December 1915)

172. *A Study in Skarlit* (Sunny South/Comedy Combine, c. December 1915)
"The Study in Skarlit is a red handkerchief, which is used by old man Moratorium, has been in the family for years, and is the only one that he can blow his nose on. Should he lose the handkerchief, he will surely die. His nephew. Professor Moratorium, knowing this, and also that the old man has left him all his money, steals his handkerchief. Consequently, old man Moratorium cannot find hanky, cannot blow nose, taken ill, has a sneeze, nearly kicks the bucket, Scherlokz Momz called in, gets a clue, starts buss., after villain, all over." Advertisement, *The Kinematograph and Lantern Weekly* (December 9, 1915): 88.

173. *Pimple in "The Whip"* (Piccadilly, c. 1915. Re-released Walturdaw, February 1917)
Pimple's Whip, "burlesque of the famous Drury Lane production" was advertised as a "coming exclusive" by Piccadilly in the supplement to *The Kinematograph and Lantern Weekly* (April 22, 1915): xxv. Earliest references to the film being publicly shown occur in the early summer of 1916.

1916

174. *Pimple Sees Ghosts* (Piccadilly/Browne, January 6, 1916)

175. *Pimple Acts* (Piccadilly/Browne, January 13)

176. *Pimple Will Treat* (Piccadilly/Browne, January 20)
"Pimple does not approve of the 'no-treating' order. With his friends he withdraws from the bar to think out a plan whereby he may defeat the law. Necessity is the mother of invention, and Pimple manages in three different ways to take in the wary barman, and so stand his appreciative friends drinks." Supplement to *The Kinematograph and Lantern Weekly* (January 1, 1916): xiii.

177. *Pimple's Artful Dodge* (Piccadilly/Browne, January 27)

178. *Pimple Gets the Hump* (Piccadilly/Browne, February 3)

179. *Pimple's Great Adventure* (Piccadilly/Browne, February 10)

180. *Pimple's Crime* (Piccadilly/Browne, February 17)

181. *Pimple Ends It* (Piccadilly/Browne, February 24)
"Jilted by the only girl, Pimple determines to commit suicide, all to no avail. Has some amusing moments, but not very successful as a comedy." Supplement to *The Bioscope* (January 13, 1916): i.

182. *Pimple's Zeppelin Scare* (Piccadilly/Browne, February 24)

183. *Pimple's Part* (Piccadilly/Browne, March 2)
Archive: BFI National Archive. Incomplete.

184. *Pimple's Double* (Piccadilly/Browne, March 30)
"Pimple and Joe are rival boarders, and to cut the former out Joe disguises himself, and, as Pimple, endeavours to estrange all the ladies. Unfortunately he succeeds in making a hero of his rival, and is forced to leave the establishment." Supplement to *The Bioscope* (February 17, 1916): i.

185. *Pimple Splits the Difference* (Piccadilly, Browne, April 6)

186. *Pimple's Pink Forms* (Piccadilly/Browne, April 13)
Archive: Archive Film Agency. Incomplete.

187. *Pimple's Arm of the Law* (Piccadilly/Browne, April 20)

188. *Pimple, Himself and Others* (Piccadilly/Browne, April 27)

189. *Pimple as Hamlet* (Piccadilly/Browne, c. April)
"'Pimple,' in his two-act burlesque on 'Hamlet,' is most amusing. He makes the house ring with laughter when he is imitating Charles Chaplin." *Lincolnshire Echo* (October 17, 1916): 2.

190. *Pimple's Midsummer Night's Dream* (Piccadilly/Browne, May 4)
"Pimple and his brother Joe partake heartily of lobster salad, and while the latter, has pleasant dreams, in which somewhat scantily-attired maidens feature, poor Pimple has a horrid nightmare of savage warriors, monkeys and boiling oil." *The Bioscope* (March 23, 1916): 1303.

191. *Pimple Poor but Dishonest* (Piccadilly/Browne, May 11)
"Pimple endeavours to make a living by playing the violin in the streets. Then a friend appears who instructs the musician in the art of deception with satisfactory pecuniary results for Pimple." *The Bioscope* (March 30, 1916): 1429

192. *Pimple's Silver Lagoon* (Piccadilly/Browne, c. May)

193. *Pimple's Woman in the Case* (Piccadilly/Browne, June 1)

194. *Diamond Cut Diamond* (Piccadilly/Browne, June 8)

195. *Pimple's Tenth Commandment* (Piccadilly/Browne, June 15)

196. *Some Monkey Business* (Piccadilly/Browne, June 22)

197. *Pimple's Clutching Hand* (Piccadilly/Browne, June 29)

198. *Pimple's Nautical Story* (Piccadilly/Kin-Ex, c. June)

199. *Pimple's Merry Wives/The Merry Wives of Pimple* (Piccadilly/Browne, July 6)

200. *Strafing the Kaiser* (Piccadilly/Walturdaw, August 21)

201. *All for Love* (Piccadilly/Walturdaw, September 16)

202. *The Match Strike* (Piccadilly/Walturdaw, September 16)

203. *What Is It?* (Piccadilly/Walturdaw, October 30)

204. *The Merchant of Venice* (Piccadilly/Walturdaw, November 13)

1917

205. *Pimple's Lady Godiva* (Piccadilly/Walturdaw, June 11, 1917)
Archive: Archive Film Agency. Incomplete.

206. *Pimple's Pitter-Patter* (Piccadilly/Walturdaw, July 23)

207. *Pimple's Motor Tour* (Piccadilly/Walturdaw, August 6)

208. *Saving Raffles* (Piccadilly/Walturdaw, September 17)

209. *Oliver Twisted* (Piccadilly/Walturdaw, October 1)
Archive: Tony Scott collection.

210. *Some Dancer* (Piccadilly/Walturdaw, October 15)

211. *Pimple's End of a Perfect Day* (first shown at the Hippodrome, Coventry on October 15, 1917)
"A great Coventry film, including all the Coventry public. Come and see yourselves in the film." Advert for the Hippodrome, *Coventry Herald* (October 13, 1917): 1.
Filmed while Fred Evans was appearing at the theater in the first week of October.
Archive: BFI National Archive.

212. *Pimple's Senseless Censoring* (Piccadilly/Walturdaw, October 29)

213. *Pimple's Romance* (Piccadilly/Walturdaw, November 5)

214. *Pimple—His Voluntary Corps* (Piccadilly/Walturdaw, November 19)

215. *Pimple's Tableaux Vivants* (Piccadilly/Walturdaw, December 31)

1918

216. *Pimple's The Woman Who Did* (Piccadilly/Walturdaw, January 14, 1918)

217. *Pimple's Mystery of the Closed Door* (Piccadilly/Walturdaw, January 28)

218. *Rations* (Ideal, c. March)
"The first of a series of Pimple comedies was shown at the Ideal Trade show last Thursday. Inasmuch as these amusing short-length films are topical reviews of modern conditions they are bound to be popular. Fun about queues reveals Pimple as a malefactor, the comic possibilities of food hoarding and the extent to which we may be card-indexed are all molded into humorous action." *The Bioscope* (April 18, 1918): 29

219. *Pimple's Better 'Ole* (Fred Evans, July)

220. *Inns and Outs* (1000) (Fred Evans/Horder, October)

1920

221. *Pimple's Topical Gazette*

1922

222. *Pimple's The Three Musketeers* (Shadow Plays, c. December)

Other Film Appearances

Although extensive, this filmography does not represent Fred Evans' screen career in its entirety. He was uncredited in an unknown number of Cricks and Martin films and may also have played in non–Pimple films released by Ec-Ko. Similarly, details of some very minor appearances in British feature films of the late 1920s and early 1930s have not been preserved. There were also actuality and newsreel items such as that showing his visit to the Vickers engineering works in February 1921. Some films were announced but were not released (and perhaps never filmed). H.A. Browne's advert in the *Kinematograph and Lantern Weekly* (March 23, 1916): 72–73, announced coming Pimple productions of *Henry VIII, The Second Mrs. Tanqueray, Sweet Nell of Old Drury, The Corsican Brothers, If I Were King, The Girl Who Took the Wrong Turning (to the left!), The Merchant of Venice, Oliver Twist, Lady Godiva, His House in Order, The Woman Who Did,* and *Macbeth* (only four of which appear to have made it to the screen).

Chapter Notes

Chapter 1

1. *Chatham News* (December 24, 1870): 2.
2. Quoted in *The Era* (September 26, 1875): 13.
3. *The Era* (March 21, 1885): 22.
4. *Ibid.* (March 2, 1932): 16.
5. *Ibid.* (September 14, 1889): 9.

Chapter 2

1. *The Era* (September 27, 1902): 20.
2. Joe Evans to Bert Langdon, November 5, 1964, published in *The Call Boy*, vol. 2, no. 2. (May 1965).
3. Harry, born 1862: Alice, 1863; Maria; 1863; Joe, 1867; Amalia Augusta, 1869; Fred, 1870; Lily, 1874; Bert, 1876; Albert 1878.
4. *The Era* (March 2, 1889): 17.
5. *Ibid.* (March 23, 1889): 14.
6. *The Stage* (July 26, 1889): 4.
7. *Pictures and the Picturegoer* (April 3, 1915): 9.
8. *Hull Daily Mail* (September 12, 1923): 3.
9. *The Era* (April 9, 1892): 16.
10. Joe Evans to Bert Langdon, September 8,1964, published in *The Call Boy*, vol. 2, no. 2. (May 1965).
11. *The Era* (December 25, 1897): 19.
12. *Ibid.* (May 17, 1902): 22.
13. Marius Leopold to Joe Evans, May 26, 1965, Denis Gifford Collection, BFI.
14. *Music Hall* (November 3, 1893): 12.
15. *The Encore* (September 4, 1902); photocopy Tony Barker collection, page number unavailable.
16. Beattie Anthony appeared with J. Hartley Milburn's "Nine Rosebuds" from the age of 14. In December 1896 she appeared with the troupe in the pantomime *Cinderella* presented at the Avenue Theatre, Sunderland, also taking the part of "Two O'clock." The role of "Dandini" in the production was played by her future husband's sister May Evans.

Chapter 3

1. *The Swindon Advertiser* (January 23, 1903): 2.

2. *Falkirk Herald* (February 10, 1904): 5.
3. *New York Clipper* (November 28, 1908): 1026.
4. *Brooklyn Daily Eagle* (January 25, 1909): 28.
5. Joe Evans to Bert Langdon. September 8, 1964, published in *The Call Boy*, vol. 2, no. 2. (May 1965).
6. *Western Mail* (May 14, 1914): 9.
7. *Ibid.*
8. Joe Evans to Bert Langdon. September 8, 1964, published in *The Call Boy*, vol. 2, no. 2. (May 1965).
9. *Ibid.*
10. *The Tatler* (July 1, 1903): 30.

Chapter 4

1. *The Sacramento Bee* (March 31, 1879): 2.
2. *Variety* (October 30, 1909): 9.
3. *Ibid.*
4. *Washington Herald* (February 1, 1910): 9.
5. *New York Clipper* (July 23, 1910): 590.
6. *Variety* (September 16, 1911): 21.

Chapter 5

1. *Croydon Guardian and Surrey County Advertiser* (September 18, 1909): 4.
2. *The Cinema News and Property Gazette* (January 8, 1913): 86.
3. *Picture Show* (May 6, 1920): 19.
4. Wood, Leslie, *The Miracle of the Movies* (London,: Burke, 1947): 142.
5. Release dates for subsequent films are given in brackets. The date of filming was usually some weeks before release.
6. *Kinematograph and Lantern Weekly* (April 7, 1910): 1235.
7. "The Society Idol" (written and composed by C.G. Coates).
8. *The Bioscope* (August 18, 1910): 35.
9. Aylott, Dave, *From Flicker Alley to Wardour Street* (unpublished manuscript, BFI), 42–45.
10. *Kinematograph and Lantern Weekly* (December 1, 1910): 121.
11. *Pictures and the Picturegoer* (week ending April 13, 1915): 10.

12. *The Bioscope* (October 26, 1911): 147.

13. Denis Gifford taped interview with Joe Evans, Denis Gifford Collection, BFI. Following Denis Gifford's death, his collection of taped interviews and correspondence with Joe Evans and other cinema veterans was rescued by Tony Fletcher who subsequently donated it to the British Film Institute.

14. *Kinematograph and Lantern Weekly* (October 20, 1932): 56.

Chapter 6

1. Denis Gifford taped interview with Joe Evans, Denis Gifford Collection, BFI.

Chapter 7

1. BT 31 123429/20830, National Archives.

2. *The Encore* (June 1, 1894): 496.

3. *The Bioscope* (September 10, 1914): 949.

4. Written and composed by W.W. Rogers.

5. *East London Observer* (August 17, 1901): 8.

6. Denis Gifford taped interview with Joe Evans, Denis Gifford Collection, BFI.

7. Mayhew, Henry, *London Labour and the London Poor*, Vol. III (London: N.p., 1861): 144–148.

8. *The Cinema* (September 12, 1912): 16.

9. *The Bioscope* (October 31, 1912): 99.

10. *Ibid.* (November 14, 1912): 113.

11. *Ibid.* (November 21, 1912): 98.

Chapter 8

1. Joe Evans to Denis Gifford, September 1, 1964, Denis Gifford Collection, BFI.

2. Supplement to *The Bioscope* (February 6, 1913): xiii.

3. *The Bioscope* (July 3, 1913): 53.

4. *The Cinema* (August 13, 1913): 135.

5. *Bexhill-on-Sea Observer* (December 13, 1913): 8.

6. *Kinematograph and Lantern Weekly* (October 16, 1913): 2638.

Chapter 9

1. Gerry Turvey, "The Battle of Waterloo (1913): The First British Epic" in Alan Burton and Laraine Porter (eds.), *The Showman, the Spectacle and the Two Minute Silence* (Trowbridge: Flicks, 2001): 40.

2. Speaight, George, *Juvenile Drama* (London: N.p., 1946): 37.

3. Supplement to *The Bioscope* (October 31, 1912): xxxviii.

4. *Leeds Mercury* (January 7, 1913): 6.

5. *Ealing Gazette and West Middlesex Observer* (August 16, 1913): 3.

6. *The Kineograph and Lantern Weekly* (October 2, 1913): 2436.

7. *The Bioscope* (December 24, 1914): 74.

8. *Kinematograph and Lantern Weekly* (June 10, 1915): 59.

9. Supplement to *The Bioscope* (August 14, 1913): xxviii.

10. *The Cinema* (January 1, 1914): 19.

11. *The Middlesex Chronicle* (October 3, 1914): 5.

12. *Ibid.* (October 17, 1914): 6.

13. *Ibid.* (April 18, 1914): 3

14. *Ibid.* (May 23, 1914): 1.

Chapter 10

1. Supplement to the *Bioscope* (December 25, 1913): xxxi.

2. *Ibid.*

3. *The Times* (January 24, 1914): 3.

4. *Ibid.* (November 21, 1914): 3.

5. *The Kinematograph and Lantern Weekly* (December 17, 1914): 23.

6. Wolters, Neb, *Bungalow Town: Theatre and Film Colony* (Shoreham: Wolters, 1995): 30.

7. "The Value of Local Topicals," in *How to Run a Picture Theatre* (London: Kinematograph, 1912): 121–125.

8. *Ibid.*, 30.

9. *The Cinema* (December 18, 1913): 41.

10. *Ibid.* (December 24, 1914): 26.

11. The partnership between Evans and Lyndhurst was apparently dissolved on June 21, 1915, and *A Study in Skarlit* and *Some Fun*, released in December 1915 by Comedy Combine Films, Climax Studios.

12. *Kinematograph and Lantern Weekly* (December 2, 1915): 96.

13. *Ibid.* (July 15, 1915): 75.

14. *Ibid.* (December 30, 1915): 2.

15. *Hull Daily Mail* (September 12, 1923): 3.

Chapter 11

1. Hepworth, Cecil, *Came the Dawn* (London: Phoenix House, 1951): 81.

2. *The Sphere* (December 6, 1913): 12.

3. *The Bioscope* (February 11, 1915): 493.

4. *Hull Daily Mail* (March 7, 1914): 2.

5. *Pictures and the Picturegoer* (June 19, 1915): 216.

6. *Ibid.* (August 7, 1915): 363.

7. *Ibid.* (July 3, 1915): 249.

8. McKernan, Dr. Luke, "Diverting Time: London's Cinemas and Their Audiences, 1906–1914," *The London Journal*, vol. 32 no. 2 (July 2007): 142.

9. *Yorkshire Evening Post* (February 7, 1913): 5.

10. *Middlesex Chronicle* (June 13, 1914): 5.

11. *North Devon Journal* (January 11, 1912): 7.

12. *The Scotsman* (April 14, 1913): 8.

13. *Derby Daily Telegraph* (January 3, 1913): 2.

14. *Falkirk Herald* (May 6, 1914): 3.
15. *Leigh Chronicle and Weekly Advertiser* (December 19, 1913): 5.

Chapter 12

1. Written and composed by Fred Godfrey and Billy Williams, 1911.
2. Andy Medhurst, "Music Hall and British Cinema," in Charles Barr (editor), *All Our Yesterdays: 90 Years of British Cinema* (London: BFI, 1986): 185.
3. Written and composed by Harry Wincott, 1895.
4. Written and composed by R.P. Weston and Fred J. Barnes.
5. Written and composed by A.J. Mills and Albert Perry, 1900.
6. Written and composed by T.W. Connor.
7. Written and composed by George D'Albert, Fred Godfrey and Billy Williams, 1909.
8. *The Era* (June 19, 1913): 87.
9. Midwinter, Eric, *Make 'Em Laugh* (London: Allen and Unwin, 1979): 13–14.

Chapter 13

1. *Wigan Observer and District Advertiser* (September 26, 1914): 1.
2. *The Kinematograph and Lantern Weekly* (June 25, 1914): 75.
3. *The Bioscope* (October 1, 1914): 78–79.
4. *The Kinematograph and Lantern Weekly* (November 12, 1914): 57.
5. *Pictures and the Picturegoer* (week ending April 10, 1915): 51.
6. Joe Evans to Denis Gifford, September 3, 1962, Denis Gifford Collection BFI.
7. Supplement to *The Kinematograph and Lantern Weekly* (April 1,1915): xiv.
8. *Hastings and St. Leonards Observer* (July 3, 1915): 4.
9. *Pictures and the Picturegoer* (week ending August 28, 1915): 421.
10. *Motion Picture News* (September 18, 1915): 62.
11. *Sheffield Daily Telegraph* (June 11, 1918): 1.
12. Robinson, David, *Chaplin: His Life and Art* (London: Penguin, 2001): 194.
13. *Pictures and the Picturegoer* (week ending December 11, 1915): 229.
14. *The Bioscope* (April 6, 1916): 58.
15. Ancestry.co.uk—British Army WWI Pension Records 1914–1920. Original Data: The National Archives of the UK.
16. *The Manchester Guardian* (June 4, 1917): 5.
17. *The Burnley News* (April 10, 1918): 2.
18. *Burnley Express and Advertiser* (April 13, 1918): 3.

Chapter 14

1. *The Stage* (December 23, 1915): 27.
2. *Ibid.*
3. *Birmingham Daily Gazette* (November 6, 1915): 7.
4. *The Globe* (November 5, 1915): 8.
5. *The Stage* (November 11, 1915): 25.
6. *Ibid.* (December 23, 1915): 27.
7. *Yorkshire Post and Leeds Intelligencer* (December 22, 1915): 7.
8. *The Stage* (December 23, 1915): 27.
9. *Ibid.* (November 11, 1915) 25.
10. *Ibid.* (December 23, 1915): 27.
11. *Yorkshire Post and Leeds Intelligencer* (November 6, 1915): 9.

Chapter 15

1. *London Daily News* (September 10, 1909): 3.
2. The actor playing Charles Peace bears a strong resemblance to the well-known music-hall comedian Sam Poluski.
3. *Portsmouth Evening News* (May 15, 1894): 1.

Chapter 16

1. Joe Evans to Denis Gifford, September 1, 1964, Denis Gifford Collection, BFI.
2. *Chicago Daily Tribune* (January 11, 1916): 14.
3. Musser, Charles, *The Emergence of Cinema: The American Screen to 1907* (Berkeley: University of California Press, 1994): 494.
4. McKernan, Dr. Luke, "Diverting Time: London's Cinemas and Their Audiences, 1906–1914." *London Journal* 32 no. 2: 142.
5. At the time of writing the street is little changed. Thanks to Joy and John Relph for taking to their own bikes to make this identification.
6. Low, Rachael, *The History of the British Film: 1906–1914* (London: Allen and Unwin, 1949): 175.
7. *The Bioscope* (February 18, 1915): 21.
8. *Coventry Evening Telegraph* (October 2, 1917): 2.
9. *Pictures and the Picturegoer* (April 3, 1915): 9.
10. *The Era* (September 25, 1918): 14.
11. *The Bioscope* (January 23, 1913): 91.
12. *Alley Sloper's Half Holiday* (September 23, 1893): 1. "Professor" Sloper's deception is laid bare, by the actions of a dog who drags the boy from his hiding place.
13. Supplement to *The Kinematograph and Lantern Weekly* (March 16, 1916): xvi.
14. *The Bioscope* (December 2, 1915): 119.
15. 11, if *Pimple's End of a Perfect Day* is included.
16. *Hull Daily Mail* (September 12, 1923): 3.
17. *The Bioscope* (January 1, 1917): 91.
18. *Ibid.* (April 18, 1918): 29.

Chapter 17

1. *Picture Show* (May 6, 1920): 19.
2. Joe Evans to Denis Gifford, August 25, 1962, Denis Gifford Collection, BFI.
3. *The Era* (July 23, 1919): 22.
4. National Archive, B9/877.
5. *Nottingham Evening Post* (November 5, 1919): 2.
6. *The Stage* (February 9, 1922): 10.
7. Tony Barker Archive.
8. *The Era* (November 2, 1922): 21.
9. *Ibid.* (June 18, 1922): 4.
10. *The Stage* (May 20, 1926): 6.
11. *Burnley Express* (August 25, 1926): 5.
12. *The Era* (April 19, 1922): 14.
13. Quoted in Peter Honri, *Working the Halls* (London: Futura, 1973): 136.
14. *Western Morning News* (February 4, 1929): 4.

Chapter 18

1. Joe Evans to Denis Gifford, August 25, 1962, Denis Gifford Collection, BFI.
2. *The Kinematograph and Lantern Weekly* (June 25, 1914): 75.
3. *The Bioscope* (June 18, 1814): 8.
4. *Ibid.* (May 9, 1914): 701.
5. *Ibid.* (February 3, 1916): 79.
6. *Ealing Gazette and West Middlesex Observer* (December 25, 1915): 2.
7. *The Bioscope* (May 4, 1916): 551.
8. *The Kinematograph and Lantern Weekly* (April 19, 1917): 5.
9. *The Era* (August 18, 1929): 19.
10. *The Bioscope* (July 9, 1914): 101.
11. Supplement to *The Bioscope* (January 21, 1915): vii.
12. *The Bioscope* (October 22, 1914): 109.
13. *Ibid.*, April 23, 1925): 66.
14. *The Bioscope Service Supplement* (November 21, 1928): ii.
15. *The Daily Colonist*, B.C. (December 28, 1924): 25.
16. *Winnipeg Free Press* (December 28, 1928): 21.

Chapter 19

1. *Portsmouth Evening News* (April 27, 1929): 8.
2. *The Era* (January 1, 1919): 8.
3. *Ibid.* (February 12, 1919): 24.
4. *Ibid.* (March 17, 1920): 18.
5. *Portmouth Evening News* (June 12, 1920): 1.
6. *Derby Evening Telegraph* (June 26, 1920): 1; *ibid..* (June 30, 1920): 1.
7. *Ibid.* (July 1, 1920): 3.
8. *Nottingham Journal* (August 17, 1920): 5.
9. *Nottingham Evening Post* (August 18, 1920): 1.

10. *Sheffield Daily Telegraph* (February 17, 1921): 3.
11. *Kinematograph and Lantern Weekly* (October 14, 1920): 125.
12. *The Era* (March 2, 1921): 16.
13. *Daily Herald* (December 20, 1921): 5.
14. *The Era* (March 15, 1922): 12.
15. *Ibid.* (July 19, 1922): 19.
16. *Ibid.* (August 9, 1922): 16.
17. *Hull Daily Mail* (April 9, 1924): 7.
18. *The Stage* (May 7, 1931): 12.
19. Charlie Chaplin Archive, Fondazione Cineteca di Bologna.
20. *The Stage* (August 27, 1931): 20.
21. *The Glamorgan Advertiser* (February 26, 1926): 8.
22. *Ibid.* (July 7, 1932): 8; *Lancashire Evening Post* (July 2, 1932): 3.
23. *Birmingham Daily Gazette* (December 19. 1932): 8.
24. *The Stage* (March 7, 1935): 2.
25. *Ibid.* (April 27, 1933): 16.
26. Denis Gifford taped interview with Joe Evans, Denis Gifford Collection, BFI.
27. *Daily Herald* (March 11, 1933): 6. *The Kinematograph Weekly* (March 16, 1933): 43, reported that the proposed studio was in Killorgan Road, Dublin.
28. *Western Morning News* (November 24, 1933): 6.
29. Wilton, Carol, *Inside the Law: Canadian Law Firms in Historical Perspective* (Toronto: University of Toronto Press, 1996): 345.
30. Howard, H. Bannister, *Fifty Years a Showman* (London: Hutchinson, 1938): 186–187.
31. *Daily Herald* (December 19, 1944): 3.
32. *Ibid.* (September 28, 1944): 3.
33. *Cornishman* (June 15, 1944): 3.
34. *Ibid.* (August 3. 1944): 8.
35. *Western Times* (May 4, 1945): 7.
36. *The Stage* (December 19, 1946): 5.
37. *Ballymena Observer* (February 25, 1949): 8.
38. *Cornish Guardian* (February 17, 1944): 8.
39. *Wells Journal* (January 4,1946): 1.
40. *The Stage* (September 6, 1951): 4.

Chapter 20

1. *Yorkshire Evening Post* (March 28, 1908): 3.
2. *The Era* (March 24, 1900): 14.
3. *Ibid.* (September 4, 1909): 18.
4. *Coventry Evening Telegraph* (December 5, 1927): 5.
5. Barbara Tibbetts to Denis Gifford, November 30, 1967, Denis Gifford Collection, BFI.

Chapter 21

1. Gifford, Denis, "Pimple," *The Silent Picture*, issue no. 6 (Spring 1970).

Bibliography

Anthony, Barry. "Evans, Fred (1889–1951) and Evans, Joe (1891–1967)," in Robert Murphy, ed., *Directors in British and Irish Cinema. A Reference Companion*. London: BFI, 2006.

Aylott, Dave. *From Flicker Alley to Wardour Street*. Unpublished manuscript. BFI, London.

British Newspaper Archive (for many digitized newspaper reports)

Dixon, Bryony. "Pimple and the Tramp: The Fickle Fortune of a Silent Comedy Star." *Sight and Sound* (March 10, 2021).

Evans, Joe. "A Great Music Hall Family." *The Call Boy*, vol. 2, no. 2 (May 1965).

Gifford, Denis. *The British Film Catalogue, 1895–1970: A Guide to Entertainment Films*. Newton Abbot: David and Charles, 1973.

_____. "Pimple." *The Silent Picture*, no. 6 (Spring 1970).

Gillis, Stacy. "Pimple's Three Weeks (Without the Option), with Apologies to Elinor Glyn." *Early Popular Visual Culture*, Vol. 12, No. 3 (2014): 378–391.

Hammond, Michael. "'Cultivating Pimple': Performance Traditions and the Film Comedy of Fred and Joe Evans," in Alan Burton and Laraine Porter, eds., *Pimple, Pranks and Pratfalls: British Film Comedy Before 1930*. Trowbridge: Flicks, 2000.

Lamb, Catherine. "Britain's Greatest Film Comedian." *The Call Boy* (Autumn 1988).

Low, Rachael. *The History of the British Film, 1906–1914*. London: Allen and Unwin, 1946.

St. Pierre, Paul Matthew. *Music Hall Mimesis in British Film, 1895–1960. On the Halls on the Screen*. Madison: University of Wisconsin Press, 2009.

Wolters, N.E.B. *Bungalow Town. Theatre and Film Colony*. Shoreham: Wolters, 1985.

Index

Numbers in **bold italics** indicate pages with illustrations